Mastering AWS CloudForı

Build resilient and production-ready infrastructure in Amazon
Web Services with CloudFormation

Karen Tovmasyan

BIRMINGHAM—MUMBAI

Mastering AWS CloudFormation

Copyright © 2023 Packt Publishing

Group Product Manager: Preet Ahuja

Publishing Product Manager: Surbhi Suman

Book Project Manager: Ashwini C

Senior Editor: Romy Dias

Technical Editor: Irfa Ansari

Copy Editor: Safis Editing

Proofreader: Safis Editing

Indexer: Subalakshmi Govindhan

Production Designer: Vijay Kamble

Senior DRME: Linda Pearlson

DRME: Rohan Dhobal

First published: May 2020

Second edition: November 2023

Production reference: 1121023

Published by Packt Publishing Ltd.

Grosvenor House

11 St Paul's Square

Birmingham

B3 1RB, UK.

ISBN 978-1-80512-390-3

www.packtpub.com

To my muse, Natalia, for fueling my dedication to the cause.

Contributors

About the author

Karen Tovmasyan is a senior software engineer at Uber, specializing in cloud infrastructure and distributed systems. Karen is a key member of a few Russian-speaking AWS communities, and he holds multiple certifications in cloud technologies and payments security. He shares his knowledge using his public channels on Telegram and Medium, as well as speaking at various conferences and events such as HighLoad, DevOpsConf, and AWS Community Day.

I want to thank my family for their continued support throughout writing this book. And also thanks to my readers from the AWS community for keeping the friendly and inclusive atmosphere.

About the reviewers

Aleksandr Patrushev is an AI/ML specialist solutions architect at AWS, based in Luxembourg. He is passionate about cloud and machine learning and how they could change the world. Outside work, he enjoys hiking, sports, and spending time with his family.

Vasily Pantyukhin is an IT veteran with 24 years in the industry. He has traveled an exciting path from Unix admin to Principal Solutions Architect and Director of Product Integration in various companies, including Amazon, EMC, and Gcore. Vasily is a passionate speaker at international conferences and a brain-friendly, knowledge-sharing evangelist.

Table of Contents

Part 2: Provisioning and Deployment at Scale

3

Validation, Linting, and Deploying the Stack   51

4

Continuous Integration and Deployment   75

5

Deploying to Multiple Regions and Accounts Using StackSets   101

6

Configuration Management of EC2 Instances Using cfn-init   123

Part 3: Extending CloudFormation

7

Creating Resources Outside AWS Using Custom Resources   141

8

Creating Your Own Resource Registry for CloudFormation   161

9

Scale Your Templates Using Macros, Nested Stacks, and Modules   189

10

Generating CloudFormation Templates Using AWS CDK   223

11

Deploying Serverless Applications Using AWS SAM   245

12

What's Next?   265

Preface

Released in 2011, AWS CloudFormation was the first response to **Infrastructure as Code** – an emerging approach to managing modern applications, systems, and servers.

In this book, you will learn how to apply infrastructure as code on AWS using CloudFormation in the most effective way.

By the end of this book, you will have learned about all of the internals of CloudFormation, how it is used in practice, related best practices, and various ways to extend its features using template macros and custom resources.

You will also learn about its alternative for serverless applications, the Serverless Application Model, and its possible future successor, **Cloud Development Kit**.

Who this book is for

This book is for engineers who work with AWS on a daily basis. Although you will find broad and deep explanations for most of the examples and code blocks in the book, I expect you to have basic knowledge of programming (preferably Python), general IT, and especially of AWS, as well as an understanding of RESTful APIs, JSON, and YAML.

What this book covers

Chapter 1, Working with CloudFormation, reminds you what CloudFormation is and how it works.

Chapter 2, Advanced Template Development, covers every single piece of a template – a core component of CloudFormation.

Chapter 3, Validation, Linting, and Deploying the Stack, teaches you about best practices for stack operations, from validation to running the stack in production.

Chapter 4, Continuous Integration and Deployment, covers another concept of continuous delivery and how it is applied with CloudFormation.

Chapter 5, Deploying to Multiple Regions and Accounts Using StackSets, explains how to manage stacks in a multi-region and multi-account environment.

Chapter 6, Configuration Management of EC2 Instances Using cfn-init, explains how to install software and apply configuration management to EC2 instances using CloudFormation.

Chapter 7, Creating Resources Outside AWS Using Custom Resources, explains how to create resources outside of CloudFormation.

Chapter 8, Creating Your Own Resource Registry for CloudFormation, shows a newer way of using and creating custom resource types.

Chapter 9, Scale Your Templates Using Template Macros, Nested Stacks, and Modules, covers macros, nested stacks, and modules, and how, when, and why to use them.

Chapter 10, Generating CloudFormation Templates Using AWS CDK, introduces Cloud Development Kit – a framework supporting multiple languages that is used to generate CloudFormation templates and operate stacks.

Chapter 11, Deploying Serverless Applications Using AWS SAM, teaches you how to provision resources for serverless applications using the Serverless Application Model – a simplified implementation of CloudFormation.

Chapter 12, What's Next?, gives a sneak peek of what we can expect from the future of infrastructure as code.

To get the most out of this book

In order to write and test the code in this book, you will need a Linux, macOS, or Windows machine with **Windows Subsystem for Linux (WSL)**. You will need the AWS CLI, Python, and obviously an AWS account. You can use any IDE or code editor you prefer. To write the code for this book, I used JetBrain's PyCharm and Visual Studio Code, since they have nice plugins for CloudFormation.

For the CDK and SAM, you will additionally need Docker, Homebrew, and **Node Package Manager (NPM)**.

All code examples were written on macOS, but they can easily run on a Linux system or WSL.

Software/hardware covered in the book	Operating system requirements
AWS CLI 1.18 or later	macOS or Linux
Python 3.6 or later	Windows, macOS, or Linux
Homebrew 2.2 or later	Windows, macOS, or Linux
Docker 19.03.5 or later	Windows, macOS, or Linux

If you are using the digital version of this book, we advise you to type the code yourself or access the code from the book's GitHub repository (a link is available in the next section). Doing so will help you avoid any potential errors related to the copying and pasting of code.

Keep in mind that using CloudFormation on AWS is free but you will need to pay for the resources it creates. In this book, I tried to use the smallest amount of resources possible (such as `t2.micro` instances), but always keep an eye on your AWS account and don't forget to delete the stack and other resources once you are done practicing.

Download the example code files

You can download the example code files for this book from GitHub at `https://github.com/PacktPublishing/Mastering-AWS-CloudFormation-Second-Edition`. If there's an update to the code, it will be updated in the GitHub repository.

We also have other code bundles from our rich catalog of books and videos available at `https://github.com/PacktPublishing/`. Check them out!

Code in Action

The Code in Action videos for this book can be viewed at `https://packt.link/1sSQs`

Conventions used

There are a number of text conventions used throughout this book.

`Code in text`: Indicates code words in text, database table names, folder names, filenames, file extensions, pathnames, dummy URLs, user input, and Twitter handles. Here is an example: "We also specify the `AWS::AccountId` pseudo parameter because in the next section, we will deploy the StackSet in multiple regions but in the same account, so we won't need to expose the AWS account ID in the template."

A block of code is set as follows:

```
import boto3
def check_if_key_exists():
    client = boto3.client(<ec2>)
    try:
        resp = client.describe_key_pairs(KeyNames=[«mykey»])
    except Exception:
```

When we wish to draw your attention to a particular part of a code block, the relevant lines or items are set in bold:

```
        return False
    if len(resp['KeyPairs']) == 0:
        return False
    return True
```

Any command-line input or output is written as follows:

```
$ aws cloudformation deploy \
                --stack-name tag \
                --template-file tag.yaml \
                --capabilities CAPABILITY_IAM
```

Bold: Indicates a new term, an important word, or words that you see onscreen. For instance, words in menus or dialog boxes appear in **bold**. Here is an example: "Once both stack instances are created, we will see that their status is **CURRENT** in the **Stack instances** section."

> **Tips or important notes**
> Appear like this.

Get in touch

Feedback from our readers is always welcome.

General feedback: If you have questions about any aspect of this book, email us at customercare@packtpub.com and mention the book title in the subject of your message.

Errata: Although we have taken every care to ensure the accuracy of our content, mistakes do happen. If you have found a mistake in this book, we would be grateful if you would report this to us. Please visit www.packtpub.com/support/errata and fill in the form.

Piracy: If you come across any illegal copies of our works in any form on the internet, we would be grateful if you would provide us with the location address or website name. Please contact us at copyright@packt.com with a link to the material.

If you are interested in becoming an author: If there is a topic that you have expertise in and you are interested in either writing or contributing to a book, please visit authors.packtpub.com.

Share your thoughts

Once you've read *Mastering AWS CloudFormation – Second Edition*, we'd love to hear your thoughts! Scan the QR code below to go straight to the Amazon review page for this book and share your feedback.

https://packt.link/r/1805123904

Your review is important to us and the tech community and will help us make sure we're delivering excellent quality content.

Download a free PDF copy of this book

Thanks for purchasing this book!

Do you like to read on the go but are unable to carry your print books everywhere?

Is your eBook purchase not compatible with the device of your choice?

Don't worry, now with every Packt book you get a DRM-free PDF version of that book at no cost.

Read anywhere, any place, on any device. Search, copy, and paste code from your favorite technical books directly into your application.

The perks don't stop there, you can get exclusive access to discounts, newsletters, and great free content in your inbox daily

Follow these simple steps to get the benefits:

1.   Scan the QR code or visit the link below

https://packt.link/free-ebook/9781805123903

2.   Submit your proof of purchase
3.   That's it! We'll send your free PDF and other benefits to your email directly

Part 1: CloudFormation Internals

In the first part, we will do a small refresher on CloudFormation. Later, we will dive deep into its core component – a template – and learn how to write universal, redundant, and reusable templates.

The following chapters will be covered in this part:

- *Chapter 1, Working with CloudFormation*
- *Chapter 2, Advanced Template Development*

Working with CloudFormation

Cloud computing introduced a brand-new way of managing infrastructure.

As the usage of the **AWS cloud** grew, the usual routine and operational tasks became troublesome. The AWS cloud allowed any type of business to rapidly grow and solve all the business needs regarding compute power; however, the need to maintain a certain stack of resources was hard.

DevOps culture brought a set of methodologies and ways of working, and one of those is called **Infrastructure as Code** (**IaC**). This process is about treating your infrastructure – network, virtual machines, storage, databases, and so on – as a computer program.

AWS **CloudFormation** was developed to solve this kind of problem.

I expect that you already have some working knowledge of CloudFormation, but let's quickly refresh our memory and look again at what CloudFormation is and how we use it.

Later, we will dive deep into learning advanced template development and how to provision at scale, use CloudFormation with CI/CD pipelines, and extend its features.

In this chapter, we will learn about the following:

- Understanding the internals of AWS CloudFormation
- Creating and updating a CloudFormation stack
- Managing CloudFormation IAM permissions
- Drift detection

Technical requirements

The code for this chapter can be found in this book's GitHub repository at `https://github.com/PacktPublishing/Mastering-AWS-CloudFormation-Second-Edition/tree/main/Chapter01`.

Check out the following video to see the Code in Action: `https://packt.link/efSwY`.

Understanding the internals of AWS CloudFormation

AWS services consist of three parts:

- API
- Backend
- Storage

We interact with AWS by making calls to its API services. If we want to create an EC2 instance, we need to perform an `ec2:RunInstances` call.

When we develop our template and create a stack, we invoke the `cloudformation:CreateStack` API method. AWS CloudFormation will receive the command along with the template, validate it, and start creating resources, making API calls to various AWS services, depending on what we have declared for it.

If the creation of any resource fails, then CloudFormation will roll back the changes and delete the resources that were created before the failure. But if there are no errors during the creation process, we will see our resources provisioned across the account.

If we want to make changes to our stack, then all we need to do is update the template file and invoke the `cloudformation:UpdateStack` API method. CloudFormation will then update only those resources that have been changed. If the update process fails, then CloudFormation will roll the changes back and return the stack to the previous, healthy state.

Now that we have this covered, let's start creating our stack.

Creating and updating a CloudFormation stack

I'm sure you've done this before.

We begin by developing our template first. This is going to be a simple S3 bucket. I'm going to use **YAML** template formatting, but you may use **JSON** formatting if you wish:

```
// my_bucket.yaml
AWSTemplateFormatVersion: "2010-09-09"
Description: This is my first bucket
Resources:
  MyBucket:
    Type: AWS::S3::Bucket
```

Now, we just need to create the stack with `awscli`:

```
$ aws cloudformation create-stack \
    --stack-name mybucket \
    --template-body file://my_bucket.yaml
```

After a while, we will see that our bucket has been created if we go to the AWS console or run `aws s3 ls` in the terminal.

Now, let's add some public access to our bucket:

```
// my_bucket.yaml
AWSTemplateFormatVersion: "2010-09-09"
Description: This is my first bucket
Resources:
  MyBucket:
    Type: AWS::S3::Bucket
    Properties:
      AccessControl: PublicRead
```

> **Important note**
> While the preceding change is for demonstration purposes, general usage of S3 ACLs is deprecated, and the `PublicRead` ACL is considered not secure.

Let's run the `update` operation:

```
$ aws cloudformation update-stack \
    --stack-name mybucket \
    --template-body file://my_bucket.yaml
```

We will see that the bucket we created now has a new access control policy.

Finally, to clean up your workspace, simply delete your stack using the following command:

```
$ aws cloudformation delete-stack --stack-name mybucket
```

Now, let's look at the CloudFormation IAM permissions.

Managing CloudFormation IAM permissions

We already know that CloudFormation performs API calls when we create or update the stack. Now, the question is, does CloudFormation have the same powers as a *root* user?

When you work with production-grade AWS accounts, you need to control access to your environment for humans (yourself and your co-workers) and machines (build systems, other AWS services or resources, and so on). Ignoring the least privilege principle may lead to disastrous security breaches, which is why controlling access for CloudFormation is important.

By default, when the user runs stack creation, they invoke the `cloudformation:CreateStack` API method. CloudFormation will use that user's permissions to invoke other API methods during stack creation.

This means that if our user has an IAM policy with an allowed action of `ec2:*` but attempts to create an RDS instance with CloudFormation, the stack will fail to create, with an error stating that the `User is unauthorized to perform this action`.

Let's try this. We will create an IAM role with `ec2:*`, assume that role, and try to create the same bucket stack:

```yaml
// iam_role.yaml
AWSTemplateFormatVersion: "2010-09-09"
Description: "This is a dummy role"
Resources:
  IamRole:
    Type: AWS::IAM::Role
    Properties:
      AssumeRolePolicyDocument:
        Version: 2012-10-17
        Statement:
          - Sid: AllowAssumeRole
            Effect: Allow
            Principal:
              AWS:
                - !Ref «AWS::AccountId»
            Action: «sts:AssumeRole»
      ManagedPolicyArns:
        - «arn:aws:iam::aws:policy/AmazonEC2FullAccess"
        - «arn:aws:iam::aws:policy/AWSCloudformationFullAccess»
Outputs:
  IamRole:
    Value: !GetAtt IamRole.Arn
```

If we create this stack, assume that role, and try to create the previous `mybucket` stack, it will fail to create with an error. Let's take a look:

```
$ aws cloudformation create-stack \
                  --stack-name iamrole \
                  --capabilities CAPABILITY_IAM \
                  --template-body file://iam_role.yaml
```

Note `CAPABILITY_IAM` in the preceding command. For some stack operations, we need to explicitly allow CloudFormation to perform specific steps, such as creating IAM roles or policies. Passing `CAPABILITY_IAM` as an argument means that we explicitly allow CloudFormation to create IAM resources.

Let's continue:

```
$ IAM_ROLE_ARN=$(aws cloudformation describe-stacks \
                                --stack-name iamrole \
--query "Stacks[0].Outputs[?OutputKey=='IamRole'].OutputValue" \
--output text)
$ aws sts assume-role --role-arn $IAM_ROLE_ARN \
                        --role-session-name tmp
# Here goes the output of the command. I will store the access
credentials in the env vars
$ export AWS_ACCESS_KEY_ID=…
$ export AWS_SECRET_ACCESS_KEY=…
$ export AWS_SESSION_TOKEN=…
$ aws cloudformation create-stack \
        --stack-name mybucket \
        --template-body file://my_bucket.yaml
```

We will see the following error on the AWS console:

Logical ID	Status	Status reason
mybucket	⊗ ROLLBACK_COMPLETE	-
MyBucket	⊘ DELETE_COMPLETE	-
mybucket	⊗ ROLLBACK_IN_PROGRESS	The following resource(s) failed to create: [MyBucket]. . Rollback requested by user.
MyBucket	⊗ CREATE_FAILED	API: s3:CreateBucket Access Denied
MyBucket	ⓘ CREATE_IN_PROGRESS	-
mybucket	ⓘ CREATE_IN_PROGRESS	User Initiated

Figure 1.1 – CloudFormation console – stack events

CloudFormation tried to create an S3 bucket but failed with an Access Denied exception. This is because CloudFormation used our role's credentials to run AWS API calls, and the role can only manipulate EC2 resources, such as EBS volumes or EC2 instances.

On the other hand, we cannot provide everyone with an AdminAccess policy. Hence, we need to find a way to use CloudFormation with the necessary permissions while only letting CloudFormation use those permissions.

CloudFormation supports **service roles**. Service roles are the IAM roles used by different AWS services (such as EC2, ECS, Lambda, and so on). CloudFormation service roles are used by CloudFormation during stacks and StackSets operations – creation, update, and deletion.

Here is a diagram that explains this concept:

Figure 1.2 – CloudFormation service role flow

Let's see how this works:

1. The AWS user runs a stack operation specifying the service role, such as `CreateStack` or `UpdateStack`.

2. CloudFormation assumes the role and obtains session credentials.

3. Using these credentials, CloudFormation calls API services, managing the resources in the stack.

Now that we understand the relationship between CloudFormation and IAM, let's continue and create the service role:

1. Let's create a specific role for CloudFormation:

    ```
    // cfn_iam_role.yaml
    AWSTemplateFormatVersion: "2010-09-09"
    Description: "This is a CFN role"
    Resources:
      IamRole:
        Type: AWS::IAM::Role
        Properties:
    ```

```
    AssumeRolePolicyDocument:
      Version: 2012-10-17
      Statement:
        - Sid: AllowAssumeRole
          Effect: Allow
          Principal:
            Service: «cloudformation.amazonaws.com»
          Action: «sts:AssumeRole»
      ManagedPolicyArns:
        - «arn:aws:iam::aws:policy/AdministratorAccess»
Outputs:
  IamRole:
    Value: !GetAtt IamRole.Arn
```

2. We create this stack for the service role and obtain the CloudFormation Role ARN:

```
$ aws cloudformation create-stack \
    --stack-name cfniamrole \
    --capabilities CAPABILITY_IAM \
    --template-body file://cfn_iam_role.yaml
$ IAM_ROLE_ARN=$(aws cloudformation describe-stacks \
                            --stack-name cfniamrole \
--query "Stacks[0].Outputs[?OutputKey=='IamRole'].OutputValue" \
--output text)
```

3. Now, we must run the code to create the stack. This will use our role, specifying Role ARN:

```
$ aws cloudformation create-stack \
    --stack-name mybucket \
    --template-body file://my_bucket.yaml \
    --role-arn $IAM_ROLE_ARN
```

4. After a while, we can verify that our stack has been created, and we will see our bucket!

```
$ aws s3 ls
# Output
2019-10-16 14:14:24 mybucket-mybucket-jqjpr6wmz19q
```

Before we continue, don't forget to delete the resources you created in this exercise from your account:

```
$ for i in mybucket iamrole cfniamrole; do aws cloudformation
delete-stack --stack-name $i ; done
```

> **Important note**
>
> Note that in the preceding example, we provided the CloudFormation role with `AdminPolicy` (the one that is provided by AWS by default).

In production-grade systems, we want to allow CloudFormation to have only those privileges that are required for the stack.

Two permission schemas are applied for CloudFormation roles:

- We have a certain list of services that we can use (for example, EC2, RDS, VPC, DynamoDB, S3, and so on)

- Each template/stack combination will use only those services it needs – for example, if we declare Lambda functions with **Simple Notification Service** (**SNS**), then we should create the role with policies only for Lambda and SNS

Depending on your organizational structure and engineering culture, you will be able to choose the right approach.

Drift detection

CloudFormation, as a service, often refers to the term **state**. The state is inventory information that contains a pair of values: the logical resource name, such as what name we define in the template, and the physical resource ID that is assigned by AWS, such as the EC2 Instance ID, DynamoDB table name, and so on.

CloudFormation uses its state to understand which resources to create or update. If we create a stack with a resource with a logical name of `foo`, change the property of this resource (`foo`) in a template, and run an update, then CloudFormation will change the corresponding physical resource in the account.

CloudFormation has a set of constraints. For example, it will not update the stack if we do not introduce changes to it. If we make manual changes to the resource, then CloudFormation will change them only when we make changes to the template.

Cloud engineers had to rethink their way of managing the infrastructure once they started using CloudFormation, but we will get to that in the later chapters. For now, let's look at a feature that doesn't solve problems regarding manual intervention but at least notifies us when they happen. This feature is called **drift detection**:

1. For this example, we will use the same template (dummy IAM role) as we did in the previous section:

    ```
    $ aws cloudformation create-stack \
          --stack-name iamrole \
          --template-body file://iam_role.yaml \
          --capabilities CAPABILITY_IAM
    ```

After a while, we will see that our stack has been created:

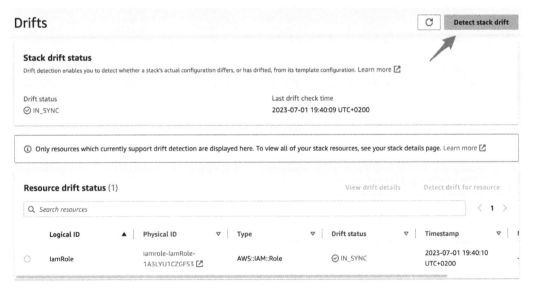

CloudFormation   ✕

Stacks
   Stack details
   Drifts
StackSet
Exports

Designer

▼ **Registry**
   Public extensions
   Activated extensions

CloudFormation > Stacks > **iamrole**

⊟ **Stacks** (1)   [C]

🔍 *Filter by stack name*

[Active ▼]   ⬤ View nested

〈 **1** 〉

Stacks

⦿   **iamrole**
    2023-07-01 19:25:06 UTC+0200
    ⊘ CREATE_COMPLETE

Figure 1.3 – The CloudFormation console

2. Note the menu item on the left called **Drifts**. If we follow that link, we will see the **Drifts** menu, and under that, **Drift status | NOT_CHECKED**. At the time of writing, we will have to run drift detection manually, so we need to run drift detection on our stack. I'm going to run **Detect stack drifts** and verify that my stack is compliant with what has been declared in the template:

Drifts
             [C] [**Detect stack drift**]

Stack drift status

Drift detection enables you to detect whether a stack's actual configuration differs, or has drifted, from its template configuration. Learn more ☑

Drift status   Last drift check time
⊘ IN_SYNC   2023-07-01 19:40:09 UTC+0200

ⓘ Only resources which currently support drift detection are displayed here. To view all of your stack resources, see your stack details page. Learn more ☑

Resource drift status (1)   View drift details   Detect drift for resource

🔍 *Search resources*   〈 **1** 〉

	Logical ID ▲	Physical ID ▽	Type ▽	Drift status ▽	Timestamp ▽	
○	IamRole	iamrole-IamRole-1A3LYU1CZGFS3 ☑	AWS::IAM::Role	⊘ IN_SYNC	2023-07-01 19:40:10 UTC+0200	

Figure 1.4 – The CloudFormation console – Drifts

3. Now, what we will do is add an extra policy to our role and rerun drift detection:

```
$ ROLENAME=$(aws cloudformation describe-stack-resources
--stack-name iamrole --query "StackResources[0].
PhysicalResourceId" --output text)
$ aws iam attach-role-policy --role-name $ROLENAME --policy-arn
"arn:aws:iam::aws:policy/AdministratorAccess"
```

4. We can now run drift detection again:

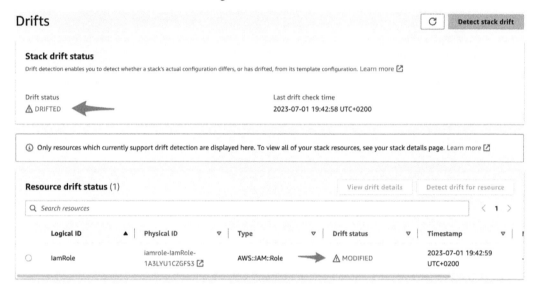

Figure 1.5 – The CloudFormation console – drift detected

5. If we check our **IamRole** resource and click **View drift details**, we will see what exactly has been changed and differs from the CloudFormation stack's state:

Details

Expected

```
{
  "AssumeRolePolicyDocument": {
    "Statement": [
      {
        "Action": "sts:AssumeRole",
        "Effect": "Allow",
        "Principal": {
          "AWS": "arn:aws:iam::            :user/Admin"
        },
        "Sid": "AllowAssumeRole"
      }
    ],
    "Version": "2012-10-17"
  },
  "ManagedPolicyArns": [
    "arn:aws:iam::aws:policy/AmazonEC2FullAccess",
    "arn:aws:iam::aws:policy/AWSCloudFormationFullAccess"
  ]
}
```

Actual

```
{
  "AssumeRolePolicyDocument": {
    "Statement": [
      {
        "Action": "sts:AssumeRole",
        "Effect": "Allow",
        "Principal": {
          "AWS": "arn:aws:iam::            :user/Admin"
        },
        "Sid": "AllowAssumeRole"
      }
    ],
    "Version": "2012-10-17"
  },
  "ManagedPolicyArns": [
    "arn:aws:iam::aws:policy/AmazonEC2FullAccess",
    "arn:aws:iam::aws:policy/AWSCloudFormationFullAccess",
    "arn:aws:iam::aws:policy/AdministratorAccess"
  ]
}
```

Figure 1.6 – The CloudFormation console – actual modification

Now, we have two options: manually roll back the change to the resource or add any dummy property to the template and run `update-stack`.

With that, we've learned about CloudFormation drifts, how to run drift detection, and the actions that must be taken afterward. But don't worry – we will revisit drifts in the following chapters.

Summary

In this refresher chapter, we renewed our knowledge as to what CloudFormation is, how we create and update stacks, why service roles are important, and how to implement them. We also remembered what drifts in CloudFormation are, when they occur, and how to detect them.

While this was an introductory chapter, we covered the fundamental building blocks of CloudFormation. In the following chapters, we will use service roles and drift detection again, but first, we need to dive deep into the internals of the CloudFormation template, which is what we will do in the next chapter.

Questions

1. Which API method is invoked when we create a CloudFormation stack?
2. What is a CloudFormation service role?
3. Which IAM policies are used if we do not specify the CloudFormation service role?

4. How is the information about stack resources stored in CloudFormation?

5. What happens if we delete the resource created by CloudFormation and try to create the same stack?

6. What happens if we delete the resource created by CloudFormation and try to update the same stack?

7. Why can't CloudFormation recreate the deleted resource?

Further reading

- CloudFormation service roles: `https://docs.aws.amazon.com/AWSCloudFormation/latest/UserGuide/using-iam-servicerole.html`

- Drift detection in CloudFormation: `https://docs.aws.amazon.com/AWSCloudFormation/latest/UserGuide/using-cfn-stack-drift.html`

2
Advanced Template Development

Bearing in mind the basics of CloudFormation, let's now move on to advanced development techniques.

In this chapter, we will learn more about the core parts of CloudFormation templates, and we will do so by building a three-tier application consisting of a web tier (our customer-facing frontend), a middleware tier (processing commands coming from the frontend), and a storage tier (the database where we will store records).

Figure 2.1 – Application architecture

Don't worry! We're not going to write any software yet (only templates for CloudFormation). For now, we will focus on provisioning our infrastructure.

We will cover the following topics in this chapter:

- Going through the internals of the template
- Creating reusable templates
- Using conditional elements
- Deletion policies
- Referring to existing stacks
- AWS pseudo parameters
- Dynamic references with AWS Systems Manager Parameter Store and Secrets Manager
- Using CloudFormation language extensions

Technical requirements

The code used in this chapter can be found in the book's GitHub repository at `https://github.com/PacktPublishing/Mastering-AWS-CloudFormation-Second-Edition/tree/main/Chapter02`.

Going through the internals of the template

The template is the main building block of CloudFormation. We can consider the template as a declarative instruction for CloudFormation—for example, what to create and how many.

The template file, whether in JSON or YAML format, consists of several elements, which we will describe in the rest of this section.

AWSTemplateFormatVersion

The `AWSTemplateFormatVersion` section is responsible for instructing CloudFormation as to what version of the template we are going to supply it with.

Not to be confused with the API version of CloudFormation, `AWSTemplateFormatVersion` is about the structure of the template.

When AWS has added this block to resolve potential breaking changes to CloudFormation, it can only have one value: `"2010-09-09"`. This version is there from the very beginning of CloudFormation, but there is always a chance that AWS will add newer versions for template formatting. Until then, this section is optional, and if it is not provided, CloudFormation will assume that your template has the default format version mentioned previously.

Description

The `Description` section is optional and serves only one purpose—to explain what your template is and what it is going to create if you push it to CloudFormation. It doesn't allow you to refer to parameters and supports single-line or multiline values.

Your description can be like this:

```
Description: Core network template consisting of VPC, IGW,
RouteTables, and Subnets
```

It can also be multiline, like this:

```
Description: >
Core network template. Consists of:
- VPC
- IGW
- Subnets
- RouteTables
```

There are no specific rules, but keep in mind that, unlike comments in your template, the description is also seen in CloudFormation services if you access it via the API, AWS CLI, or the AWS Console.

All in all, the best practice for the description is to store useful information for CloudFormation users.

Metadata

While the metadata section might not seem useful, it adds additional configuration capabilities.

You can use metadata in conjunction with CloudFormation-specific resources, such as the following:

- `AWS::CloudFormation::Init`
- `AWS::CloudFormation::Interface`
- `AWS::CloudFormation::Designer`

We will cover these in more detail later.

Parameters

One of the most important – yet optional – sections, `Parameters`, allows us to make our template customizable. Think of parameters as variables for your stack: CIDR ranges for your VPC and subnets, instance types for your EC2 and RDS instances, and so on.

The use of parameters differs in different cases. One of the most popular ways of using parameters is to allow the creation of different stacks without changing the template resources.

For example, look at the following code:

```
Parameters:
  InstanceType:
    Type: String
Resources:
  Ec2Instance:
    Type: AWS::EC2::Instance
    Properties:
    # …
      InstanceType: !Ref InstanceType
    # …
```

In this case, you define `InstanceType` for your EC2 separately from the actual template, meaning that you can choose different types for different environments (development, testing, production) or other cases.

It is important to know that parameters have the following properties: `Default`, `AllowedValues`, and `AllowedPattern`.

These properties are not mandatory, but it is best practice to use them.

For example, say that you want to specify the `Environment` tag as a parameter and have the environments `dev`, `test`, and `prod`. You will likely want to prevent the template user from having to specify the tag that should not be there (such as `foo` or `bar`). For this, you will want to use `AllowedValues`:

```
Parameters:
  Environment:
    Type: String
    AllowedValues: ["dev", "test", "prod"]
```

`AllowedPattern` should be used when you want to match your parameter within a specific regular expression. For a case when you need to supply an IP address or a CIDR range, you want to make sure that you pass exactly the following:

```
Parameters:
  SubnetCidr:
    Type: String
    AllowedPattern: '(\d{1,3})\.){3}\d{1,3}/\d{1,2})'
```

> **Important note**
> You have to make sure that you follow the Java regular expression syntax!

`Default` is a property that helps you to ensure that your parameter always has a value. By design, when you try to create a stack and don't specify a parameter value, the validation of the template (in the pre-creation step) will fail.

In this example, we pass a Docker Image tag as a parameter for the **ECS Task Definition – Container Definition**. To make sure there is an image, we set the default value to `latest` in any case:

```
Parameters:
  DockerImageVersion:
    Type: String
    Default: latest
```

On the other hand, sometimes you need to double-check that the template user always knows what they are doing, so it is up to you as a template developer to decide whether you want to have the default values.

Needless to say, parameters have types, such as strings, for the naming of properties, integers, for defining amounts and sizes, arrays, and so on. The list of types is available on the CloudFormation documentation page at `https://docs.aws.amazon.com/AWSCloudFormation/latest/UserGuide/parameters-section-structure.html`.

One of the most frequently used types is `String` because most of the property values of `Resources` require this data type.

AWS-specific parameter types

It is handy to use AWS-specific parameter types such as `AWS::EC2::AvailabilityZone::Name`, `AWS::EC2::Image::Id`, `AWS::EC2::Instance::Id`, `AWS::EC2::KeyPair::KeyName`, and `AWS::EC2::VPC::Id`. The benefit here is that CloudFormation will check whether the value supplied to this specific parameter type is valid for this kind of resource during validation.

For example, if you want to specify the subnet ID as a parameter, you will have to write a correct regular expression for it, while `AWS::EC2::Subnet::Id` already has this check built in.

In addition to assigning parameters directly, we can refer to parameters via SSM Parameter Store parameters. For example, we can refer to a public parameter from AWS to identify the latest Amazon Linux AMI:

```
Parameters:
  ImageId:
    Type: AWS::SSM::Parameter::Value<AWS::EC2::Image::Id>
    Default: "/aws/service/ami-amazon-linux-latest/amzn2-ami-hvm-
x86_64-gp2"
```

In the preceding code, we tell CloudFormation to pick the parameter that holds an AMI type.

Mappings

We can treat mappings the same way as parameters. The only difference is that they are provided in a dictionary format.

> **Mapping intrinsic functions**
>
> Unlike parameters, whose values are obtained with `Fn::Ref`, values for mappings can be referenced using the `Fn::FindInMap` function.

The most common usage for mappings is when you want to specify the AMI ID for different regions:

```
Mappings:
  RegionMap:
    us-east-1:
      HVM64: «ami-0ff8a91507f77f867»
      HVMG2: «ami-0a584ac55a7631c0c»
    us-west-1:
      HVM64: «ami-0bdb828fd58c52235»
      HVMG2: «ami-066ee5fd4a9ef77f1»
    eu-west-1:
      HVM64: «ami-047bb4163c506cd98»
      HVMG2: «ami-0a7c483d527806435»
Resources:
  Ec2Instance:
    Type: «AWS::EC2::Instance"
    Properties:
      ImageId: !FindInMap [RegionMap, !Ref "AWS::Region", HVM64]
```

Maintaining mappings can be troublesome, especially for frequently updated items like AMI IDs. Mappings' power is unleashed when we use them to store **constant** values that are rarely changed.

Conditions

Conditions are similar to parameters, but their value is `true` or `false`. Conditions have their own block in the template; we refer to them in the resource declaration and its attributes.

> **Important note**
>
> Note that `Conditions` in a declaration cannot be set to `true` or `false` manually. The Boolean value is obtained only from a result of intrinsic functions, such as `Fn::Equals`, `Fn::If`, `Fn::Not`, `Fn::And`, and `Fn::Or`!

For example, look at the following code:

```
---
AWSTemplateFormatVersion: '2010-09-09'
Parameters:
  Env:
    Default: «dev»
    Description: «Define the environment (dev, test, or prod)"
    Type: String
    AllowedValues: ["dev", "test", "prod"]
Conditions:
  IsProd: !Equals [!Ref Env, 'prod']
Resources:
  Bucket:
    Type: «AWS::S3::Bucket"
    Condition: IsProd
```

In this case, we have to manually provide the Env parameter, which must be equal to prod; otherwise, the resource will *not* be created.

Conditions work along with specific Boolean intrinsic functions, but those functions also work outside of the conditional block. We will cover these in greater detail when we start the development of our template.

Transform

The Transform block is declared when we want to run CloudFormation-specific macros in our template. At the end of this chapter, we will make use of a macro called LanguageExtensions (https://docs.aws.amazon.com/AWSCloudFormation/latest/UserGuide/transform-aws-languageextensions.html), newly developed by AWS.

All in all, this is a deep topic that we will cover the rest of in the last part of this book, *Extending CloudFormation*.

Resources

This is the main and only required block in the template file. As indicated by its name, the Resources section provides resources that we want to provision.

The resources that we create can vary. Some think that any AWS resource can be created by CloudFormation, but there are multiple services (such as AWS Organizations, Control Tower, and many others) that do not support CloudFormation.

Before starting to create the stack, you must first review the resource and property reference in the CloudFormation documentation to make sure that the services you want to use are supported by CloudFormation. For more information, go to https://docs.aws.amazon.com/ AWSCloudFormation/latest/UserGuide/aws-template-resource-type-ref. html.

Resources have multiple attributes, listed as follows:

- Type: The type of the resource (instance, subnet, DynamoDB table, lambda function, and so on).

- Properties: The configuration of the resource.

- DependsOn: Used for adding indirect dependencies.

- CreationPolicy: Used for notifying CloudFormation to wait for the signal of completion (we will cover this when we create Auto Scaling groups).

- DeletionPolicy: Used to instruct CloudFormation what to do with the resource when we delete it from the stack (or with the stack)—for example, from the *state*. This is used for important resources, such as storage backends.

- UpdatePolicy: Used to instruct CloudFormation on handling indirect updates of Auto Scaling groups, ElastiCache replication groups, and Lambda function aliases.

- UpdateReplacePolicy: Similar to DeletionPolicy, UpdateReplacePolicy is used to manage leftover resources when they have to be replaced with a new one. It works within the same logical resource and default policy as Delete.

Outputs

Outputs are the resource identifiers and attributes that we *export* after stack creation.

The outputs do not bring many benefits on their own, but in the previous chapter, we used outputs to automatically get the ARN of the IAM role we created.

For example, we can retrieve the API key and secret for an IAM user when we create it and supply our end users with it:

```
Resources:
  Bob:
    Type: AWS::IAM::User
    Properties:
      UserName: "Bob"
  BobApiKey:
    Type: AWS::IAM::AccessKey
    Properties:
      UserName: !Ref Bob
Outputs:
```

```
BobKey:
  Value: !Ref BobApiKey
BobSecret:
  Value: !GetAttBobApiKey.SecretAccessKey
```

As you can see, we retrieved Bob's API key and secret and exposed it to the outputs.

Important note

Note that outputs are accessible to anyone who is authorized to read the stacks' description, so exposing security credentials is a risky operation. In case you need to use outputs for that, make sure that only authorized users will have access to your stacks, even if they are read-only.

Outputs also have a powerful feature called **exports**. Exports allow the template developer to refer to the existing resources created in another stack. Using exports is best practice for large workloads where you often have a shared stack (resources used by many applications) and application-specific stacks.

Now, let's start developing our template. Before proceeding, make sure that you understand all the preceding sections because we will rely on them heavily in the coming sections.

Creating reusable templates

We already know that we are going to deploy a three-tier application, but we're going to have more than three stacks.

The first stack we will create is our core stack.

This stack will consist of the following:

- Network (VPC, subnets, and so on)
- IAM (roles and users)

We will have two environments for our application: **test** and **production**. These environments will differ in terms of size, the amount of resources, and security settings.

The code of our templates is going to be huge, so you will only see blocks that are specific to the topic; the entire source code can be found in Packt's repository.

Before we start, let's think about how we are going to organize the template and its parameters. Since we are going to reuse the same template for two different stacks (production and test), we will need to separate the network ranges and use different naming conventions.

In terms of network, our stack will have the following resources:

- 1 VPC
- 3 public subnets
- 3 WebTier subnets
- 3 middleware subnets
- 3 database subnets
- 1 internet gateway
- 1 NAT gateway
- 1 public route table
- 1 private route table
- 2 IAM roles (for administrators and developers)

These resources will have tags such as Name and Env.

In this case, we want to parametrize the properties for our resources, such as CIDR ranges and tags, so we will have the following parameters:

- VPC CIDR range
- Public subnet 1 CIDR range
- Public subnet 2 CIDR range
- Public subnet 3 CIDR range
- WebTier subnet 1 CIDR range
- WebTier subnet 2 CIDR range
- WebTier subnet 3 CIDR range
- Middleware subnet 1 CIDR range
- Middleware subnet 2 CIDR range
- Middleware subnet 3 CIDR range
- Database subnet 1 CIDR range
- Database subnet 2 CIDR range
- Database subnet 3 CIDR range
- Environment

All these parameters will have the type `String`. Let's write our `Parameters` section:

```
Parameters:
  VpcCidr:
    Type: String
    AllowedPattern: '(\d{1,3})\.){3}\d{1,3}/\d{1,2})'
  PublicSubnetCidr1:
    Type: String
    AllowedPattern: '(\d{1,3})\.){3}\d{1,3}/\d{1,2})'
  PublicSubnetCidr2:
    Type: String
    AllowedPattern: '(\d{1,3})\.){3}\d{1,3}/\d{1,2})'
  PublicSubnetCidr3:
    Type: String
    AllowedPattern: '(\d{1,3})\.){3}\d{1,3}/\d{1,2})'
# And so on...
  DatabaseSubnetCidr1:
    Type: String
    AllowedPattern: '(\d{1,3})\.){3}\d{1,3}/\d{1,2})'
  DatabaseSubnetCidr2:
    Type: String
    AllowedPattern: '(\d{1,3})\.){3}\d{1,3}/\d{1,2})'
  DatabaseSubnetCidr3:
    Type: String
    AllowedPattern: '(\d{1,3})\.){3}\d{1,3}/\d{1,2})'
  Environment:
    Type: String
    AllowedValues: ["prod", "test"]
```

This is it for our core stack. Now, in our resources, we will use `Fn::Ref` to inject the parameter value in the resource property. We will also use another intrinsic function, `Fn::Sub`, to concatenate a nice string name for our VPC:

```
Resources:
  Vpc:
    Type: "AWS::EC2::VPC"
    Properties:
      CidrBlock: !Ref "VpcCidr"
      EnableDnsHostnames: True
      EnableDnsSupport: True
      InstanceTenancy: Default
      Tags:
        - Key: "Name"
          Value: !Sub "${Environment}-vpc"
```

```
        - Key: «Env»
          Value: !Ref "Environment
```

A similar pattern will be used for the remaining resources.

> **Important note**
> The Fn::Ref function can also be used to refer to certain attributes from one resource in the stack to another. In this case, we supply Fn::Ref with the logical name of the resource instead of the parameter.

In the following example, we use Fn::Ref to refer to VpcId with the subnet we will create next:

```
PublicSubnet1:
   Type: «AWS::EC2::Subnet"
   Properties:
      CidrBlock: !Ref PublicSubnetCidr1
      VpcId: !Ref Vpc
```

Note that I didn't specify the default values for parameters in the template file. In this case, I'm forced to provide them within the create-stack command; otherwise, the validation will not pass.

There are two ways to supply CloudFormation with parameters: as a JSON file or as a positional argument.

For large templates with plenty of parameters, you are advised to use JSON files:

```
[
  {
    «ParameterKey": "...",
    «ParameterValue": "..."
  }
]
```

In our case, it will look like the following:

```
// testing.json
[
  {
    «ParameterKey": "Environment",
    «ParameterValue": "Testing"
  },
  {
    «ParameterKey": "VpcCidr",
    «ParameterValue": "10.0.0.0/16"
  },
```

```
{
    «ParameterKey": "PublicSubnetCidr1",
    «ParameterValue": "10.0.1.0/24"
},
{
    «ParameterKey": "PublicSubnetCidr2",
    «ParameterValue": "10.0.2.0/24"
},
// And so on...
]
```

When we create a template, we specify the parameter file in the argument:

```
$ aws cloudformation create-stack \
                    --stack-name core \
                    --template-body file://core.yaml \
                    --parameters file://testing.json
```

In the case that we have default values and want to make a few changes, we can specify the parameters one by one as positional arguments:

```
$ aws cloudformation create-stack \
                    --stack-name core \
                    --template-body file://core.yaml \
                    --parameters \
ParameterKey="Environment",ParameterValue="Testing" ParameterKey
="VpcCid",ParameterValue="10.0.0.0/16"
```

This is suitable if we have a few parameters but is too complex for a large set of parameters.

> **Important note**
> Parameters are provided as a list, and elements are split by spaces. Pay attention to the `List` type parameters, where you will have to use double backslashes:
>
> `ParameterKey=List,ParameterValue=Element1\\,Element2`

Let's make a small change to our parameters. Since we have multiple CIDR ranges for each subnet per tier, let's use `List` parameters instead of `String`:

```
Parameters:
  VpcCidr:
    Type: String
    AllowedPattern: '(\d{1,3})\.){3}\d{1,3}/\d{1,2})'
  PublicSubnetCidrs:
    Type: List<String>
```

```
    AllowedPattern: '(\d{1,3})\.){3}\d{1,3}/\d{1,2})'
# and so on...
  MiddlewareSubnetCidrs:
    Type: List<String>
    AllowedPattern: '(\d{1,3})\.){3}\d{1,3}/\d{1,2})'
  DatabaseSubnetCidrs:
    Type: List<String>
    AllowedPattern: '(\d{1,3})\.){3}\d{1,3}/\d{1,2})'
  Environment:
    Type: String
    AllowedValues: ["prod", "test"]
```

Since we're using lists, we cannot use `Fn::Ref` anymore (technically, we can, but we would pass the whole list). Instead, we will use `Fn::Select`:

```
PublicSubnet1:
  Type: «AWS::EC2::Subnet"
  Properties:
  CidrBlock: !Select [0, PublicSubnetCidrs"]
  VpcId: !Ref Vpc
PublicSubnet2:
  Type: «AWS::EC2::Subnet"
  Properties:
  CidrBlock: !Select [1, PublicSubnetCidrs]
  VpcId: !Ref Vpc
PublicSubnet3:
  Type: «AWS::EC2::Subnet"
  Properties:
  CidrBlock: !Select [2, PublicSubnetCidrs]
  VpcId: !Ref Vpc
```

We can still use `AllowedPattern`, thereby making sure that we use the correct variables. Now, we need to change our parameters file a bit:

```
{
    «ParameterKey": "PublicSubnetCidr1",
    «ParameterValue": [
      «10.0.1.0/24»,
      «10.0.2.0/24»,
      «10.0.3.0/24»
    ]
}
```

Looks much better now, right?

On the other hand, it might be tricky and too much effort to specify CIDR ranges one by one, especially when you have lots of subnets. For subnet ranges specifically, we can use an intrinsic function called `Fn::Cidr`.

The `Fn::Cidr` function is used to break bigger subnet ranges into smaller ones. This might sound a bit hard at the beginning, but if you understand how to calculate subnet masks, you will benefit from making your parameter file smaller while keeping the logic you need in the template.

Let's get back to our VPC. We specify the VPC CIDR range in the parameter. Our parameter file should now look like the following:

```
[
  {
    «ParameterKey": "VpcCidr",
    «ParameterValue": "10.0.0.0/16"
  }
]
```

In order to break our big subnet into smaller ones (/24), we need to provide the `Fn::Cidr` function with the following arguments:

- `ipBlock`: Our CIDR range.

- `count`: The number of CIDR ranges we want to generate.

- `cidrBits`: This will tell CFN which ranges to generate. For a /24 CIDR range, we need to specify 8.

We know that we will have nine subnets (three for each public, middleware, and database subnet), so our intrinsic function will appear as follows:

```
Fn::Cidr:
  - !RefVpcCidr
  - 9
  - 8
```

Or, in short-form syntax, it will look as follows:

```
!Cidr [ !Ref VpcCidr, 9, 8 ]
```

This function returns a list of CIDR ranges, so we need to combine it with `Fn::Select` when we declare our subnets. This is how our template will look:

```
PublicSubnet1:
  Type: «AWS::EC2::Subnet"
  Properties:
  CidrBlock: !Select [0, !Cidr [ !GetAtt VpcCidr, 9, 8 ]]
```

```
        VpcId: !Ref Vpc
    PublicSubnet2:
        Type: «AWS::EC2::Subnet"
        Properties:
        CidrBlock: !Select [1, !Cidr [ !GetAtt VpcCidr, 9, 8 ]]
        VpcId: !Ref Vpc
    PublicSubnet3:
        Type: «AWS::EC2::Subnet"
        Properties:
        CidrBlock: !Select [2, !Cidr [ !GetAtt VpcCidr, 9, 8 ]]
        VpcId: !Ref Vpc
```

Using `Fn::Cidr` will allow you to avoid specifying CIDR ranges in the parameters one by one.

> **Important note**
>
> You should be careful when using this function because it expects you to prepare and design your network really well.
>
> You will use `Fn::Cidr` each time you create a subnet, and each time, you need to make sure that the count of CIDR range blocks is the same; otherwise, you will have a subnetting issue, and your stack deployment will fail.
>
> If you are creating a network stack separately, your architecture is well designed, and you know what you are doing, then stick to using `Fn::Cidr`.

We will use parameters and intrinsic functions a lot, but let's now learn about another important feature of CloudFormation called conditions.

Using conditional elements

We want to have reusable templates, but sometimes, we need to create a resource in one case and don't need to create one in another, or perhaps we need to create one with different attributes.

Conditions are handy to solve that kind of problem. They can be used in two ways: to specify the condition under the resource or to use the conditional intrinsic function in the resource properties.

We already know that `Conditions` is a strict Boolean variable, which is evaluated by parameters and conditional functions. We have already learned how conditions are used in resource declaration (jump to the *Going through the internals of the template* section if you need a refresher), so let's look at another useful example.

Say that we have an Auto Scaling group that is built from a launch template. We expect to have a different load on test and production, so we want to adjust the size of the EC2 instance accordingly. For now, we are happy with `t3.micro` on test and `m5.large` on production.

Since we will only have two environments, we can stick to only one condition—`ProdEnv`. Why? Because, in the resource attribute, we use a condition function, `Fn::If`. We use `Fn::If` as it is quite obvious that it has three inputs: condition, value when `True`, and value when `False`. So, if it's not production, we definitely know it is a test.

Let's develop our template:

```
Parameters:
  Env:
    Type: String
    Default: test
    AllowedValues: [ "test", "prod" ]
  ImageId:
    Type: AWS::SSM::Parameter::Value<AWS::EC2::Image::Id>
    Default: /aws/service/ami-amazon-linux-latest/amzn2-  ami-hvm-
x86_64-gp2
Conditions:
  IsProd: !Equals [ !Ref Env, "prod" ]
Resources:
  WebLt:
    Type: «AWS::EC2::LaunchTemplate"
    Properties:
      LaunchTemplateName: "web"
      LaunchTemplateData:
      ImageId: !Ref ImageId
      InstanceType: !If [ IsProd, "m5.large", "t3.micro" ]
```

The long syntax format for the last line would look like this:

```
InstanceType:
  Fn::If:
    - IsProd
    - «m5.large"
    - «t3.micro"
```

The `Fn::If` function also supports inheritance. If we had three environments (test, staging, and production), then we would need to have different instance types on those environments, and we would need extra conditions and a slightly longer condition function:

```
Conditions:
  IsProd: !Equals [ !Ref Env, "prod" ]
  IsStaging: !Equals [!Ref Env, "stage" ]
Resources:
  WebLt:
    Type: AWS::EC2::LaunchTemplate
```

```
    Properties:
      LaunchTemplateName: web
      LaunchTemplateData:
        ImageId: !Ref ImageId
        InstanceType: !If [ IsProd, "m5.large", !If [ IsStaging, "t3.
  large", "t3.micro "] ]
```

Conditions have various use cases; most of them show up when you start building a big infrastructure on AWS. While you will often find conditions handy, keep in mind the limitations and usage examples from this book.

Let's now move on to another important topic—deletion policies.

Deletion policies

When we create our stack, we need to make sure that mission-critical resources are protected from accidental deletion.

In some cases, this is enabled by `EnableTerminationProtection` for services such as EC2 and RDS. S3 buckets, when filled with objects, will fail to delete because they have to be emptied first.

Deletion policies allow you to mitigate this risk within CloudFormation. In addition, deletion policies give you a few more features in addition to basic termination protection.

For example, say that you have created a testing stack that you don't need once the testing phase is finished, but you need the dump of the database (which is actually a snapshot of the RDS instance). Sometimes, you don't want to recreate the same data structure, or the database already has important data that you want to move to the production environment.

Let's see whether deletion policies can help us:

```
  Resources:
    VeryImportantDb:
      Type: «AWS::RDS::Instance"
      DeletionPolicy: Snapshot
      Properties:
        # Here, you set properties for your RDS instance.
```

When we remove this resource from the template or delete the stack, CloudFormation will signal RDS to take a final snapshot of the instance and then delete it.

> **Important note**
>
> The deletion policy snapshot is not available for every single resource. At the time of writing, the supported resources are `AWS::EC2::Volume`, `AWS::ElastiCache::CacheCluster`, `AWS::ElastiCache::ReplicationGroup`, `AWS::Neptune::DBCluster`, `AWS::RDS::DBCluster`, `AWS::RDS::DBInstance`, and `AWS::Redshift::Cluster`.
>
> Bear that in mind when you design your infrastructure. To keep yourself up to date, refer to this part of the CloudFormation documentation: `https://docs.aws.amazon.com/AWSCloudFormation/latest/UserGuide/aws-attribute-deletionpolicy.html#aws-attribute-deletionpolicy-options`.

Another situation is when we want to retain some of the resources when we delete the stack. Here, we use the deletion policy called `Retain`:

```
Resources:
  EvenMoreImportantDb:
    Type: «AWS::RDS::Instance"
    DeletionPolicy: Retain
    Properties:
      # Here, you set properties for your RDS instance.
```

In case of deletion, what will happen is that this DB instance will be removed from CloudFormation's state, but the resource itself will stay in our account.

Another deletion policy is, obviously, `Delete`, which is a default policy for all the resources in the template. If we do not specify any deletion policy for the resource, it will be deleted from the stack or with the stack.

Fortunately, deletion policies can be combined with conditions. What do we need to do if we want different deletion policies for different conditions?

Well, this will require us to use Language Extensions, which we briefly covered in the previous section about `Transform`!

We will add a `Transform` section at the beginning of our template:

```
// database.yaml
AWSTemplateFormatVersion: "2010-09-09"
Transform: AWS::LanguageExtensions
Description: Database template
Parameters:
  Environment:
    Type: String
    AllowedValued: [ "dev", "test", "prod" ]
    Default: «dev»
Conditions:
```

```
    ProdEnv: !Equals [ !Ref Environment, "prod" ]
    TestEnv: !Equals [ !Ref Environment, "test" ]
    DevEnv: !Equals [ !Ref Environment, "dev" ]
```

Then, our `Resources` section will look like the following:

```
Resources:
  Database:
    DeletionPolicy: !If [ProdEnv, "Retain", "Delete"]
    Type: "AWS::RDS::DBCluster"
    Properties:
       # Properties for production database
```

This does not introduce extra complexity for our template and still makes it universal!

Protecting your data is important, so always make sure that you use deletion policies for storage services, such as databases, and storage backends, such as S3 buckets or EBS volumes.

Now that we know how to mitigate the risk of data loss let's move on to the next topic.

Referring to existing stacks

In large environments with shared responsibility models, where different teams manage their own stack resources, we sometimes have a situation where resources or resource attributes (RDS instance endpoints, for example) have to be shared between different stacks.

Remember that we have a network stack in our application. Resources from this stack, such as subnets, are used in the application templates.

Whenever you deploy a virtual machine, an Auto Scaling group, a load balancer, or a database cluster, you need to specify the subnet ID. We can specify that subnet ID as a parameter and then use `Fn::Ref` to map it in the resource attribute, but that will require a lot of unnecessary actions that can be avoided by using exports and `Fn::ImportValue`.

In *Chapter 1, Working with CloudFormation*, we used outputs to obtain the ARN of the IAM role, which we used in the AWS command line.

Outputs are handy for quickly accessing the attributes of created resources, but they can also be transformed into exports.

Exports are the aliases for the physical resource IDs. Each `Export` name must be unique within a region for a single account.

This means that when we want to refer to the resource attribute created in another stack, we need to create an output record with the `Export` name. Once this is done and the stack is created, we can then refer to it using an intrinsic function called `Fn::ImportValue`.

The Fn::ImportValue function will look up the necessary attribute in the CloudFormation exported values across the whole account within a region and write a necessary entry to the resource attribute.

If this sounds a bit complicated, let's look at how this works in an example. Here, we create subnets in our core stack, and we need to use their IDs in our WebTier (and other) stacks. This is what our core template will look like:

```
// core.yaml
Parameters:
# ...
Resources:
  Vpc:
    Type: «AWS::EC2::VPC"
    Properties:
      # ...
  PublicSubnet1:
    Type: «AWS::EC2::Subnet"
    Properties:
      # ...
# The rest of our resources...
```

The Outputs section is as follows:

```
Outputs:
  VpcId:
    Value: !Ref Vpc
    Export:
      Name: Vpc
  PublicSubnet1Id:
    Value: !Ref PublicSubnet1
    Export:
      Name: PublicSubnet1Id
  PublicSubnet2Id:
    Value: !Ref PublicSubnet2
    Export:
      Name: PublicSubnet2Id
  PublicSubnet3Id
    Value: !Ref PublicSubnet3
    Export:
      Name: PublicSubnet3Id
  # And so on
```

Here is how we refer to exported values from the core stack:

```
// webtier.yaml
Resources:
  WebTierAsg:
    Type: «AWS::AutoScaling::AutoScalingGroup"
    Properties:
      # Some properties...
      VpcZoneIdentifier:
        - !ImportValue PublicSubnet1Id
        - !ImportValue PublicSubnet2Id
        - !ImportValue PublicSubnet3Id
    # And so on...
```

You've noticed that I'm doing extra work here by creating additional exports and importing those values one by one.

Sometimes, you need to import single attributes, such as a shared secret or an IAM role for ECS task execution, but for listed items, such as subnets or Availability Zones, it is wise to combine them into lists and refer to them as lists.

Let's refactor the preceding example into a simpler structure:

```
// core.yaml
Outputs:
  PublicSubnetIds:
    Value: !Join [ ",", [ !Ref PublicSubnet1, !Ref PublicSubnet2, !Ref
PublicSubnet3] ]
    Export:
      Name: PublicSubnetIds
```

What we do here is make a comma-separated string with our subnet IDs and then use `Fn::Split` to turn this long string into a list. Since there is no intrinsic function to generate a list of elements, we have to use this workaround.

Now, we can import this value in a shorter form:

```
// webtier.yaml
Resources:
  WebTierAsg:
    Type: AWS::AutoScaling::AutoScalingGroup
    Properties:
      # Some properties
      VpcZoneIdentifier: !Split [ ",", !ImportValue PublicSubnetIds ]
```

Since we already pass a list of values, CloudFormation will parse it properly and create the instance's Auto Scaling group the way we need it.

Outputs/exports also support conditional functions. If we have a conditional resource (such as a hardcoded secret in one case and a generated secret in another), we can create a single export using a condition.

> **Important note**
> Note that `Outputs` does not have the `Condition` property, like resources. We have to use conditional functions in order to use the correct value for exports.

For example, to export correct database credentials (as we store them in different `SecretsManager` resources), we can use `Fn::If` to select the correct value:

```
// database.yaml
Outputs:
  DbCredentials:
    Value: !If [ProdEnv, GeneratedDatabaseSecret,
HardcodedDatabaseSecret]
    Export:
      Name: DbCredentials
```

This is one of the cases when a short syntax form makes our template almost unreadable, so let's write it in a standard syntax form:

```
Outputs:
  DbEndpoint:
    Value:
      Fn::If:
        - ProdEnv
        - GeneratedDatabaseSecret
        - HardcodedDatabaseSecret
    Export:
      Name: DbCredentials
```

Looks much more clear, right? However, it is up to you to decide which syntax form (long or short) to choose when you declare complex conditional checks. Just don't forget that you write the code not only for the machine (CloudFormation, in our case) but also for your fellow colleagues.

Now, let's move on to the next important topic, which is AWS pseudo parameters.

AWS pseudo parameters

What makes these parameters special? Well, the fact that they are obtained from AWS itself.

The current list of these parameters is as follows:

- AWS::AccountId

- AWS::NotificationARNs

- AWS::NoValue

- AWS::Region

- AWS::StackId

- AWS::StackName

- AWS::URLSuffix

- AWS::Partition

We're not going to cover all of them, only the most widely used ones.

AWS::AccountId

One of the use cases where we need to use AccountId is when we are using an IAM principal.

If you are familiar with IAM, then you know that we can set the AWS account ID as a principal element. If you need to refresh your memory regarding IAM, you can read a great blog series at https://medium.com/@thomas.storm/aws-iam-deep-dive-chapter-1-essentials-a9cfb1931a01.

At the same time, it is a security risk to expose an AWS account ID in public; for production environments, we should stick to using AWS pseudo parameters when we specify this kind of data.

An example usage of AWS::AccountId is as follows:

```
Resources:
  MyIamRole:
    Type: «AWS::IAM::Role"
    Properties:
      AssumeRolePolicyDocument:
        Version: 2012-10-17
        Statement:
          - Effect: «Allow"
            Action:
              - «sts:AssumeRole"
            Principal:
              AWS: !Ref AWS::AccountId
            Sid: «AllowRoleAssume"
      # The rest of the IAM role properties...
```

As with any other parameter, pseudo-parameters can be used in conjunction with intrinsic functions. The following is an example (you probably remember it from *Chapter 1, Working with CloudFormation*) where we specify all users within an account in `Principal`:

```
MyIamRole:
  Type: «AWS::IAM::Role"
  Properties:
    AssumeRolePolicyDocument:
      Version: 2012-10-17
      Statement:
        - Sid: «AllowAssumeRole"
          Effect: «Allow»
          Principal:
            AWS: !Sub arn:aws:iam::${AWS::AccountId}:user/${aws.
username}"
          Action: «sts:AssumeRole"
```

Note the `${aws.username}` variable. This variable is not a part of CloudFormation but a part of IAM policy variables.

When we initiate stack deployment, CloudFormation will replace the pseudo parameter with an actual value. For `AWS::AccountId`, the value will be the account where the stack is being created.

AWS::NoValue

The `AWS::NoValue` phrase is an equivalent of the *null* value. There is not much practical usage for it unless you want to combine it with conditional functions. It is important to know that if you supply your resource property with `AWS::NoValue`, it will act as if you hadn't specified this property at all.

One use case of this would be using it to create a database from a snapshot or from scratch:

```
Resources:
  MyDB:
    Type: «AWS::RDS::DBInstance"
    Properties:
      AllocatedStorage: "5"
      DBInstanceClass: "db.t3.micro"
      Engine: MySQL
      EngineVersion: "5.7"
      DBSnapshotIdentifier:
        Fn::If:
          - UseDBSnapshot
          - !Ref DBSnapshotName
          - !Ref AWS::NoValue
```

In the last few lines, we can see that if the condition is not met, then the DBSnapshotIdentifier property will not be used.

AWS::Region

Some resources require you to specify the AWS region. Hardcoding the region might not be a security issue, but will cause us trouble when we deploy the same stack in different regions. It is a best practice to use this pseudo parameter, no matter if your infrastructure may scale to multi-region deployment.

For example, when we create an ECS task definition and want to use CloudWatch logs as a log driver, we need to specify a log group and AWS region:

```
Resources:
  EcsTaskDefinition:
    Type: «AWS::ECS::TaskDefinition"
    Properties:
      # Some properties...
    ContainerDefinition:
      - Name: «mycontainer"
        # Some container properties...
        LogConfiguration:
          LogDriver: "awslogs"
          Options:
            awslogs-group: "myloggroup"
            awslogs-region: !Ref AWS::Region
            awslogs-stream-prefix: ""
```

When this stack is created, CloudFormation will create a CloudWatch log group in the stack region.

AWS::StackId and AWS::StackName

The AWS::StackId and AWS::StackName pseudo parameters are handy when you need to specify tags for your resources. An example usage is giving an application name to the name of the stack and reusing it in Tags:

```
Resources:
  SomeResource:
    Type: # any, that supports tags
    Properties:
      # Some properties..
      Tags:
        - Key: «Application»
          Value: !Ref AWS::StackName
```

Referring to `AWS::StackName` in the `Tags` value will indicate the CloudFormation stack that this resource belongs to.

AWS::URLSuffix

The `AWS::URLSuffix` pseudo parameter is used for specifying AWS service URLs. For you, it's likely going to be `amazonaws.com`, but if you plan to deploy your application to a special region, such as China or AWS GovCloud, you will have to use their own URL suffixes.

You need a URL suffix for services such as IAM roles if the role has to be assumed by AWS—for instance, ECS's task execution role:

```
Resources:
  EcsTaskExecutionRole:
    Type: AWS::IAM::Role
    Properties:
      AssumeRolePolicyDocument:
        Version: 2012-10-17
        Statement:
          - Sid: «AllowAssumeRole"
            Effect: Allow
            Principal:
              Service: !Sub "ecs-tasks.${AWS::URLSuffix}"
            Action: «sts:AssumeRole"
      # Some role properties...
```

Using pseudo parameters will make your template recyclable and flexible. If you have to deploy your application in another region or even account, the amount of refactoring will be minimal.

AWS::Partition

When we define an ARN ourselves, we often write it in the following manner: `arn:aws:service:region:account_id:...`

The word `aws` here refers to a partition – which we understand as a namespace. In most cases, you will see `aws`, but you want to know that there are other partitions as well. For example, regions in China have the partition `aws-cn`, and GovCloud regions have the partition `aws-us-gov`.

This said, let's continue with another important topic – dynamic referencing in templates.

Let's move on to the last bit of this chapter, which is about using dynamic references for your stacks with AWS SSM Parameter Store and AWS Secrets Manager.

Dynamic references with Parameter Store and Secrets Manager

At the beginning of this chapter, we looked at working with static parameters either in JSON or command-line argument form.

Although it is a known practice in infrastructure-as-code to keep parameters in a **Version Control System** (**VCS**), it introduces additional complexity.

If we store parameters in a VCS, we need to take care of encrypting sensitive data, such as passwords or other credentials. If we pass them via command-line arguments, we have to make sure we don't make a mistake or a typo (which is a common occurrence in the life of IT engineers).

To solve these issues, we can store template parameters in the SSM Parameter Store or Secrets Manager (for passwords).

They both support versioning, so we can always revert the parameters to the previous version if there was a mistake and then redeploy our stack.

Another benefit of using the Parameter Store and Secrets Manager is that we can provide developers who are not responsible for CloudFormation development with the ability to apply slight changes to the stack, such as changing the instance type or increasing the size of the Auto Scaling group.

What we are going to do now is append our core template with a few parameters for our application templates:

```
// core.yaml
Resources:
# Some resources...
  WebAsgMinSize:
    Type: «AWS::SSM::Parameter"
    Properties:
      Type: String
      Value: «1»
  WebAsgMaxSize:
    Type: «AWS::SSM::Parameter"
    Properties:
      Type: String
      Value: «1»
  WebAsgDesiredSize:
    Type: «AWS::SSM::Parameter"
    Properties:
      Type: String
      Value: «1»
# The rest...
```

Then, we will add SSM parameters to the outputs:

```
Outputs:
# Original outputs...
  WebAsgMinSize:
    Value: !Ref WebAsgMinSize
    Export:
      Name: WebAsgMinSize
  WebAsgMaxSize:
    Value: !Ref WebAsgMaxSize
    Export:
      Name: WebAsgMaxSize
  WebAsgDesiredSize:
    Value: !Ref WebAsgDesiredSize
    Export:
      Name: WebAsgDesiredSize
```

We created three parameters for the web tier stack to use. Now, we need to refer to those parameters in the web tier template. There are two ways we can do this:

- Refer to them from the parameters
- Refer to them from the resource declaration

You will recall that we used AWS-specific parameters in the `Parameters` section when we were creating our WebTier template (look at the *Using conditional elements* section if you need a refresher).

While the use of this is relatively obvious and simple, this will require us first to create a core stack and then copy and paste the SSM Parameter Store parameter's name to the `Parameters` section in the template.

To reduce the number of manual actions, it is wise to *resolve* the parameter right in the resource declaration.

This is how it works: once the parameter is created and you have its name, you can pass it to a resource property by using Jinja formatting: `"{{resolve:service-name:reference-key}}"`.

We can use the SSM parameter name or ARN.

For our case, we export the parameter's ARN. Let's now resolve it in the web tier `Auto Scaling` group resource:

```
// webtier.yaml
Resources:
# WebTier resources...
  WebTierAsg:
    Type: AWS::AutoScaling::AutoScalingGroup
    Properties:
```

```
        # Properties of ASG...
     DesiredCapacity: !Sub [ "{{resolve:ssm:${parameter}:1}}",
parameter: !ImportValue WebTierDesSizeParameter ]
      MaxSize: [ "{{resolve:ssm:${parameter}:1}}", parameter:
!ImportValue WebTierMaxSizeParameter ]
      MinSize: !Sub [ "{{resolve:ssm:${parameter}:1}}", parameter:
!ImportValue WebTierDesSizeParameter ]
```

In the preceding code, our properties refer not to the template parameters but to the values of SSM parameters.

You might wonder why we need to create an internal `Fn::Sub` inner variable called `parameter` that equals the value of the export. Well, this is because of the visibility of `Fn::Sub` – it can refer to AWS's pseudo parameters or template parameters, or resource identifiers and attributes, but not attributes exported from other stacks.

> **SSM Parameter Store limitations**
>
> At the time of writing, it is not possible to refer to the latest version of parameters in the SSM Parameter Store. If you make a change to a parameter, you will still have to change the version of it in the `resolve` block.

We can use the same method to randomly generate a DB password, so we don't have to hardcode and/or expose it:

```
// database.yaml
Resources:
  DbPwSecret:
    Type: «AWS::SecretsManager::Secret"
    Properties:
      GenerateSecretString:
      GenerateStringKey: "DbPassword"
  RdsInstance:
    Type: AWS::RDS::DBInstance
    Properties:
      # Some RDS Instance properties...
      MasterUserPassword: !Sub
"{{resolve:secretsmanager:${DbPwSecret}:SecretString: DbPassword}}"
```

Note that, unlike SSM parameters, we do not specify the secret's version but the actual key we want to refer to.

Using CloudFormation language extensions

CloudFormation templates are in YAML or JSON format, but the template itself is a DSL – domain-specific language. While we can use YAML features such as anchors and aliases, CloudFormation supercharges generic indented text with variable references with `Fn::Ref`, class attribute getters with `Fn::GetAtt`, and CIDR range generation with `Fn::Cidr` and else.

One of the unpleasant limitations is when we have to create multiple similar resources or when we need to write JSON strings in the resource properties.

While repeatability is solved with other tools such as Cloud Development Kit and Serverless Application Model, AWS keeps improving CloudFormation, and with it has recently released Language Extensions (https://aws.amazon.com/about-aws/whats-new/2022/09/aws-cloudformation-new-language-extensions-transform/).

One example usage we have already seen is the deletion policy, where we decide to retain or delete the database depending on its environment, either testing or production. Previously (and you would have seen it in the first edition of this book!), we would need to declare two of the same resources with `Condition`.

Another problem that extensions solve is the in-flight generation of JSON strings. Let's look at the example of using Secrets Manager with hardcoded data:

```
// database.yaml
Resources:
  HardcodedDatabaseSecret:
    Condition: TestEnv
    Type: "AWS::SecretsManager::Secret"
    Properties:
      Description: "Database credentials"
      # Do not do this in production!
      SecretString: '{"username":"dbuser","password":"dbpassword"}'
```

Such a setup is already uncomfortable to read and maintain. It gets even worse in JSON-formatted templates!

```
{
  "Resources": {
    "MySecret": {
      "Type": "AWS::SecretsManager::Secret",
      "Properties": {
      "SecretString": "{\"username\":\" dbuser \",\"password\":\" dbpassword \"}"
      }
    }
  }
}
```

Language extensions allow us to use `Fn::ToJsonString`, an intrinsic function that generates a JSON string from a YAML key value. Let's try it on the hardcoded secret once more:

```
// database.yaml
Resources:
  HardcodedDatabaseSecret:
    Condition: TestEnv
    Type: "AWS::SecretsManager::Secret"
    Properties:
      Description: "Database credentials"
      SecretString:
        Fn::ToJsonString:
          username: "dbuser"
          # Do not do this in production!
          password: "dbpassword"
```

While the example above is relatively simple, `Fn:: ToJsonString` is very powerful and can be used to convert complex objects, such as CloudWatch dashboards (`https://github.com/aws-cloudformation/cfn-language-discussion/blob/main/RFCs/0014-ToJsonString.md`).

Language extensions are under heavy development, and I personally am carefully looking at the proposals. One of my favorites is the `for` loop feature (`https://github.com/aws-cloudformation/cfn-language-discussion/pull/75`), which I have been waiting for too long!

This is not the only powerful feature that CloudFormation `Transform` provides. We will cover them in depth in *Chapter 9, Scale Your Templates Using Macros, Nested Stacks, and Modules*.

Summary

Although we didn't deploy any stacks, we went through every bit of the main building blocks of CloudFormation in this chapter.

We learned how to make our templates reusable and recyclable, how to control them using conditions, and how to protect stack resources from accidental or intentional deletion. We also covered dynamic parameter referencing, which we will use more and more toward the end of this book.

Before continuing to the next chapter, make sure you have gone through the templates in the repository and understood each line.

In the next chapter, we will dive into the preflight checks and various ways of provisioning stack resources.

Questions

1. Can we use intrinsic functions in the `Conditions` attribute in a resource?

2. Can we use an intrinsic function for conditions in the resource property?

3. What is the difference between `UpdatePolicy` and `UpdateReplacePolicy`?

4. Which deletion policy should be used for a mission-critical database?

5. What is `Fn::ImportValue` used for?

6. Is it possible to create multiple exports with the same name?

7. Is there a parameter data type used specifically for AMIs?

8. What is `AWS::NoValue`? What are its use cases?

Further reading

*   Template anatomy: `https://docs.aws.amazon.com/AWSCloudFormation/latest/UserGuide/template-anatomy.html`

*   Dynamic referencing: `https://docs.aws.amazon.com/AWSCloudFormation/latest/UserGuide/dynamic-references.html`

*   Deletion policies: `https://docs.aws.amazon.com/AWSCloudFormation/latest/UserGuide/aws-attribute-deletionpolicy.html`

*   Sample templates: `https://docs.aws.amazon.com/AWSCloudFormation/latest/UserGuide/cfn-sample-templates.html`

*   Language extensions: `https://docs.aws.amazon.com/AWSCloudFormation/latest/UserGuide/transform-aws-languageextensions.html`

Part 2: Provisioning and Deployment at Scale

In this part, we are going to do a lot of practice with CloudFormation stack operations and see how we can apply DevOps practices using CloudFormation and AWS.

The following chapters will be covered in this part:

3

Validation, Linting, and Deploying the Stack

So far, we have not deployed our stacks yet. While we have learned the features of the template, this knowledge has no value if we do not provision our resources.

This chapter is about the checks we need to perform before provisioning our resources, various ways to deploy the stack, and which steps are being performed.

The following topics will be covered in this chapter:

- Validating the template
- Using a linter for best practices on templates
- Provisioning our stack
- Handling errors
- Working with drifts

Technical requirements

The code that will be used in this chapter can be found in this book's GitHub repository at `https://github.com/PacktPublishing/Mastering-AWS-CloudFormation-Second-Edition/tree/main/Chapter03`.

Check out the following video to see the Code in Action: `https://packt.link/SvQ7o`.

Validating the template

Whenever we execute `aws cloudformation create-stack` (or `update-stack`), CloudFormation will first validate the template, checking whether it is a valid JSON or YAML file (a syntax check) and whether there are any critical issues, such as circular dependencies.

Although template validation is a necessary step before stack deployment, many things will break stack deployment, even if validation succeeds:

- Missing required resource properties

- Syntax errors and typos in resource property names

- Non-existent resource property values

We could continue with this list, but let's move from theory to practice.

The command that runs template validation is straightforward:

```
$ aws cloudformation validate-template --template-body file://path_to_
your_template
```

For example, if we want to validate our core template, we need to run the following command:

```
$ aws cloudformation validate-template --template-body file://core.
yaml
```

If there is an error in the template, we will see the following output (for this example, I've changed the `PublicSubnet1` resource type to something completely non-existent – that is, `AWS::EC2::DoesNotExist`):

```
An error occurred (ValidationError) when calling the ValidateTemplate
operation: Template format error: Unrecognized resource types:
[AWS::EC2::DoesNotExist]
```

If we simulate a typo error in an intrinsic function, we will get another error (for this example, I've changed the `Fn::Select` intrinsic function to the non-existent `Fn::NoSelect` intrinsic function):

```
An error occurred (ValidationError) when calling the ValidateTemplate
operation: Template format error: YAML not well-formed. (line 31,
column 18)
```

However, if the template is valid, we will see the parameters of the template, its description, and IAM capabilities and their reasons, which shows the resource that requires it:

```
{
    «Parameters»: [
        {
            «ParameterKey": "VpcCidr",
            «NoEcho": false
        },
        {
            «ParameterKey": "Environment",
            «NoEcho": false
        }
```

```
    ],
    «Description»: «Core template. Contains network and iam roles",
    «Capabilities»: [
        «CAPABILITY_IAM»
    ],
    «CapabilitiesReason": "The following resource(s) require
capabilities: [AWS::IAM::Role]"
}
```

The validator always runs before stack deployment, but to save time and catch all the errors as early as possible, you should always consider running validation before deploying the stack and using it as a step in your CI/CD pipeline (which we will cover in the next chapter).

Now, let's look at an interesting tool called `cfn-lint`.

Using a linter for best practices on templates

Let's describe a linter again. A **linter** is a tool that is used for static source code analysis to flag obvious programming errors and bugs, as well as stylistic and non-idiomatic issues. A linter generally operates on a set of predefined rules and style guides. CloudFormation has two linters available: `cfn-lint`, a previous generation yet still maintained linter, written in Python, and `cloudformation-guard`, a policy-based linter written in Rust. In this section, we will take a look at both and find out which one serves the best for our use cases.

Evaluating templates with cfn-lint

`cfn-lint` is a command-line tool that inspects your template and compares the declared resources against a wide range of written rules.

Unlike the template validator, `cfn-lint` can detect tricky issues such as missing resource properties or arguments in an intrinsic function.

CloudFormation's linter is an external tool that can be installed using `pip`:

```
$ pip install cfn-lint
```

It will automatically appear in $PATH, so we can run it right away:

```
$ cfn-lint core.yaml
```

If the template meets all the rule requirements, we will see nothing on the output (and the *return code* of the command will be 0). However, if there is an error, the linter will notify us immediately.

For this example, I've commented out the `VpcId` property and removed the mask bits in the `Fn::Cidr` function. The `PublicSubnet2` resource looks like this:

```
PublicSubnet2:
  Type: «AWS::EC2::Subnet"
  Properties:
    # Missing argument for mask bits!!!
    # This should look like this:
    # !Select [ 1, !Cidr [ !Ref VpcCidr, 12, 8 ] ]
    CidrBlock: !Select [ 1, !Cidr [ !Ref VpcCidr, 12 ] ]
    # VpcId: !Ref Vpc  # Missing property!
    MapPublicIpOnLaunch: True
    AvailabilityZone: !Select
      - 1
      - Fn::GetAZs: !Ref "AWS::Region"
    Tags:
      - Key: ‹Name›
        Value: !Sub "${Environment}-public-subnet02"
      - Key: ‹Env›
        Value: !Ref ‹Environment›
```

This is the output of running the linter:

```
$ cfn-lint core_broken.yaml
E0002 Unknown exception while processing rule E1024: list index out of
range
core.yaml:1:1
E3003 Property VpcId missing at Resources/PublicSubnet2/Properties
core.yaml:45:5
```

The *return code* will be 1 or 2 (these are common return codes for errors in Linux systems).

> **Important note**
>
> You may have noticed that `cfn-lint` also shows which lines it found a mistake on. However, when you mess around with arguments for intrinsic functions, you will see the error on the first line, which is not the case.
>
> Also, the error is not an actual error that's pointed to by the linter. This is a Python exception.

The linter doesn't only check our templates against built-in rules – it also supports tweaking and customization.

Linting against specific regions

When you run `cfn-lint`, it will check your template against the default region (which is `us-east-1`). To check against other regions, you can specify it manually:

```
$ cfn-lint core.yaml --regions 'eu-west-1'
# or...
$ cfn-lint core.yaml --regions 'eu-west-1','us-east1'
# or even...
$ cfn-lint core.yaml --regions 'ALL_REGIONS'
```

In the previous example, you will get an even more interesting result:

```
E3001 Invalid or unsupported Type AWS::SSM::Parameter for resource
MiddlewareAsgMaxSizeParameter in us-gov-west-1
core.yaml:393:5
E3001 Invalid or unsupported Type AWS::SSM::Parameter for resource
MiddlewareAsgMaxSizeParameter in us-gov-east-1
core.yaml:393:5
E3001 Invalid or unsupported Type AWS::SSM::Parameter for resource
MiddlewareAsgMaxSizeParameter in eu-north-1
core.yaml:393:5
E3001 Invalid or unsupported Type AWS::SSM::Parameter for resource
MiddlewareAsgMaxSizeParameter in ap-east-1
core.yaml:393:5
```

This error is triggered because the regions mentioned do not support this resource type. If you plan to deploy your template to various regions, it is wise to include all or a part of them in the check, so you must make sure that the services and resources you want to provision are supported by CloudFormation.

Another way to include regions to be checked against is to add them to the template's metadata:

```
// core.yaml
Metadata:
  cfn-lint:
    regions:
      - us-east-1
      - eu-west-1
      - eu-central-1
```

Then, `cfn-lint` will automatically pick these regions when you run the check.

> **Important note**
> Note that the template's metadata values are always overridden by command-line arguments.

In some cases, we cannot comply with the linter rules by default. For example, when we use Macros transformations, that cannot be parsed by the linter. Let's see how we can make `cfn-lint` ignore specific rules so we can make it less strict.

Ignoring specific rules

If you include `cfn-lint` in your CI/CD pipeline, you will get into trouble if you mark the step as failed if the return code of the linter is not 0. If `cfn-lint` fires a warning (which is not necessarily an issue), you might want to ignore it if it does not apply to your stack.

You can ignore specific rules by supplying an `--ignore-checks` argument:

```
cfn-lint core.yaml --ignore-checks 'W2001'
```

Alternatively, you can include them in the metadata:

```
Metadata:
  cfn-lint:
    regions:
      - us-east-1
      - eu-west-1
      - eu-central-1
    ignore-checks:
      - W2001
```

Ignoring the linter rule is not recommended, so only use it for specific rules, such as non-existent services, when you lint your template against all regions.

Creating custom rules

`cfn-lint` has a rich library for checks and rules. However, your organization might have its own requirements for templates (such as necessary `Tags`) that do not come out of the box.

`cfn-lint` supports the creation of custom rules. Custom rules have to be written in the same language as `cfn-lint` (for example, Python) and need to be appended when the linter is running.

Before we add our custom rules, let's develop one! Our scenario is that we want to make sure that our RDS resources (such as DB instances and DB clusters) have `DeletionPolicy`, and that `DeletionPolicy` is *not* set to `Delete`.

Part of the job is already done: `cfn-lint` has a built-in template parser, so we only need to match specific resources and check that they have the required property.

The flow of the linter rule will be as follows:

1. The rule will check whether there are resources in the template with a type of `AWS::RDS::DBInstance` or `AWS::RDS::DBCluster`.

2. The rule will then check whether that resource has `DeletionPolicy`.

3. The rule will then check whether `DeletionPolicy` is either `Retain` or `Snapshot`.

4. If `DeletionPolicy` is *not* set or is set to `Delete`, the rule will return `Warning`.

Let's create a directory called `custom_rules` and create a Python file called `rdsdeletionpolicy.py`.

> **Important note**
>
> For `cfn-lint` to process the custom rule properly, you must make sure that your class name and the rule's filename are the same.
>
> A file `myrule.py` with `class MyRule(CloudFormationLinterRule)` in it will work.
>
> A file `my_rule.py` with `class MyRule(CloudFormationLinterRule)` in it will not work.

First, we need to come up with a rule number. `cfn-lint` has a list of category rules. The category we can take is `W9001` (W stands for warning, and 9XXX is reserved for user rules).

Each custom rule is a Python class that inherits from the `CloudFormationLintRule` class. Since this class object belongs to the `cfnlint` Python module, we need to install it using `pip` and, to not mess up our system libraries, we will create a Python virtual environment using `virtualenv`:

```
$ pip install virtualenv
$ virtualenv venv
$ source venv/bin/activate
(venv)$ pip install cfnlint
```

We will start by importing the required modules and creating our rule class skeleton:

```
// rdsdeletionpolicy.py
class RdsDeletionPolicy(CloudFormationLintRule):
    id = 'W9001'
    shortdesc = 'Check RDS Deletion Policy'
    description = 'This rule checks DeletionPolicy on RDS resources to
be Snapshot or Retain'
    RDS_RESOURCES = [
        'AWS::RDS::DBInstance',
        'AWS::RDS::DBCluster'
```

```
    ]

    def match(self, cfn):
        matches = []
        # You rule code goes here
        return matches
```

We have initialized an empty array called `matches`. This array will contain resources that match our rule.

Now, we need to parse the template, obtain only the RDS resources we want to evaluate, and check whether they have `DeletionPolicy`. We need to add this code to the `match` function:

```
// rdsdeletionpolicy.py (partial)
    def match(self, cfn):
        matches = []
        resources = cfn.get_resources(self.RDS_RESOURCES)
        for resource_name, resource in resources.items():
            deletion_policy = resource.get('DeletionPolicy')
            path = ['Resources', resource_name]
            if deletion_policy is None:
                message = f'Resource {resource_name} does not have
Deletion Policy!'
                matches.append(RuleMatch(path, message))
            elif deletion_policy not in ('Snapshot', 'Retain'):
                message = f'Resource {resource_name} does not have
Deletion Policy set to Snapshot or Retain!'
                matches.append(RuleMatch(path, message))
        return matches
```

Now, let's see what our rule looks like:

```
// rdsdeletionpolicy.py
from cfnlint import CloudFormationLintRule
from cfnlint import RuleMatch

class RdsDeletionPolicy(CloudFormationLintRule):
    # ...
    RDS_RESOURCES = [
        'AWS::RDS::DBInstance',
        'AWS::RDS::DBCluster'
    ]
    def match(self, cfn):
        matches = []
        resources = cfn.get_resources(self.RDS_RESOURCES)
```

```
        for resource_name, resource in resources.items():
            deletion_policy = resource.get('DeletionPolicy')
            path = ['Resources', resource_name]
            if deletion_policy is None:
                message = f'Resource {resource_name} does not have
Deletion Policy!'
                matches.append(RuleMatch(path, message))
            elif deletion_policy not in ('Snapshot', 'Retain'):
                message = f'Resource {resource_name} does not have
Deletion Policy set to Snapshot or Retain!'
                matches.append(RuleMatch(path, message))
        return matches
```

As you can see, we are performing the actions explained previously (in the linter rule workflow). We obtain all the DB resources, and we check whether each of them has a proper Deletion Policy.

> **Important note**
>
> Do you remember that we used `Conditions` in Deletion Policy? This rule may not work as-is against the resource that we declared in *Chapter 2, Advanced Template Development*, since `cfn-lint` evaluates the value as-is.
>
> Keep this in mind when you're developing your own rule!

Now, we can check this linter rule! The following example shows how we can check our template's compliance with our own rules:

```
(venv) $ deactivate
$ cfn-lint database_failing.yaml -a custom_rules
W9001 Resource TestDatabase does not have Deletion Policy!
database_failing.yaml:42:3
W9001 Resource ProdDatabase does not have Deletion Policy set to
Snapshot or Retain!
database_failing.yaml:65:3
```

`cfn-lint` and template validation are important parts of the stack deployment process. We will return to them in the next chapter when we discuss continuous delivery. But before that, let's learn how to provision our resources.

Using a policy-based linter

When I first saw `cloudformation-guard`, my first thought was, *what's wrong with cfn-lint?!* The truth is – nothing! `cloudformation-guard` was built to make use of policy-based rules, which are smaller in size and easier to maintain. This comment summarizes my understanding: `https://github.com/aws-cloudformation/cloudformation-guard/issues/9#issuecomment-726299482`.

Guard's rules are written in DSL, and we will write our own rule a bit later. But first, we need to install `cfn-guard`!

If you are on macOS, the installation is quite trivial:

```
$ brew install cloudformation-guard
```

For other OS installations, such as Ubuntu, we need some `curl` magic:

```
$ curl --proto '=https' --tlsv1.2 -sSf https://raw.githubusercontent.
com/aws-cloudformation/cloudformation-guard/main/install-guard.sh | sh
```

For Windows installation, please check this guide: `https://github.com/aws-cloudformation/cloudformation-guard#windows-10-install-rust-and-cargo`.

`cloudformation-guard` does not have default linter rules the way `cfn-lint` does. Hence, we need to write our rule first. Guard comes with its own DSL that leverages iterating over the template and filtering on resource type.

In this example, we're filtering all VPC `Subnet` resource types:

```
Resources.*[ Type == 'AWS::EC2::Subnet' ]
```

Guard's DSL supports high-level programming language features such as variable declaration and control flow. We can declare a variable that is an array of all subnets and iterate over it:

```
let subnets = Resources.*[ Type == 'AWS::EC2::Subnet' ]
rule generic_iteration when %subnets !empty {
}
```

In this block, we declare a rule called `generic_iteration` using the `rule` keyword. The `when variable_name !empty` keyword declares iteration over an array type variable. We can treat `when ... !empty` the same way we treat a `While` loop.

Let's check whether all our subnets have the required tag keys attached:

```
let subnets = Resources.*[ Type == "AWS::EC2::Subnet" ]

rule no_tags_assigned when %subnets !empty {
    %subnets.Properties.Tags[*] {
    Key in ["Env", "Name"]
    <<
    The subnet is missing Env or Name tag key
    >>
    }
}
```

So, what are we doing here? In our loop, we iterate over the subnets and check whether the `Tags` property has the required keys present. After an evaluation, we give a custom rule message so that the template developer knows what to improve in their stack.

Let's run this rule on the working template:

```
$ cfn-guard validate \
            -d core_full.yaml \
            -r cfn_guard_rules/subnets_have_tags.guard
```

Since the template is compliant, there will be nothing in the output. Let's validate the rule against a template, where we purposely removed a tag from the resource:

```
$ cfn-guard validate \
            -d core_missing_tag.yaml \
            -r cfn_guard_rules/subnets_have_tags.guard
# ...some output...
Number of non-compliant resources 1
Resource = PublicSubnet1 {
  Type       = AWS::EC2::Subnet
  Rule = no_hardcoded_cidr {
# ...some more output...
          Code:
                28.  PublicSubnet1:
                29.    Type: "AWS::EC2::Subnet"
                30.    Properties:
                31.      CidrBlock: !Select [ 0, !Cidr [ !Ref VpcCidr,
 12, 8 ] ]
                32.      VpcId: !Ref Vpc
                33.      MapPublicIpOnLaunch: True
```

The good thing here is that Guard shows us a non-compliant code piece, so we won't spend too much time looking for it.

Since we have both `cfn-lint` and `cloudformation-guard`, you might be wondering which of them you should use. Let's make this clear.

Choosing the right linter

Both linters are extremely powerful and have their caveats. For example, authoring `cfn-lint` rules requires Python skills, while `cloudformation-guard` rules are written in plain simple DSL.

Well, I am not willing to let you think about making this choice for too long, so here's my recommendation – use both! Here's why.

You see, `cfn-lint` has a set of predefined rules, and you can run it as soon as you install it. `cloudformation-guard` does not run magically without any rule supplied, but its ease of rule writing makes it handy for in-house compliance checks. However, there is another caveat.

You might have noticed that I picked a different case for the Guard rule example, although I could have just rewritten the same RDS Deletion Policy rule. And I would love to! But at the time of writing, Guard does not support short-form intrinsic functions in the template (`https://docs.aws.amazon.com/cfn-guard/latest/ug/troubleshooting.html#troubleshooting-cfn-intrinsic-functions`). So, I could author the rule in Guard's DSL if the Deletion Policy was a plain string. Ironically, it was a plain string in the first edition of this book, but then the CloudFormation development team released Language Extensions.

So, to summarize my advice: if you run a small infrastructure and aim to run a basic sanity check, go with `cfn-lint`; if you have a strong suite of internal rules and want an easier way to author them, add `cloudformation-guard` to your linter toolbox, but keep its limits with functions in mind!

This said, let's finally deploy our infrastructure!

Provisioning our stack

In *Chapter 1, Working with CloudFormation*, we created our stack with a simple command:

```
$ aws cloudformation create-stack --stack-name ... --template-body
file://...
```

This command invokes a CloudFormation API, `CreateStack`. CloudFormation's API receives the template and parameters in the request body and starts creating the stack.

When we want to update our stack (for example, make changes to the existing resources or add new ones), we invoke another API, `UpdateStack`:

```
$ aws cloudformation update-stack --stack-name ... --template-body
file://...
```

In both cases, the AWS CLI will invoke the `ListStacks` API method to check whether the stack exists or not.

If the stack exists during the creation operation, you will receive an error:

```
An error occurred (AlreadyExistsException) when calling the
CreateStack operation: Stack [...] already exists
```

If you try to update a stack that does not exist, you will receive another error:

```
An error occurred (ValidationError) when calling the UpdateStack
operation: Stack [foo] does not exist
```

Note that this is a `ValidationError` error. As you may remember, before resources begin to be provisioned, CloudFormation always validates the template to check that the template can be used.

A long time ago, when CloudFormation only supported templates in YAML format, the `CreateStack` and `UpdateStack` API methods were the only way to provision and update resources. There were (and still are) several issues with using these methods. First, it is hard to integrate `create-stack` and `update-stack` subcommands in CI/CD pipelines when we want to make them universal and reusable pipeline templates because we don't know if we are provisioning a new stack or updating an existing one. We have to use a workaround in that we can execute the `list-stacks` subcommand to check whether the stack exists and then decide which operation to run. Another workaround is to create stacks manually first and only use `update-stack` in the CI/CD pipeline, but then we would lose our developer's autonomy.

Second, when we update the stack using atomic operations such as `update-stack`, we might have a lot of changes in one update operation and it is hard to predict what changes will apply or whether these changes will destroy important resources. We have to either make small or even granular updates or spend a lot of time on code review, thus reducing the speed of development.

To solve these problems, the CloudFormation development team has introduced a feature called **change sets**.

Deploying stacks using change sets

Change sets (as the name suggests) are the set of changes that will be applied to the stack during its deployment.

We can create, review, execute, or even delete change sets, depending on whether the changes that will be applied are desirable.

For this example, we will deploy part of our core template, create a change set for this stack (including additional resources), and then review and execute it:

```
$ aws cloudformation create-stack \
    --stack-name core \
    --template-body file://core_partial.yaml \
    --parameters file://testing.json
```

When the stack is created, we can examine the **Change sets** tab and verify that it is empty:

Figure 3.1 – CloudFormation console

Let's create a change set:

```
$ aws cloudformation create-change-set \
      --stack-name core \
      --change-set-name our-change-set \
      --template-body file://core_full.yaml \
      --parameters file://testing.json \
      --capabilities CAPABILITY_IAM
```

We will receive the following output (yours will differ):

```
{
    «Id»: «arn:aws:cloudformation:REGION:ACCT_ID:changeSet/our-change-
set/bd04aeb3-386b-44d7-a25c-5fe626c24aed»,
    «StackId": "arn:aws:cloudformation:REGION:ACCT_ID:stack/
core/00697420-1123-11ea-9d40-02433c861a1c"
}
```

We can review this change set either in the AWS Console or in the AWS CLI.

Via the AWS CLI, it will look like this (again, yours might differ because of the different AWS account and/or AWS region):

```
$ aws cloudformation describe-change-set \
                     --change-set-name
arn:aws:cloudformation:REGION:ACCT_ID:changeSet/our-change-set/
bd04aeb3-386b-44d7-a25c-5fe626c24aed
```

The output will be long because there are many changes, so I will only include part of it:

```
{
    «Changes»: [
        {
            «Type»: «Resource»,
            «ResourceChange": {
                «Action»: «Add»,
                «LogicalResourceId": "AdminRole",
                «ResourceType": "AWS::IAM::Role",
                «Scope»: [],
                «Details»: []
            }
        },
        {
            «Type»: «Resource»,
            «ResourceChange": {
                «Action»: «Add»,
                «LogicalResourceId": "DevRole",
                «ResourceType": "AWS::IAM::Role",
                «Scope»: [],
                «Details»: []
            }
        },
    # The rest of the output...
    }
```

In the second half, we have the metadata of the change set, but for now, we're interested in this bit:

```
    {
                «Type»: «Resource»,
                «ResourceChange": {
                    «Action»: «Add»,
                    «LogicalResourceId": "AdminRole",
                    «ResourceType": "AWS::IAM::Role",
                    «Scope»: [],
                    «Details»: []
    }
```

Since we added a new resource, in this change set, Action is set to Add. If we were to remove the resource from the template, we would see Remove, and if the resource had been changed in the template, we'd see Modify.

Let's examine this change set in the AWS Console:

Figure 3.2 – The CloudFormation console – the Change sets tab

When we click on **our-change-set**, we will see its internals:

Figure 3.3 – The CloudFormation console – our-change-set review

All in all, the outcome is the same but is more human-friendly to review.

Once we've reviewed the changes, we can deploy this change set:

```
$ aws cloudformation execute-change-set --change-set-name our-change-
set --stack-name core
```

Last but not least, another useful subcommand called `deploy` is used like this:

```
$ aws cloudformation deploy --stack-name foo --template-file bar
```

The difference between `deploy` and `create-stack` or `update-stack` is that `deploy` is immutable. If you run `deploy` on the non-existing stack, CloudFormation will create it. If the stack already exists, CloudFormation will update it.

The main differences are as follows:

- `deploy` runs stack provisioning using change sets.

- `deploy` uses the `--template-file` argument instead of `--template-body`.

- `deploy` doesn't support parameter files. Instead, you have to specify parameters in the `--parameter-overrides` argument.

- `deploy` will not just return `stackId` in response; instead, it will wait until the stack is created or fails (which comes in handy when we include CloudFormation commands in the CI/CD pipeline).

To provision the core stack using `deploy`, we need to run the following command:

```
$ aws cloudformation deploy \
                    --stack-name core \
                    --template-file core_full.yaml \
                    --capabilities CAPABILITY_IAM \
                    --parameter-overrides \
                    VpcCidr="10.1.0.0/16" \
                    Environment=»test»
```

Since the `deploy` subcommand is the easiest and most redundant way to provision stacks and resources, we will stick to it in the upcoming chapters.

Handling errors

The default behavior of CloudFormation stack deployment in response to errors is to roll back to the previous state.

While this is the proper way to manage a production infrastructure, it might introduce various issues. For example, if you create resources with termination protection and the creation of those resources fails, CloudFormation won't be able to clean up.

For example, let's say we create the WebTier stack, enabling deletion protection on the load balancer.

This is what our load balancer resource looks like:

```
// webtier_failing.yaml
  WebTierLoadBalancer:
```

```
    Type: «AWS::ElasticLoadBalancingV2::LoadBalancer"
    Properties:
      Type: application
      LoadBalancerAttributes:
        - Key: «deletion_protection.enabled"
          Value: True
  # the rest of properties...
```

At the same time, we have a `WebInstance` security group that contains a mistake. It will fail to create and therefore trigger the rollback:

```
// webtier_failing.yaml
  WebInstanceSg:
    Type: «AWS::EC2::SecurityGroup"
    DependsOn: WebTierLoadBalancer
    Properties:
      GroupDescription: WebTier Instance SG
      SecurityGroupIngress:
        - IpProtocol: notexist # will fail
          SourceSecurityGroupId: !Ref WebTierLbSg
          FromPort: 80
          ToPort: 80
      # the rest of the properties...
```

What we know for sure is that CloudFormation will roll back the stack deployment as soon as it receives an error when creating the security group. However, if the load balancer is created before the security group creation starts, CloudFormation will fail to delete the load balancer because of deletion protection. If we try deleting the stack, we will still hit the same problem.

We would be stuck. We can't re-update the stack and we can't delete the stack at the same time! To get rid of this situation, all we have to do is remove termination protection from the balancer manually and delete the stack again. Another option is to retain those resources, but we won't want to do that when the initial stack creation fails.

However, for change sets, we can add another argument called `--disable-rollback`. This argument lets the stack remain in the failed state until the bug is fixed and we roll out the new change.

This would improve the performance of creating stacks from scratch, but I would discourage you from doing this by updating existing stacks. Rollback is a core feature of CloudFormation to preserve the safety of the infrastructure and disabling rollbacks on updates may result in the infrastructure failing.

Working with drifts

We covered drifts in *Chapter 1, Working with CloudFormation*. A **drift** is a change in a CloudFormation resource that was not applied by CloudFormation. Although most drifts are created by changes made in the AWS Console or API, some drifts appear even if we provision resources with CloudFormation.

Let's look at the example in the `core` stack. First, we need to deploy the stack:

```
$ aws cloudformation deploy \
                    --template-file core_full.yaml \
                    --stack-name core \
                    --parameter-overrides \
                    VpcCidr=10.1.0.0/16 \
                    Environment=test \
                    --capabilities CAPABILITY_IAM
```

When the stack is created, we can run drift detection from `awscli`:

```
$ aws cloudformation detect-stack-resource-drift \
                    --stack-name core \
                    --logical-resource-id DevRole
```

In the long output, we will see an interesting change:

```
{
    «StackResourceDrift": {
        «StackId": "arn:aws:cloudformation:REGION:ACCT_ID:stack/
core/32861920-16a7-11ea-bd3e-064a8d32fc9e",
        «LogicalResourceId": "DevRole",
        «PhysicalResourceId": "core-DevRole-G5L6EMSFH153",
        «ResourceType": "AWS::IAM::Role",
        «ExpectedProperties": ...,
        «ActualProperties": ...,
        «PropertyDifferences": [
            {
                «PropertyPath": "/AssumeRolePolicyDocument/
Statement/0/Principal/AWS",
                «ExpectedValue": "ACCT_ID",
                «ActualValue": "arn:aws:iam::ACCT_ID:root",
                «DifferenceType": "NOT_EQUAL"
            }
        ],
        «StackResourceDriftStatus": "MODIFIED",
        «Timestamp»: «...»
    }
}
```

So, what happened? When we set `Principal` for the IAM role to `DevRole`, we set its `Principal` attribute to the value of `!Ref "AWS::AccountId"`. But when the stack is created, CloudFormation (or IAM) rewrites it to the full path to the root user (which is essentially the same as storing the AWS account ID when IAM needs to authenticate the API call).

Although this doesn't introduce many issues, we want to keep our stack drift clean. So, in this case, the only thing we can do is set the right `Principal` value so that it doesn't get rewritten.

Another situation is when there is an unintended change. Let's add another policy to our IAM role:

```
$ aws iam attach-role-policy \
        --role-name core-DevRole-G5L6EMSFH153 \
        --policy-arn \
        arn:aws:iam::aws:policy/AmazonEC2FullAccess
```

For ease of understanding, let's run drift detection from the console:

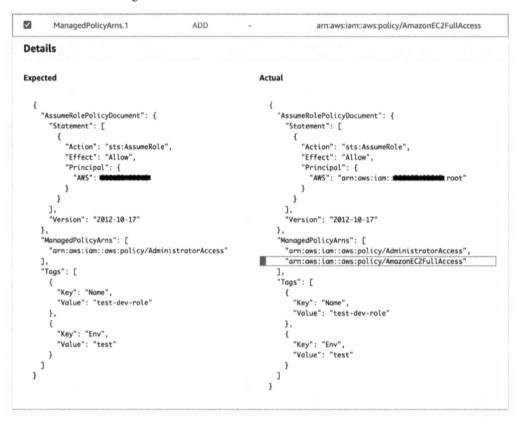

Figure 3.4 – The CloudFormation console

What we can do is remove that policy manually. But if for some reason we can't do that (let's say we have no access to the API), then we can make this change by adding this policy to the template and executing the deployment again:

```
// core_drift.yaml
  DevRole:
```

```
    Type: «AWS::IAM::Role"
    Properties:
      # some properties...
      ManagedPolicyArns:
        - !If [ ProdEnv, "arn:aws:iam::aws:policy/ReadOnlyAccess",
"arn:aws:iam::aws:policy/AdministratorAccess"]
        - «arn:aws:iam::aws:policy/AmazonEC2FullAccess"
```

Let's update the stack one more time:

```
$ aws cloudformation deploy \
                    --template-file core_drift.yaml \
                    --stack-name core \
                    --parameter-overrides \
                    VpcCidr=10.1.0.0/16 \
                    Environment=test \
                    --capabilities CAPABILITY_IAM
```

As we can see, the drift is gone:

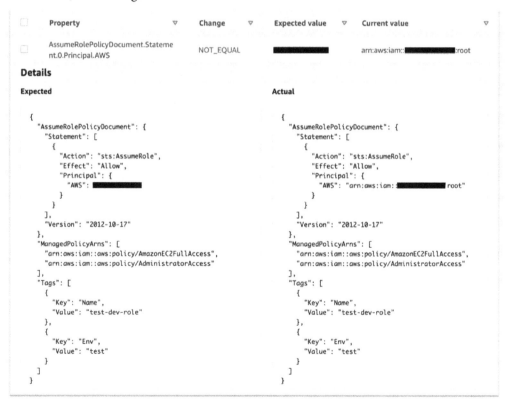

Figure 3.5 – The drift is gone

If this is an undesired change, all we have to do is delete the policy from the role in the template, and it will be removed in IAM.

We were able to resolve this drift by adding the policy to the CloudFormation template.

> **Important note**
>
> At the time of writing, the AWS CloudFormation team has released a new feature called **Resource Import**, which allows you to add existing resources to your stack.
>
> This is a long-awaited functionality that helps us migrate to **Infrastructure as Code (IaC)** practices with few issues. However, at the time of writing, it is impossible to import drifts into the CloudFormation stack. But stay tuned!

Drift management is a complex task. As AWS engineers, we want to expect that CloudFormation developers will add more features, but it is our job to make sure that all the changes in the infrastructure are done only via CloudFormation.

Summary

In this chapter, we covered various ways of provisioning a stack.

We learned how to make sure that our stack will not fail to deploy, and that our resources will provision as we want. We also wrote our very first (but not our last) linter rules, making our infrastructure code more reliable and our development process more efficient.

Then, we learned about change sets and how they advance the manner of stack deployments. We now know how to handle errors and how we can import the changes manually.

In the next chapter, we will reuse our knowledge and apply automation to CloudFormation using AWS development services such as **CodeCommit**, **CodeBuild**, and **CodePipeline**.

Questions

1. Which category in `cfn-lint` is reserved for custom rules?
2. What is the difference between template linting and validation?
3. What happens when you run `aws cloudformation deploy ...`?
4. Can you have two different change sets with the same name?
5. What are the requirements for naming custom rules in `cfn-lint`?
6. How can you move the detected drift in the stack if the unmanaged change is desirable?

Further reading

- CloudFormation linter: `https://github.com/aws-cloudformation/cfn-python-lint`

- CloudFormation Guard: `https://github.com/aws-cloudformation/cloudformation-guard`

- Importing resources in the stack: `https://docs.aws.amazon.com/AWSCloudFormation/latest/UserGuide/resource-import.html`

- Working with drifts: `https://docs.aws.amazon.com/AWSCloudFormation/latest/UserGuide/using-cfn-stack-drift.html`

4

Continuous Integration and Deployment

We know how to build our templates, and we know how to make sure they are valid and how to deploy them. Now it is time to apply another block of DevOps, called **Continuous Delivery** (**CD**). CD is used to test our applications against real-life scenarios and deploy them seamlessly so that the end user notices the changes once they refresh the page. This means no downtime and no *the page is under maintenance* messages.

In **Infrastructure as Code** (**IaC**), you treat your infrastructure and resources as a computer application. Although you cannot perform unit tests against your templates, you still have various options for how to run a proper CD pipeline.

In this chapter, we will learn how to include our templates in our applications. We will also learn how we can test our stacks and how we can apply **Amazon Web Services CloudFormation** (**AWS CloudFormation**) within our CD practices. By the end of this chapter, we will be able to apply a CI/CD pipeline with CloudFormation.

We will look at the following topics in this chapter:

- Including a template in your application
- Running smoke tests on your stack
- Best practices for the release management of CloudFormation stacks
- Creating a CI/CD pipeline with CloudFormation and CodePipeline

Technical requirements

The code used in this chapter can be found in the book's GitHub repository at `https://github.com/PacktPublishing/Mastering-AWS-CloudFormation-Second-Edition/tree/main/Chapter04`.

Check out the following video to see the Code in Action: `https://packt.link/S9auv`.

Including a template in your application

You will recall from the previous chapters that we had several templates for different tiers. We had **core** (network and security), **web** (frontend), **middleware** (backend), and **database** tiers.

So far, we haven't stored our templates in the version control system, but since we need to apply CD, we need to figure out the proper way to store them. Normally, it all depends on how you want to organize your workflow. If you have a separate *operations* or *cloud* team that is responsible for infrastructure and operations, it is wise to keep all the templates in a single repository. Developers will then supply you with any desired changes to the infrastructure or with the new version of the application.

Our flow is as follows:

1. The developer publishes a new version of an app.
2. The developer provides the operations team with the new version and/or changes.
3. The operations team makes changes to parameters and/or templates.
4. The operations team deploys the changes to the stack.

Although this sounds logical, just think about how this flow would work in the real world. It could take several hours—or even days—for the new version to move to production! DevOps culture is all about collaboration between developers and operations, which is why it is wise to mix the flow and let both parties take responsibility for the infrastructure.

So, it is wise to *include* the template in the application repository. Look at the template as the configuration of your application. We know what our application needs to have in order to run, so why not include it?

The repository for this kind of application, including the app and the configuration files, would look like the following:

```
my_app/
|----.git/
|----config
|    |----test
|    |    |----config.ini
|    |----prod
|         |----config.ini
|----src/
|    |---- # your source code here
|----tests/
|    |---- # your tests here
|----cloudformation/
     |----template.yaml
```

This will require your developers to learn how to use AWS CloudFormation, but their hard work will definitely pay off.

For some resources, this method will not work. For example, the core stack is not a part of any application, so we will have to keep it in a separate repository.

In this chapter, we will cover both scenarios, but before we build our first pipeline, we need to understand two core concepts – first, what the steps for deployment are, for example, what we run and in what order, and second, how we can understand whether our infrastructure is deployed and operating as expected. Let's dive right into it.

Running smoke tests on your stack

How do we know whether our application is healthy once it is deployed?

In addition to monitoring, logging, and alerting, there is a method called **smoke testing**.

Smoke testing is a method of testing that is applied during or after an application's release. It helps us to understand whether the current release is functional or whether it contains several bugs or failures that require immediate rollback.

CloudFormation has an out-of-the-box rollback feature. As we know, it will roll back our stack to the previous healthy state if at least one of the changes cannot be applied or a resource cannot be created. From the perspective of AWS, it is usually an AWS service that reports that the resource creation has failed and that the error we are seeing is actually an error message from AWS' API. However, some resources do not report back to CloudFormation if they have failed to be created. Let me explain in the following example.

Smoke testing for EC2 auto scaling groups

For example, we provision an **auto scaling group** (**ASG**) with an **Elastic Load Balancer** (**ELB**). An ASG will run one or more instances from either the launch configuration or the launch template. The launch configuration might have a set of commands to run during the creation of an **EC2** instance. We can install web server software on an instance while provisioning and set the ASG to replace an instance if the ELB health checks fail for it. We can provision all of this with CloudFormation.

The following is an example template (part of the resources is missing because I'm using a **default VPC**). For the full template, look at the following source code:

```
// broken_asg.yaml (partial)
AWSTemplateFormatVersion: "2010-09-09"
Parameters:
  # ...
Resources:
  Lc:
```

```
        Type: "AWS::AutoScaling::LaunchConfiguration"
        Properties:
          ImageId: !Ref AmiId
          InstanceType: "t2.micro"
          UserData: # can you find a mistake in this UserData?
            Fn::Base64: |
              #!/bin/bash
              yum -y install yolo
              systemctl start yolo
          SecurityGroups:
            - !Ref Sg
      Asg:
        Type: "AWS::AutoScaling::AutoScalingGroup"
        Properties:
          # ...
          LaunchConfigurationName: !Ref Lc
          # ...
  # The rest of the resources...
  Outputs:
    Dns:
      Value: !GetAtt Elb.DNSName
```

When we deploy this template, CloudFormation will report that the creation of the stack is complete:

```
$ aws cloudformation deploy \
                    --template-file broken_asg.yaml \
                    --stack-name broken \
                    --parameter-overrides VpcId=vpc-12345678\
                    SubnetIds=subnet-123,subnet-456,subnet-
789,subnet-012,subnet-345,subnet-678
Waiting for changeset to be created..
Waiting for stack create/update to complete
Successfully created/updated stack - broken
```

However, if we try to go via the URL of the ELB from the CloudFormation output, we will see the following:

```
$ aws cloudformation describe-stacks \
      --stack-name broken \
      --query 'Stacks[0].Outputs[0].OutputValue' \
      --output text
broken-Elb-157OHF7S5UYIC-1875871321.us-east-1.elb.amazonaws.com
$ curl broken-Elb-157OHF7S5UYIC-1875871321.us-east-1.elb.amazonaws.com
<html>
```

```
<head><title>503 Service Temporarily Unavailable</title></head>
<body bgcolor="white">
<center><h1>503 Service Temporarily Unavailable</h1></center>
</body>
</html>
```

Why does this happen? If the stack is created, that means the infrastructure is in place and everything *should* be fine. However, if we open the EC2 console, we can see that the instances are being terminated one by one:

Figure 4.1 – The AWS EC2 console

This occurs because the launch configuration's user data is malfunctioning (as you may have noticed, I haven't installed any web server software). An ASG has also been created and the instances are being launched and terminated, but CloudFormation is not aware of that; it received the API response from EC2 and the ASG.

There is an easy way to solve this problem using ASGs (we will look into this in *Chapter 6, Configuration Management of EC2 Instances Using cfn-init*), but for now, just keep in mind that these kinds of issues might occur and CloudFormation cannot deal with them out of the box.

Another problem with testing our templates is that CloudFormation doesn't have any unit testing abilities, such as common programming languages. The only way to test them is to provision the stack from the template and run tests against the stack and its resources.

There are several ways to check application stacks, but the simplest is to make an HTTP request to a health check endpoint (in our case, /).

Our test suite will be a small Python script, which will do the following:

1. Parse the argument (the stack name).

2. Make a request to the CloudFormation API to get the stack output (the ELB DNS name).

3. Make an HTTP request to that DNS name.

4. If the script doesn't receive a `200 OK` HTTP response, it will print `Stack deployment failed!` and exit with code `1`.

This is how our testing script will look:

```
// asg_test.py
# imports ...
try:
    stack = sys.argv[1]
except IndexError:
    print('Please provide a stack name')
    sys.exit(1)
cfn_client = boto3.client('cloudformation')
try:
    stack = cfn_client.describe_stacks(StackName=stack)
except botocore.exceptions.ClientError:
    print('This stack does not exist or region is incorrect')
    sys.exit(1)
elb_dns = stack['Stacks'][0]['Outputs'][0]['OutputValue']
for _ in range(0, 2):
    resp = requests.get(f'http://{elb_dns}')
    if resp.status_code == 200:
        print('Test succeeded')
        sys.exit(0)
    sleep(5)
print(f'Result of test: {resp.content}')
print(f'HTTP Response code: {resp.status_code}')
print('Test did not succeed')
sys.exit(1)
```

If we run it against our stack again, we will get the following result:

```
$ python asg_test.py broken
Result of test: b'<html>\r\n<head><title>503 Service Temporarily
Unavailable</title></head>\r\n<body bgcolor="white">\r\
n<center><h1>503 Service Temporarily Unavailable</h1></center>\r\n</
body>\r\n</html>\r\n'
HTTP Response code: 503
Test did not succeed
```

Now, we have to figure out what went wrong with the template. Once we find a problem (which, in this case, is in the launch configuration's user data), we can fix it, rerun the stack deployment, and test our resources again:

```
// working_asg.yaml
# Parameters section...
Resources:
  Lc:
```

```
    Type: "AWS::AutoScaling::LaunchConfiguration"
    Properties:
      ImageId: !Ref AmiId
      InstanceType: "t2.micro"
      UserData:
        Fn::Base64: |
          #!/bin/bash
          amazon-linux-extras install -y epel
          yum -y install nginx
          systemctl start nginx
      SecurityGroups:
        - !Ref Sg
# the rest of the template...
```

Once the working template is deployed, we can run our script again:

```
$ python asg_test.py broken
Test succeeded
```

While this is just an example of this case, we know that we cannot use this test suite for other stacks and resources. Depending on what we are building, we must create a new test case for every application or infrastructure that we deploy.

For services such as VPC networks, IAM roles, and DynamoDB tables, CloudFormation can ensure that resources are properly configured. However, how do we know that they are doing what they are supposed to do?

Smoke-testing VPC resources

Let's look again at our **core** template. We know it has **private** and **public** subnets. Let's say we want to check whether subnets that are supposed to be private are associated with a private route table (the one that routes traffic through a NAT gateway).

To carry out this test, we need to do the following:

1. First, append your subnet resources with an extra tag.

    Use the following tag for public subnets:

    ```
    - Key: "Private"
      Value: "False"
    ```

    Use the following tag for private subnets:

    ```
    - Key: "Private"
      Value: "True"
    ```

2. Our script will gather the stack's resources, not its outputs. Filter the resources to be of the `AWS::EC2::Subnet` type and make the value of the `Private` tag "True".

3. Obtain the ID of the private route table and then check whether private subnets are associated with the private route table ID.

The following steps will give us a test suite for the VPC subnets:

1. First, parse the arguments and verify that the stack exists:

```
// core_subnets.py
# imports...
matches = []
try:
    stack = sys.argv[1]
except IndexError:
    print('Please provide a stack name')
    sys.exit(1)
cfn_client = boto3.client('cloudformation')
try:
    resources = cfn_client.describe_stack_
resources(StackName=stack)
except botocore.exceptions.ClientError:
    print('This stack does not exist or region is incorrect')
    sys.exit(1)
```

2. Then, obtain the ID of the private route table and all of the subnets in the stack:

```
// core_subnets.py
subnets_in_stack = []
for resource in resources['StackResources']:
    if resource[<LogicalResourceId>] == 'PrivateRouteTable':
        private_route_table = resource['PhysicalResourceId']
    if resource[<ResourceType>] == 'AWS::EC2::Subnet':
        subnets_in_stack.append(resource[<PhysicalResourceId>])
```

3. Finally, obtain the subnets' association using the EC2 API, match their tags, and check that they have the necessary route table association:

```
// core_subnets.py
ec2_client = boto3.client('ec2')
subnets_to_check = []
for subnet in subnets_in_stack:
    resp = ec2_client.describe_subnets(SubnetIds=[subnet])
    for tag in resp[<Subnets>][0][<Tags>]:
        if tag[<Key>] == 'Private' and tag['Value'] == 'True':
```

```
                    subnets_to_check.append(subnet)
    route_table = ec2_client.describe_route_
    tables(RouteTableIds=[private_route_table])
    private_subnets = []
    for assoc in route_table['RouteTables'][0]['Associations']:
        private_subnets.append(assoc[<SubnetId>])
    for subnet in subnets_to_check:
        if subnet not in private_subnets:
            matches.append(subnet)
    if matches:
        print('One or more private subnets are not associated with
    proper route table!')
        print(f'Non-compliant subnets: {matches}')
        sys.exit(1)
    print('All subnets are compliant!')
    exit(0)
```

4. Let's deploy our stack and try this test case:

```
$ aws cloudformation deploy --stack-name core --template-file
core_non_compliant.yaml --capabilities CAPABILITY_IAM
Waiting for changeset to be created..
Waiting for stack create/update to complete
Successfully created/updated stack - core
$ python core_subnets.py core
One or more private subnets are not associated with proper route
table!
Non-compliant subnets: ['subnet-0b087c910c675cd5d', 'subnet-
037acf2fce30c38fd', 'subnet-041e96329b5d1449a']
```

We've received an error, which means our core stack has non-compliant subnets! Let's now deploy a stack with proper association and try this test again:

```
$ aws cloudformation deploy --stack-name core --template-file
core_compliant.yaml --capabilities CAPABILITY_IAM
Waiting for changeset to be created..
Waiting for stack create/update to complete
Successfully created/updated stack - core
$ python core_subnets.py core
All subnets are compliant!
```

Again, this is just an example of a particular case. Depending on how you organize your CloudFormation templates, you will figure out how to carry out proper testing.

> **Important note**
>
> Do we really need to perform these actions during stack operations? Try to work out how you can avoid carrying out these tests once the stack is deployed. By the end, we are making sure that the resources have proper attributes and/or associations. Think about how you can come to a solution by using `cfn-lint`.

We now know how to perform testing on a stack, so let's move on to the next topic.

Best practices for the release management of CloudFormation stacks

Before we build our very first pipeline for CD, I want to focus on this important topic. In this section, we will go through the best practices for the release management of CloudFormation stacks.

By the end, we want to treat our infrastructure like a computer program, so let's use the experience of software development!

Always use version control systems

Your infrastructure is now code. So, you need to have version control on it. **Version Control Systems (VCS)** have several benefits, including code collaboration, change history, centralized storage for source code, integration with build systems, and much more.

In order to keep your infrastructure clean and well maintained and your changes well observed, always keep your CloudFormation templates in VCS.

Ensure that your dependencies can be easily retrieved

In this and the previous chapter, we developed several scripts for our templates, including custom linter rules and smoke tests.

These scripts have external dependencies (`pip` packages, in our case), so you want to make sure that they can be installed and resolved easily.

Keep your code base clean

Make sure you properly organize your CloudFormation repository. Store smoke tests in the `tests` folder, parameters where they should be, and custom linter rules in a proper directory (such as `custom_rules`). If you store your template with a *monorepo* model, create a subdirectory for each group or project so they can be easily maintained.

Choose a proper branching model

In most software projects, the *master* branch is considered to be a production branch. It is important to choose your branching model wisely so that you can integrate your source code with the CI/CD systems.

You can break up your workflow in the dev/test/master branches so that the CI/CD system runs specific stages on specific branches. You don't need to deploy each commit to the production stack, so for the dev branch, you are likely to only do validation and linting.

If you use project management tools, such as **Jira**, make sure that you add the issue key to a commit message:

```
git commit -m "PROJ-1234 add extra subnets for databases"
```

Making clear comments and including project or issue keys will help you to keep the code base clean and the development process transparent.

Always perform a code review

Do not allow a direct push to main and use pull requests to control upcoming changes. Even if the linter is happy and all the tests pass, there may be a case in which a faulty configuration gets into the production stack. Even if CloudFormation is able to roll back, it is always wise to prevent this from happening by reviewing each change.

Have full test coverage

You must always perform linting and template validation before deploying changes to the stack. You cannot perform unit testing against CloudFormation templates, but you still need to ensure that as few errors are reaching CloudFormation as possible. Focus on developing custom rules for cfn-lint so that you can implement best practices for your organization.

Don't forget to use a CloudFormation IAM role

As you remember, when we deploy a stack, we use our own IAM privileges. This means that we must have at least an administrator access policy on AWS, which is not secure. In addition, since we expect more people to collaborate on the infrastructure, we need to use a CloudFormation IAM role so that we don't provide each template developer with administrator access to AWS.

Always perform smoke testing

If we manage critical infrastructure, we need to ensure that every change will not cause a failure or misconfiguration. Deploying a temporary stack with the latest changes in a separate environment (or even separate AWS accounts) and running smoke tests against our stack, combined with proper linting and validation, is the best practice to prevent mistakes.

Use the correct CI/CD instruments

Stack operations (validation, linting, and deployment) are basic commands. However, we need to be sure that CI/CD systems can perform them. We need to choose functionality and costs wisely. Moreover, we need to think about security because we are providing access to our AWS account. If we have strict security requirements, we'll likely want to provision a CI/CD system (such as GitLab or Jenkins) in our AWS environment or use AWS-managed services, such as CodeBuild or CodePipeline.

Keep up the good work

Practices and methodologies are evolving and so are instruments. We want to revise the way we carry out CD and see whether there is any room for improvement. Long story short, there always is.

This said, let's move on to the last section of this chapter and build our own CD pipeline for CloudFormation!

Creating a CI/CD pipeline with CloudFormation and CodePipeline

Before we begin creating the pipeline, let's revise what a CI/CD pipeline actually is. Any CI/CD pipeline (in terms of software development) consists of stages.

Those stages are usually as follows (we will practice all of these steps later):

1. **Pre-build**: Pull the code from source code management and install the dependencies.
2. **Build**: Run the build and retrieve the artifacts.
3. **Test**: Run a test suite against the build.
4. **Package**: Store the build artifacts in the artifact storage.
5. **Deploy**: Deploy a new version on the environment.

If any of these steps fail, the build system will trigger an error.

So, how can we apply the same steps on CloudFormation? Usually, it depends on the **Continuous Integration (CI)** system. In our case, these stages will do the following:

1. **Pre-build**: Store the code (for example, the templates) in AWS CodeCommit and use AWS CodeBuild as a build system. We will also pull the code from CodeCommit and install the necessary dependency packages, including the following:

    - `cfn-lint`
    - `awscli`
    - `boto3` and `botocore` (an AWS SDK for Python)

2. **Build**: This stage will be skipped. Why? Because CloudFormation templates aren't like any software source code. For example, we do not need to compile them. Instead, we can run a validation check:

```
aws cloudformation validate-template --template-body ...
```

At this stage, this will be enough. The reason we don't run validation checks during the test phase is that validation is a simple syntax check, which is similar to code compilation in the context of CloudFormation.

3. **Test**: In this step, we will run `cfn-lint` against our template. If the linter check doesn't fail, we will deploy the new template to a testing environment, run the smoke test, and then terminate it.

4. **Package**: In this step, we want to store the artifact (which, in our case, is a template file) in the artifact storage. Since, as a service, AWS CloudFormation uses the template from S3 (a particular bucket), S3 will act as artifact storage for us.

Once the testing phase is complete, we will upload the changed (or new) template to the S3 bucket.

5. **Deploy**: In this step, we will just run the production deployment using the template that was packaged and stored on S3.

Scenario – core stack

We decided to store the core stack as a separate entity of our AWS environment. For the core stack, our flow will look as follows:

Figure 4.2 – The core CI/CD pipeline workflow

If any of these steps fail, the CI/CD system will fire an error and cancel the build.

To perform this task, we will use CodeCommit (the SCM), CodeBuild (the build system), and CodePipeline (the actual CI/CD *connector* system).

We will have to configure the files. The first one will be `buildspec.yaml`—the build specification file with instructions and build stages (this is similar to `Jenkinsfile` in Jenkins). The second will be a CloudFormation template, which contains all the building blocks for our pipeline: the source code repository, the build project, and the pipeline.

Let's start with `buildspec.yml`. This is how it is going to look in our case:

```
// buildspec.yml
version: 0.2
phases:
```

```
install:
  runtime-versions:
    python: 3.8
  commands:
    - pip install awscli cfn-lint
build:
  commands:
    - aws cloudformation validate-template --template-body file://
core.yaml
    - cfn-lint core.yaml
post_build:
  commands:
    - aws cloudformation deploy --template-file core.yaml --stack-
name core-tmp --capabilities CAPABILITY_NAMED_IAM --role-arn $CFN_ROLE
    - python tests/core_subnets.py core-tmp
  finally:
    - aws cloudformation delete-stack --stack-name core-tmp --role-
arn $CFN_ROLE
artifacts:
  files:
    - core.yaml
```

We will include this file in the repository; otherwise, CodeBuild won't know which actions to perform.

The instructions for CodeBuild are specified in the build specification. The build specification consists of several phases: `install`, `build`, and `post_build`.

During the `install` phase, we install the necessary dependencies, such as `cfn-lint` and `awscli`. During the `build` phase, we run validation and linting. During the `post_build` phase, we run the deployment of a temporary stack, run smoke tests, and delete the stack. If all of the steps are completed successfully, the core template and its parameters are uploaded to S3 (this is defined in the `artifacts` section, but the actual path to S3 is managed in CodePipeline).

If the `post_build` step fails (let's say the temporary stack deployment failed or the tests didn't succeed), we stop right there and clean up the temporary stack.

We are going to perform the following actions to get a working CI/CD pipeline:

1. We'll start by looking at our CI/CD template. This template contains the following resources:

    • A repository (CodeCommit)

    • A build project (CodeBuild)

    • Artifact storage (an S3 bucket)

- A pipeline (CodePipeline)

- IAM roles (for CodeBuild, CodePipeline, and, of course, CloudFormation)

2. Let's focus on the important sections of the template. The following code block declares the CodeCommit repository and S3 bucket (which will act as artifact storage for CodePipeline):

```
// cicd.yaml (the SCM repo and artifacts storage)
Repository:
  Type: "AWS::CodeCommit::Repository"
  Properties:
    RepositoryName: "core"
TemplateBucket:
  Type: "AWS::S3::Bucket"
```

We don't have to configure much here since the creation of the S3 bucket and CodeCommit repository is a trivial task. However, CodeBuild is a bit more challenging.

3. In the CodeBuild declaration, we need to explicitly declare that the source for the build jobs will be CodePipeline. This instructs CodeBuild to accept API calls from CodePipeline in order to run build jobs:

```
// cicd.yaml (the build project)
Build:
  Type: "AWS::CodeBuild::Project"
  Properties:
    Artifacts:
      Type: "CODEPIPELINE"
    ServiceRole: !GetAtt BuildRole.Arn
    Name: "Core"
    Source:
      Type: "CODEPIPELINE"
    Environment:
      Type: "LINUX_CONTAINER"
      ComputeType: "BUILD_GENERAL1_SMALL"
      Image: "aws/codebuild/amazonlinux2-x86_64-standard:2.0"
```

> **Important note**
>
> For `Source` and `Artifacts`, we set the type to CodePipeline. This is because the input and the output are supplied to and from CodePipeline, which will act as the arbiter and the manager. We don't specify any build steps in the template itself. This is because the build steps for CodeBuild are declared in `buildspec.yml`.

4. Now, let's investigate what is in our pipeline resource. The pipeline consists of three major stages. The first is `Clone`. At this stage, source code is pulled from CodeCommit and stored on S3. The S3 object key (for example, the path to the code) is also stored as an output artifact:

```
// cicd.yaml (the pipeline)
# ...
        - Name: "Clone"
          Actions:
            - ActionTypeId:
                Category: "Source"
                Owner: "AWS"
                Provider: "CodeCommit"
                Version: «1»
              Name: "Clone"
              OutputArtifacts:
                - Name: "CloneOutput"
              Configuration:
                BranchName: "main:
                RepositoryName: !GetAtt Repository.Name
              RunOrder: 1
```

5. The second stage is `Build`. This stage will take the code from S3 (the output artifact from the previous stage) and run the CodeBuild project. If the build's job is successful, the template will also be stored on S3 as an output artifact:

```
// cicd.yaml (the pipeline)
        - Name: "Build"
          Actions:
            - Name: "Build"
              InputArtifacts:
                - Name: "CloneOutput"
              ActionTypeId:
                Category: "Build"
                Owner: "AWS"
                Version: «1»
                Provider: "CodeBuild"
              OutputArtifacts:
                - Name: "BuildOutput"
              Configuration:
                ProjectName: !Ref Build
              RunOrder: 1
```

6. The last stage is `Deploy`. During this stage, CodePipeline will run stack creation (or updating a stack) using the template from the output of the build step:

```
// cicd.yaml (the pipeline)
        - Name: "Deploy"
          Actions:
            - Name: "Deploy"
              InputArtifacts:
                - Name: "BuildOutput"
              ActionTypeId:
                Category: "Deploy"
                Owner: "AWS"
                Version: «1»
                Provider: "CloudFormation"
              OutputArtifacts:
                - Name: "DeployOutput"
              Configuration:
                ActionMode: "CREATE_UPDATE"
                RoleArn: !GetAtt CfnRole.Arn
                Capabilities: "CAPABILITY_NAMED_IAM"
                StackName: "Core"
                TemplatePath: "BuildOutput::core.yaml"
```

All these stages happen automatically; CodePipeline listens to the repository and launches every time there is a change.

7. Now, let's deploy the CI/CD stack and experiment a bit:

```
aws cloudformation deploy \
                --stack-name cicd \
                --template-file cicd.yaml \
                --capabilities CAPABILITY_IAM
```

Once the stack is deployed, we can add the templates and other files one by one to the repository, but let's first take a look at our pipeline:

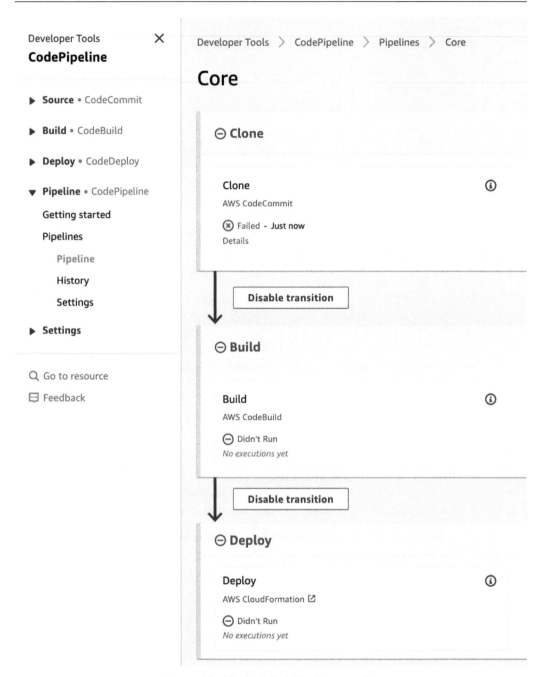

Figure 4.3 – The AWS CodePipeline console

We can already see that it has failed. This is because CodePipeline runs immediately after creation but our repository is empty and there is nothing to pull.

8. Now, let's add the necessary files to the repository. For ease, we'll do it manually, but in production, it will be carried out using `git` commands.

    We need to go to **Source** | **Repositories** | **Code**. What we see are instructions on how to clone the repository. We can ignore them for now and click **Add file** | **Upload file**:

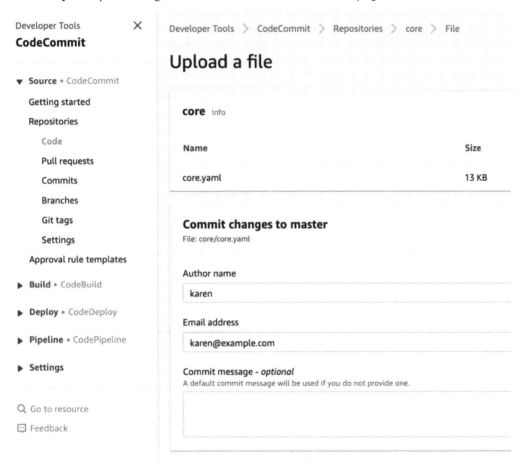

Figure 4.4 – The AWS CodeCommit console

9. We will do the same for the other files we need for the pipeline, or alternatively, we can use Git to add the content to the repository. After setting up a local Git client for working with the CodeCommit repo (`https://docs.aws.amazon.com/codecommit/latest/userguide/setting-up.html`), we can do the following:

```
$ git add .
$ git commit -m "Ready for deployment"
$ git push
```

10. By the end, our repository will look like this:

Figure 4.5 – The AWS CodeCommit console

11. Let's go back to CodePipeline:

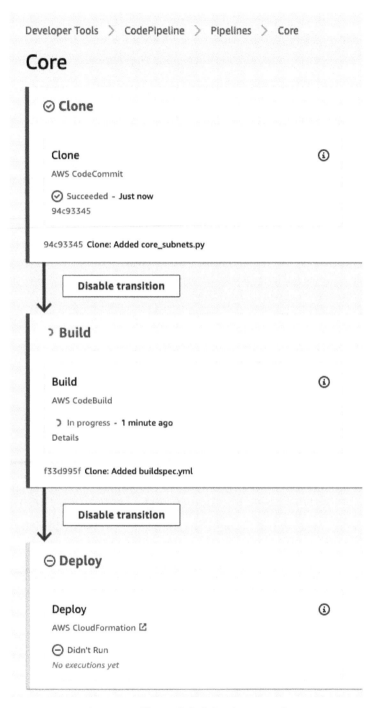

Figure 4.6 – The AWS CodePipeline console

We can already see some action! However, unfortunately, these builds are going to fail because the repository isn't complete. Meanwhile, we can look at the build project logs:

```
[Container] 2019/12/19 15:03:19 Running command cfn-lint core.
yaml
[Container] 2019/12/19 15:03:20 Phase complete: BUILD State:
SUCCEEDED
[Container] 2019/12/19 15:03:20 Phase context status
code:  Message:
[Container] 2019/12/19 15:03:21 Entering phase POST_BUILD
[Container] 2019/12/19 15:03:21 Running command aws
cloudformation deploy --template-file core.yaml --stack-name
core-tmp --capabilities CAPABILITY_NAMED_IAM --role-arn $CFN_
ROLE
Waiting for changeset to be created..
Waiting for stack create/update to complete
```

The build system is busy creating the stack. If you were adding the files one by one using the CodeCommit, it would fail afterward because the test suite was uploaded after `buildspec.yml`. We will see an error such as the following:

```
[Container] 2019/12/19 15:06:18 Running command python tests/
core_subnets.py core-tmp
python: can't open file 'tests/core_subnets.py': [Errno 2] No
such file or directory
[Container] 2019/12/19 15:06:18 Command did not exit
successfully python tests/core_subnets.py core-tmp exit status 2
[Container] 2019/12/19 15:06:18 Running command aws
cloudformation delete-stack --stack-name core-tmp --role-arn
$CFN_ROLE
[Container] 2019/12/19 15:06:19 Phase complete: POST_BUILD
State: FAILED
[Container] 2019/12/19 15:06:19 Phase context status code:
COMMAND_EXECUTION_ERROR Message: Error while executing command:
python tests/core_subnets.py core-tmp. Reason: exit status 2
```

The next error is as follows (for the pipeline running once we have added the test suite, the error is different):

```
[Container] 2019/12/19 15:06:57 Running command aws
cloudformation deploy --template-file core.yaml --stack-name
core-tmp --capabilities CAPABILITY_NAMED_IAM --role-arn $CFN_
ROLE
An error occurred (ValidationError) when
calling the CreateChangeSet operation:
Stack:arn:aws:cloudformation:REGIOS:ACCT_ID:stack/core-tmp/
b2960880-2270-11ea-90be-06bc90058f1a is in DELETE_IN_PROGRESS
state and can not be updated.
```

This is because the previous step started deleting the template and the new one tried to deploy the same template. The pipeline now looks really bad:

Figure 4.7 – The AWS CodePipeline console

12. However, there is no need to worry! Let's run the whole pipeline again by hitting **Retry** on the **Build** stage. After a while, we can see that the pipeline has succeeded:

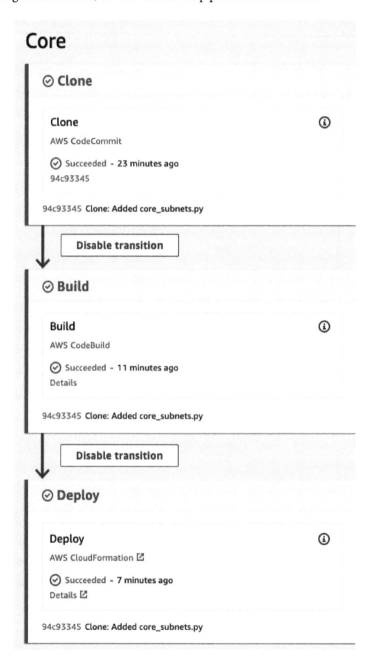

Figure 4.8 – The AWS CodePipeline console

13. We can also see our **Core** stack:

CloudFormation > **Stacks**

Stacks (2)

Q *Filter by stack name*

	Stack name	Status
○	Core	⊘ CREATE_COMPLETE
○	cicd	⊘ CREATE_COMPLETE

Figure 4.9 – The AWS CloudFormation console

That's it! We now have a fully functional CD pipeline with test coverage!

Summary

In this chapter, we learned how to perform testing against CloudFormation stacks and what the best practices are for CD with CloudFormation.

We also created our very first pipeline using development services in AWS, such as CodeCommit, CodeBuild, and CodePipeline.

Although this pipeline is working and doing what it is supposed to do, there is always room for improvement. Ask yourself what you could add to the pipeline or change to make it more effective.

We should move the creation of the temporary stack from CodeBuild to CodePipeline as an extra stage so we can save some money since, in CodeBuild, you pay for build execution time. Simply put, while CodeBuild waits until the temporary stack has been created, the build job is being billed.

Another thing is that by using the same temporary stack name (`core-tmp`), we are not able to run multiple builds at the same time. If another build runs while `core-tmp` is being deleted by a previous build, we will receive an error.

As mentioned in the *Best practices for the release management of CloudFormation stacks* section, there is always room for improvement.

In the next chapter, we will cover another important topic: **StackSets**. We will learn how to deploy the same stacks in different regions and even accounts!

Questions

1. What is `buildspec.yml`?

2. What are CloudFormation artifacts? Where are they stored?

3. How can you inform CloudFormation about instances where ASGs are not properly provisioned?

4. How can a CloudFormation API provide a list of resources that are provisioned within a stack?

5. What are the building blocks of CodePipeline? Which AWS services are used?

Further reading

- *Continuous Delivery with CodePipeline*: `https://docs.aws.amazon.com/AWSCloudFormation/latest/UserGuide/continuous-delivery-codepipeline.html`

- *Infrastructure Continuous Delivery Using AWS CloudFormation*: `https://www.slideshare.net/AmazonWebServices/infrastructure-continuous-delivery-using-aws-cloudformation-73808130`

5

Deploying to Multiple Regions and Accounts Using StackSets

In this chapter, we are going to learn about StackSets—a part of CloudFormation that allows us to deploy stacks to different regions and accounts. StackSets are useful when it comes to managing big and enterprise-class infrastructure worldwide, whether you are hosting a **Software as a Service** (**SaaS**) platform globally or are running distributed systems in the **Amazon Web Services** (**AWS**) cloud.

In this chapter, we will learn about StackSets and how to deploy them to multiple regions and accounts. By the end of this chapter, we will have learned how to prevent failures of multiple StackSet deployments using **Target Account Gates** (**TAGs**).

We will cover the following topics in this chapter:

- The legacy way of multi-regional and multi-account infrastructure management
- Introducing StackSets
- Deploying to multiple regions
- Best practices for StackSets
- Deploying to multiple accounts
- Preventing failures of multiple StackSet deployments using TAGs

Technical requirements

The code used in this chapter can be found in the book's GitHub repository at `https://github.com/PacktPublishing/Mastering-AWS-CloudFormation-Second-Edition/tree/main/Chapter05`.

Check out the following video to see the code in action:

`https://packt.link/OoXwT`

The legacy way of multi-regional and multi-account infrastructure management

Until now, our stack deployment was primarily focused on provisioning resources within a single AWS account and region. But what if we needed to provision the same stack in several regions? Let's say we need to provision the same stack in Ireland, North Virginia, and Frankfurt.

Usually, the default region (for example, the API endpoint that we want to connect to) is chosen either from environment variables or from a local config file. When you invoke any command via `awscli`, it will connect to that specific default region.

We can also specify the region manually as an argument. So, if we want to provision the same stack in different regions, we have to repeat the same command that changes the argument value, as illustrated here:

```
aws cloudformation deploy --region eu-west-1 --template-file foo.yaml
aws cloudformation deploy --region us-east-1 --template-file foo.yaml
aws cloudformation deploy --region eu-central-1 --template-file foo.
yaml
```

But that brings us extra complexity. What if one of the deployments fails? If one stack is provisioned for more than 30 minutes, then the whole operation will take hours! We of course can parallelize the execution using Linux tools such as `parallel` or `xargs`, but that does not protect us from a stack failing to create in one region and succeeding in others. In such a scenario, we introduce inconsistency in the infrastructure.

We might also need to deploy the same stack to multiple accounts. We will have to store multiple credentials and profiles in our local configuration file for `awscli` and specify the profiles one by one! You can see an example here:

```
aws cloudformation deploy --profile dev
aws cloudformation deploy --profile test
aws cloudformation deploy --profile prod
```

And again, we have the same issue as we had with the regions.

Previously we would use *nested stacks* to declare region-wide stacks within a single stack. Nested stacks are a feature of CloudFormation that allows the template developer to specify the CloudFormation stack as a resource in the CloudFormation template. The initial idea was to have a workaround for AWS's limits on the number of resources per stack, but now nested stacks can also be used for this particular case. For more information, you can read AWS's blog at `https://aws.amazon.com/blogs/infrastructure-and-automation/multiple-account-multiple-region-aws-cloudformation/`.

In 2017, the CloudFormation development team introduced a feature called **StackSets** that solves all these problems. Let's dive into it.

Introducing StackSets

The result of CloudFormation stack deployment is always a bunch of resources, grouped in a single stack. We can consider a StackSet as a group of stacks deployed from the same template, with the same or different parameters, in multiple regions in a single account, in a single region for multiple accounts, or even multiple regions for multiple accounts! StackSets can be deployed to target regions or even accounts (whether in your AWS organization or just a separate account), as shown in the following diagram:

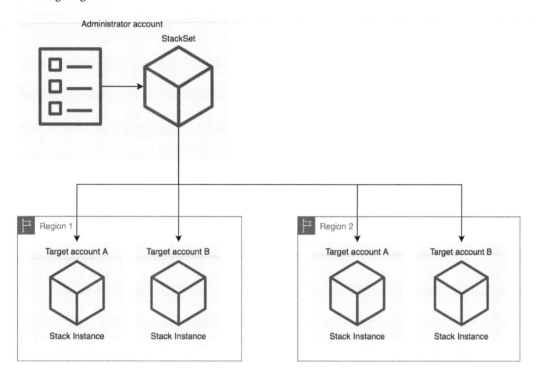

Figure 5.1 – StackSet architecture

As you can see in the preceding diagram, each StackSet consists of one or more stacks, provisioned from the same template. Those stacks are referred to as stack instances and are distributed among various accounts and regions. This is the first concept that we need to know.

Another concept is administrator and target accounts. An administrator account is an account where StackSets are managed. Whenever we want to create or update StackSets, we need to use an administrator account. This account must be granted to create stacks in other accounts (which is handled by **Identity and Access Management (IAM)**). The accounts in which stacks are being created are target accounts.

If you want to use StackSets to provision stacks to different regions, but in a single account, then your administrator and target accounts will be the same.

If the creation of one of the stack instances fails, then that won't affect other stack instances.

Let's look at a simple case: You deploy a stack with resources from services that for now are not supported in some of AWS's regions. In those regions, the stack creation will obviously fail. CloudFormation, by design, will start to roll back the changes. We might think that all other stack instances will roll back too, but that's not going to happen. Only the affected stack instance will be reverted, while the others will be deployed with no issues. This behavior is maintained by failure tolerance, which we will cover in the next section.

> **Important note**
>
> If we delete a StackSet, then *all* of the stack instances should be deleted. In order to keep some of the stack instances, we need to delete them *from* the StackSet with an option to *retain* them. That will remove the stack instance from the StackSet, but the stack on its own will stay.

That sounds complicated and increases the chance of accidental deletion. To prevent this from happening, AWS won't allow you to delete the StackSet. First, you must delete the stack instances, and when the StackSet is *empty*, it can be deleted.

Yet another thing to know about StackSets is the so-called StackSet operation options.

While the StackSet operation terms are fairly simple (the operations are *create*, *update*, and *delete*), the options might be tricky.

StackSets deployments are based on rolling the update out of the box. To configure the deployment behavior, we can set the **Maximum concurrent accounts**, **Failure tolerance**, and **Retain stacks** options, as detailed here:

- **Maximum concurrent accounts** defines the amount of parallel deployments per account. That said, if we deploy five stack instances within a StackSet, then we can define the number of concurrent deployments or a percentage. If we set this value to 2 (as a number) or 40 (as a percentage), then a deployment will occur in two accounts at the same time. Increasing this figure will improve the speed of stack provisioning, but if there is a mistake in a template that may lead to a failure, it will affect more target regions and accounts.

- **Failure tolerance** is an option that defines how we want to handle failure per deployment. This works only on a per-region basis and defines how many stack deployment failures we can ignore.

- **Retain stacks** is used only when we initiate the deletion of the stack instance from the StackSet. We cannot delete a StackSet when it's not empty. If we want to remove a stack instance from the StackSet but want to keep it in the target account or region, then we need to check this box.

The last thing to learn about before we start is the permissions that we need to grant to the administrator and target accounts.

Permissions

Stack instances within a StackSet can be deployed only using CloudFormation service roles. At the same time, the administrator account must have a role that allows the creation of stack instances. Before we proceed, let's configure those permissions for our account.

> **Important note**
>
> StackSet management roles must have a name:
> `AWSCloudFormationStackSetAdministrationRole` for administrator accounts and `AWSCloudFormationStackSetExecutionRole` for target accounts. This is not a string but is recommended, and is defined in the CloudFormation's documentation at `https://docs.aws.amazon.com/AWSCloudFormation/latest/UserGuide/stacksets-prereqs.html`.

To deploy these roles in our account (which will act as an administrator and target account at the same time), we will use the following code:

```
// CloudFormation:StackSetPermissions.yaml (admin account)
  StackSetAdministratorRole:
    Type: AWS::IAM::Role
    Properties:
      RoleName: «AWSCloudFormationStackSetAdministrationRole»
      AssumeRolePolicyDocument:
        # ...
      Policies:
        - PolicyName: StackSetAdministratorPolicy
          PolicyDocument:
            Version: 2012-10-17
            Statement:
              Effect: Allow
              Action: «sts:AssumeRole»
              Resource:
                - «arn:aws:iam::*:role/
AWSCloudFormationStackSetExecutionRole»
```

The administrator role only has one action that is allowed, and this is to assume the role in a target account:

```
// StackSetPermissions.yaml (target account)
  StackSetExecutionRole:
    Type: AWS::IAM::Role
    Properties:
      RoleName: AWSCloudFormationStackSetExecutionRole
      AssumeRolePolicyDocument:
        Version: 2012-10-17
        Statement:
          Effect: Allow
          Action: «sts:AssumeRole»
          Principal:
            AWS: !Sub «arn:aws:iam::${AWS::AccountId}:root»
      ManagedPolicyArns:
        - «arn:aws:iam::aws:policy/AdministratorAccess»
```

The role in a target role will do all of the jobs, and so it must have enough permissions, so we grant administrator access to the execution role for the target account.

We also specify the AWS::AccountId pseudo parameter because, for the next section, we will deploy a StackSet in multiple regions but in the same account, so we won't need to expose the AWS account ID in the template. We just need to deploy the stack using this template:

```
$ aws cloudformation deploy \
      --stack-name StackSet-Permissions \
      --template-file StackSetPermissions.yaml \
      --capabilities CAPABILITY_NAMED_IAM
```

Once the stack is created, we are all set and ready to go. We've prepared IAM roles in order to allow StackSets to be created and provisioned. Now, let's deploy our core stack to multiple regions!

Deploying to multiple regions

We are now going to start creating a StackSet for a single account but in multiple regions. We will begin with the AWS Management Console.

Using the AWS console

Let's start by deploying a StackSet with the core template in a single account (for example, our main account). We'll begin with the AWS console. Follow these steps:

1. Once we log in to the console, we will go to **CloudFormation - StackSets** and click on **Create StackSet**. We will choose **Template is ready**, upload our `core.yaml` file (which you will find in the GitHub repository), and click **Next**. The template will be uploaded to **Simple Storage Service (S3)** automatically:

Choose a template

Prerequisite - Prepare template

Prepare template
Every stack is based on a template. A template is a JSON or YAML file that contains configuration information about the AWS resources you want to include in the stack.

● Template is ready	○ Use a sample template

Specify template
A template is a JSON or YAML file that describes your stack's resources and properties.

Template source
Selecting a template generates an Amazon S3 URL where it will be stored.

○ Amazon S3 URL	● Upload a template file

Upload a template file

Choose file 🔼	core.yaml

JSON or YAML formatted file

S3 URL: https://s3.eu-central-1.amazonaws.com/cf-templates-1jztmpgj6dq2l-eu-central-1/2019365AVb-core.yaml | View in Designer |

Cancel   Next

Figure 5.2 – CloudFormation StackSet console – Template selection

2.   Now, we need to supply the StackSet name and parameters and hit **Next**:

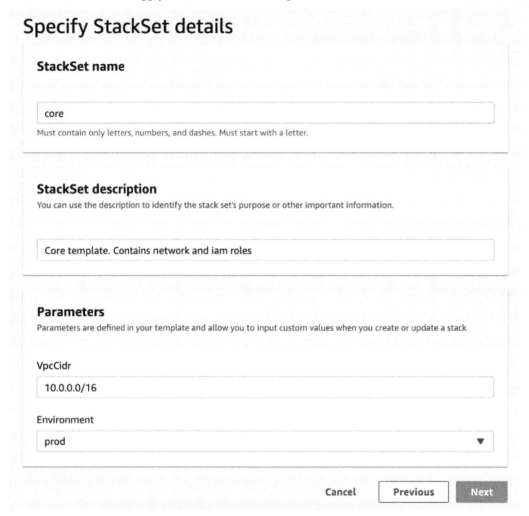

Figure 5.3 – CloudFormation StackSet console – StackSet details

> **Important note**
>
> We insert parameter values for the StackSet, and these parameters will be inherited by stack instances. It is not yet possible to add unique parameters per stack instance during StackSet creation, since all stack instances by design are meant to be the same. Alternatively, we can create one stack instance for the StackSet in the beginning, and then use `--parameter-overrides` when we add stack instances.

3. For this example, we are not going to provide any TAGs, but we must specify the administrator role for the StackSet. We will leave the execution role unchanged and hit **Next**:

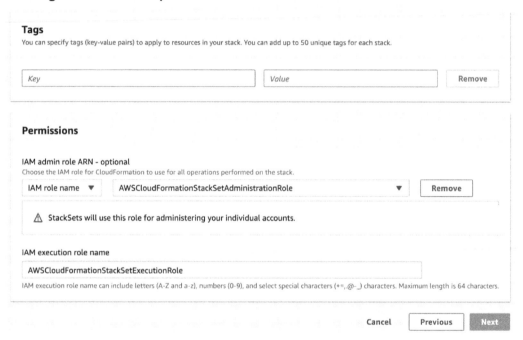

Figure 5.4 – CloudFormation StackSet console – StackSet options

4. Now, we need to enter values for AWS accounts, regions, and deployment options. Since we're only creating a StackSet in our main accounts, we will choose **Deploy stacks in accounts** and add the account ID:

Set deployment options

Accounts

Identify accounts or organizational units in which you want to modify stacks

Deployment locations

StackSets can be deployed into accounts or an organizational unit.

- ● **Deploy stacks in accounts**
- ○ **Deploy stacks in organizational units**

Account numbers

Enter account numbers or populate from a file.

```
ACCT_ID
```

12-Digit account numbers separated by commas.

| Upload .csv file ⬆ | *No file chosen* |

Figure 5.5 – CloudFormation StackSet console – Deployment options (account)

5. Next, we need to specify the regions we will deploy our stacks to. We will choose **US East (N. Virginia)** (us-east-1) and **EU (Ireland)** (eu-west-1):

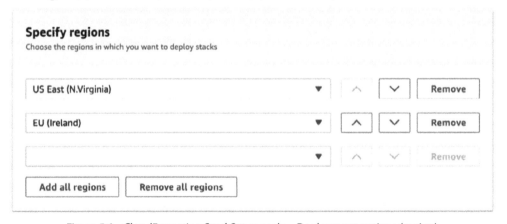

Figure 5.6 – CloudFormation StackSet console – Deployment options (region)

We can change the order of regions if we wish, given that CloudFormation will deploy the stack instances in the order that they are specified here. If we made Ireland our *test* region and North Virginia our *prod* region, it would be wise to deploy first to test and then to production. But for this example, we will keep things as they are.

Now, let's look at our deployment options.

6. We will set **Maximum concurrent accounts** to 1 (since we will only deploy to our account) and **Failure tolerance** to 0—we don't want to proceed if one of the stack instances fails to be provisioned. Then, we hit **Next** one last time:

Deployment options

Maximum concurrent accounts - optional
Number of accounts per region to which you can deploy stacks at one time. The higher the number, the faster the operation

| Number ▼ | 1 |

Failure tolerance - optional
Number of account, per region, for which stacks can fail before CloudFormation stops the operation in that region. If the operation is stopped in one region, it does not continue in other regions. The lower the number the safer the operation.

| Number ▼ | 0 |

Figure 5.7 – CloudFormation StackSet console – Deployment options (deployment preferences)

7. We need to review the summary and check **I acknowledge that AWS CloudFormation might create IAM resources** (this is like setting CAPABILITY_IAM in awscli). If there is something that we want to change, then we can click **Edit** on any of the steps in the **Summary** section. If everything is set in order, then all we need to do is click **Submit**. Now, we can review our StackSet:

Figure 5.8 – CloudFormation StackSet console – Main page

In the StackSet information, we will see the summary and other properties of the StackSet. What we're interested in is **stack instances**:

AWS region	Stack ID	Detailed Status
eu-west-1	arn:aws:cloudformation:eu-west-1:⬛⬛⬛⬛:stack/StackSet-core-3bd7d958-71a5-4836-ad18-ece380835965/5ed18030-3298-11ee-adf6-06db57156585	ⓘ RUNNING
us-east-1	-	⊘ PENDING

Figure 5.9 – CloudFormation StackSet console – Stack instances

8. We can see that only one stack is being provisioned. This is because we set **Maximum concurrent accounts** to **1**, and deployment to Ireland will not begin until the stack instance in North Virginia is provisioned. We can't see CloudFormation events from this menu, so we will have to switch to the North Virginia region and look them up there, as shown in the following screenshot:

Stacks

○   **StackSet-core-f875d322-ad70-4f98-b81d-25dd34b9fd2c**
     2023-08-04 09:29:40 UTC+0200
     ⊘ CREATE_COMPLETE

Figure 5.10 – CloudFormation StackSet console - Stacks

9. We can see that this stack instance is created. Once both stack instances are created, we will see that their **Status** value is **CURRENT** in the stack instances section:

into the stack instance's account, navigate to the appropriate region, and then select the desired stack

AWS region	Stack ID	Status
eu-west-1	arn:aws:cloudf…	⊘ CURRENT
us-east-1	arn:aws:cloudf…	⊘ CURRENT

Figure 5.11 – CloudFormation StackSet console – Stack instances

Now, let's do the same using `awscli`. To clean up, we need to delete the stack instances from the StackSet and then the StackSet itself.

Using awscli

Creating StackSets using `awscli` introduces a few differences. One of them is that the creation of a StackSet *and* stack instances is a different and independent operation. This means that we can easily use specific parameters per stack instance, which is helpful when we want to have slight changes in stack instances within a single StackSet.

By going through the following steps, we will be able to achieve multi-region deployment:

1. We begin by creating a StackSet, like so:

```
$ aws cloudformation create-stack-set \
      --stack-set-name core \
      --template-body file://core.yaml \
      --capabilities CAPABILITY_NAMED_IAM
```

We will see `StackSetId` in response. If we go to the AWS console, we will see the active StackSet with no stack instances; however, the parameters will be set (with the default values, unless we specify otherwise).

2. Now, we create the first stack instance. We will still use our account, choose Ireland as the region, and override the parameters for `VpcCidr` and `Environment`:

```
$ aws cloudformation create-stack-instances \
      --stack-set-name core \
      --accounts ACCT_ID \
      --regions eu-west-1 \
      --parameter-overrides \
ParameterKey=VpcCidr,ParameterValue=10.1.0.0/16 \
ParameterKey=Environment,ParameterValue=test
# Response
{
    "OperationId": "7643d973-1358-475d-b148-5e096f9a44b9"
}
```

3. `awscli` will return an `OperationId` value, and we can review our stack instance in the AWS console or using the command-line interface:

```
$ aws cloudformation list-stack-instances \
      --stack-set-name core
{
    "Summaries": [
        {
```

```
            "StackSetId": "core:ec0e8256-dcc9-4dd0-b074-
aee9721ed949",
            "Region": "eu-west-1",
            "Account": "ACCT_ID",
            "StackId": "arn:aws:cloudformation:eu-west-
1:ACCT_ID:stack/StackSet-core-f8b4d34b-abaf-4e97-b004-
9309ea693803/124e9400-2bc6-11ea-8c11-0abd335268a4",
            "Status": "OUTDATED",
            "StatusReason": "User Initiated",
            "DriftStatus": "NOT_CHECKED"
        }
    ]
}
```

4. We don't have to wait until this stack instance is created. Let's create a production stack instance:

```
$ aws cloudformation create-stack-instances \
    --stack-set-name core \
    --accounts ACCT_ID \
    --regions us-east-1 \
    --parameter-overrides \
ParameterKey=VpcCidr,ParameterValue=10.0.0.0/16 \
ParameterKey=Environment,ParameterValue=prod
```

Voilà! Using `awscli`, we were able to work around the issue with inherited parameters from StackSets! Now, let's check how StackSets work in a multi-account environment.

Best practices for StackSets

Before we begin, we need to learn a bit about best practices for StackSets. This is crucial, because we don't want to make a monstrous zoo instead of a properly organized infrastructure, and we want to have efficiency and transparency for stack operations. The most important of these are listed as follows:

- **Develop universal templates**: By default, a StackSet deploys the same template and parameter set in all the regions and accounts. To allow this process to be as automated as possible, we must focus on the reusability of our template. Do not hardcode regions and Availability Zones; instead, use AWS **Systems Manager** (**SSM**) parameter stores in every account and region to ease the deployment of the StackSet. Don't set names for global resources such as IAM roles, users, groups, policies, S3 buckets, and so on to avoid naming conflicts.

  Think big, start small. If you are asked to create a StackSet for an application that will serve tens of accounts and regions, it is wise to start with only a few of them. Get some hands-on experience, improve your template, and continue growing.

- **Don't forget about deployment performance**: It will take a lot of time to perform rolling updates on a StackSet. You can speed up this process if you set your maximum concurrent operations accordingly.

- **Don't forget about validation and linting**: Even if the StackSet stops operating in case of failure and rollback, we don't want to slow down. Doing preflight checks using linting and validation will save us a lot of time.

Make sure you look up the best practices for StackSets in the AWS documentation (you will find a link in the *Further reading* section). Meanwhile, let's continue looking at how to deploy to multiple accounts.

Deploying to multiple accounts

Now, let's begin working with multiple accounts. For this section, I've created two additional accounts in AWS Organizations: testing and production.

> **Important note**
>
> Since this book is not about **Multi-Account Strategies** (**MAS**), we're not going to cover the creation of child accounts and **Organizational Units** (**OUs**) in this book. If you need to learn about these, then you can start looking at AWS Organizations (`https://aws.amazon.com/organizations/`). If you don't use a MAS and don't plan to, then you may skip this section.

Since we will work in various accounts, we need to tweak our StackSet permissions template. We've separated it into two templates—one for an administrator role and one for an execution role. We don't need to create an execution role in our main (or to use the terms of AWS, our payer) account, because no stack instance will be created in it.

Our StackSet administrator role is the same, but the StackSet execution role will be a bit different, as shown here:

```
// StackSetExecution.yaml
AWSTemplateFormatVersion: "2010-09-09"
Description: StackSet IAM roles
Parameters:
  AdminAcctId:
    Type: String
    AllowedPattern: «(\d+)$»
Resources:
  StackSetExecutionRole:
    Type: AWS::IAM::Role
    Properties:
      # ...
          Principal:
```

```
            AWS:
              - !Sub "arn:aws:iam::${AdminAcctId}:root"
        # ...
```

Here, we add an `AdminAcctId` parameter, which we will enter manually. This parameter will be used to set a proper `Principal` value for the execution role.

To deploy this stack in all the child accounts, we will add an API key and secret to `~/.aws/credentials` under different profiles and use those profiles to provision execution roles:

```
$ aws cloudformation deploy \
      --stack-name Admin-Role \
      --template-file StackSetAdmin.yaml \
      --capabilities CAPABILITY_NAMED_IAM
$ aws cloudformation deploy \
      --stack-name Exec-Role \
      --profile test \
      --template-file StackSetExec.yaml \
      --parameter-overrides AdminAcctId=ACCT_ID \
      --capabilities CAPABILITY_NAMED_IAM
$ aws cloudformation deploy \
      --stack-name Exec-Role \
      --profile prod \
      --template-file StackSetExec.yaml \
      --parameter-overrides AdminAcctId=ACCT_ID \
      --capabilities CAPABILITY_NAMED_IAM
```

Once this is done, we can start by creating a StackSet with multiple accounts. We've altered our core template as well: now, it will have a single `VpcCidr` value, which defaults to `10.0.0.0/16`, as we don't expect our production and testing environment to interact with each other, and we have removed the `Environment` parameter since we separated testing and production on the AWS account level. This will reduce the number of steps we need to take when we deploy StackSets across different accounts.

Following the next steps, we will deploy a multi-account infrastructure, as follows:

1. Again, we first create a StackSet:

    ```
    $ aws cloudformation create-stack-set \
          --stack-set-name core \
          --template-body file://core.yaml \
          --capabilities CAPABILITY_NAMED_IAM
    ```

2. Then, we create stack instances, but this time, we will change the arguments a bit. First, we will specify two child accounts—testing and production—and set maximum concurrent operations to `100` in order to deploy to both accounts in parallel:

```
$ aws cloudformation create-stack-instances \
      --stack-set-name core \
      --accounts ACCT_ID_PROD ACCT_ID_TEST \
      --regions REGION \
      --operation-preferences \
      MaxConcurrentPercentage=100
```

One thing we need to remember is that the number of concurrent deployments is defined per account per region. This means that if we work with two accounts and three regions, then the first batch will be done in one account, then another, and then in the third.

Let's move on to the next topic.

Preventing failures of multiple StackSet deployments using TAGs

When we want to deploy StackSets where stack instances in one StackSet depend on the stack instances in another, then we need to make sure that these deployments do not fail.

Although there is a failure-tolerance option in implementing StackSet operations, we need to catch and handle all possible exceptions before the actual operation.

StackSets have an optional feature called a TAG. A TAG is a Lambda function that is executed on a target account before a StackSet operation and checks whether a target account is *ready* to perform this operation—for example, if the required resources exist or if there is no other ongoing StackSet operation.

TAGs must be developed by us, but their outcome is quite simple: if all checks pass, then it should return `SUCCESS`, or `FAIL` if one or more checks do not pass.

For this chapter, we will develop a TAG function that will check the following:

-   Whether a core stack exists
-   Whether the necessary exports from the core stack also exist
-   Whether the **Secure Shell** (**SSH**) key exists on **Elastic Compute Cloud** (**EC2**)

We need this because we will deploy a web tier StackSet on top of the core StackSet. As we remember from *Chapter 2*, *Advanced Template Development*, WebTier resources are created in subnets, which are a part of the core stack.

Since our TAG will invoke CloudFormation's and EC2's API, it must have an IAM role that allows `Get*` and `Describe*` calls to those services.

We will deploy our TAG function in a single-account environment (to make it possible for those readers who do not yet use multi-account strategies and AWS Organizations).

> **Important note**
>
> The TAG function must have a name such as `AWSCloudFormationStackSetAccountGate`. While it is possible to override the default names for the StackSet administrator and execution roles, it is not yet possible to set a custom name for the TAG. If the TAG function name is different, or this function cannot be invoked, the StackSet will ignore the TAG's check.

Our TAG will have a handler (which is a `"main"` function for Lambda) and three functions: `check_if_key_exists`, `check_if_core_stack_exists`, and `check_if_exports_exist`.

Our script should look like the following:

- The following function connects to the EC2 service and checks whether the `"mykey"` SSH key is present:

```
// tag.py
import boto3
def check_if_key_exists():
    client = boto3.client(<ec2>)
    try:
        resp = client.describe_key_pairs(KeyNames=[«mykey»])
    except Exception:
        return False
    if len(resp[<KeyPairs>]) == 0:
        return False
    return True
```

- The following function connects to the CloudFormation service and requests information on the core stack:

```
// tag.py
def check_if_core_stack_exists():
    client = boto3.client(<cloudformation>)
    try:
        resp = client.describe_stacks(StackName=»core»)
    except Exception:
        return False
    if len(resp[<Stacks>]) == 0:
        return False
    return True
```

- The following function connects to the CloudFormation service too, but runs a different API call to obtain exported outputs:

```python
// tag.py
def check_if_exports_exist():
    to_check = [«WebTierSubnet1Id»,
                <WebTierSubnet2Id>,
                «WebTierSubnet3Id»,
                «VpcId»,
                «WebTierMaxSizeParameter»,
                «WebTierMinSizeParameter»,
                «WebTierDesSizeParameter»]
    exports = []
    client = boto3.client(<cloudformation>)
    try:
        resp = client.list_exports()
    except Exception:
        return False
    for export in resp[<Exports>]:
        exports.append(export[<Name>])
    if not all(exp in exports for exp in to_check):
        return False
    return True
```

Lastly, we define a Lambda handler, which will invoke all the functions above tag.py:

```python
def lambda_handler(event, context):
    status = «SUCCEEDED»
    if not (check_if_key_exists() and check_if_core_stack_exists() and
check_if_exports_exist()):
        status = «FAILED»
    return {
        <Status>: status
    }
```

As we can see in the lambda_handler function, if any of those functions return False, then the TAG result is FAILED.

Let's package our TAG into the CloudFormation template, like so:

```yaml
// tag.yaml
AWSTemplateFormatVersion: "2010-09-09"
Resources:
  AccountGateFunctionRole:
    Type: <AWS::IAM::Role>
```

```
    Properties:
      # ...
  AccountGateFunction:
    Type: <AWS::Lambda::Function>
    Properties:
      FunctionName: <AWSCloudFormationStackSetsAccountGate>
      Code:
        ZipFile: |
          # source code of our function...
      Handler: lambda_function.lambda_handler
      MemorySize: 128
      Runtime: python3.7
      Timeout: 30
      Role: !GetAtt AccountGateFunctionRole.Arn
```

Now, we just need to deploy this TAG, as follows:

```
$ aws cloudformation deploy \
    --stack-name tag \
    --template-file tag.yaml \
    --capabilities CAPABILITY_IAM
```

Note that the TAG function must be deployed in every account *and* region where stack instances will be created. Once the TAG stack is deployed, we can create a StackSet for the web tier (the same way we did before for the core StackSet), as follows:

```
$ aws cloudformation create-stack-set \
    --stack-set-name webtier \
    --template-body file://webtier.yaml
$ aws cloudformation create-stack-instances \
    --stack-set-name webtier \
    --accounts ACCT_ID \
    --regions eu-central-1
```

What we will see is obviously an error:

Status	Status Reason
⊗ OUTDATED	AccountGate check failed

Figure 5.12 – CloudFormation StackSet console

This is because the core stack doesn't exist.

Checking by TAG doesn't show enough information, as we can see here. (Try to find out which check failed exactly. The first thing it looks up is the TAG function logs.) However, it can help us to prevent failures before the StackSet operations initiate, thereby protecting us from unexpected downtime.

What we also must remember is that TAG is only done during create and update operations and *not* for the deletion of stack instances.

Summary

In this chapter, we've learned about StackSets, their use cases, how to deploy them, and how to work with failures.

StackSets are a promising feature, although they introduce some complexity, and it is not easy to integrate them with **Continuous Delivery** (**CD**) systems. Nevertheless, they come in handy when you want to provision the same stacks across multiple regions or even accounts.

Consider using StackSets when you are tasked to deploy the same environment and resources to your customers—for example, if you provide a **Business-to-Business** (**B2B**) SaaS platform or want to automate deployment for development, test, staging, and production environments. StackSets are also useful for replicating your applications across multiple regions if you need to have a **Point of Presence** (**PoP**) in various countries and continents.

In the next chapter, we will use `cfn-init`, CloudFormation's helper script, to install software on EC2 resources. Stay tuned!

Questions

1. Is it possible to have custom names for administrator and execution roles?
2. If you create a StackSet in a single account, is it possible to create stack instances in multiple regions at the same time?
3. In which order are stack instances created?
4. Is it possible to delete a StackSet if it has stack instances in it?
5. What are the required actions allowed for the administrator IAM role in a StackSet?

Further reading

- StackSets best practices: `https://docs.aws.amazon.com/AWSCloudFormation/latest/UserGuide/stacksets-bestpractices.html`
- Configuring a TAG: `https://docs.aws.amazon.com/AWSCloudFormation/latest/UserGuide/stacksets-account-gating.html`

6

Configuration Management of EC2 Instances Using cfn-init

There are multiple ways to manage the configuration of your EC2 instances and applications on AWS. There is `UserData`, a basic shell script that runs during the launch of an EC2 instance. You can use configuration management systems, such as Ansible, Puppet, Chef, and SaltStack, to manage your resources. AWS provides a service called **OpsWorks**—a managed Chef or Puppet server.

We are going to learn about `cfn-init` (CloudFormation's own configuration management tool) and how can we use it to deploy applications on EC2 resources. We are going to cover `cfn-init` along with `AWS::CloudFormation:Init`, CloudFormation's metadata key, which actually declares configuration items for EC2 resources.

In this chapter, we will cover the following topics:

- Introducing `cfn-init`
- Deploying your application on EC2 during stack creation
- Using `cfn-signal` to inform CloudFormation of resource readiness

Technical requirements

The code used in this chapter can be found in the book's GitHub repository at `https://github.com/PacktPublishing/Mastering-AWS-CloudFormation-Second-Edition/tree/main/Chapter06`.

Check out the following video to see the Code in Action:

`https://packt.link/J0FUQ`

Introducing cfn-init

CloudFormation is a declarative instrument. This means that everything in your template is a declaration of what should be there in CloudFormation's state. And since you use resource attributes to declare your infrastructure, you must store your configuration in it as well, whether it's a source code in a Lambda function or UserData in an EC2 launch template, launch configuration, or instance.

Using UserData is a very simple process, but it is hard to declare a configuration in it. In the end, you will do a lot of shell programming, which is not as reliable as configuration management should be.

Luckily, CloudFormation has a set of so-called *helper scripts*—instruments that can get the data from CloudFormation's metadata or a stack, process it, and perform operations on your resources. One of them is called cfn-init.

> **Important note**
>
> The cfn-init instrument (and any other helper script) is only included in Amazon Linux AMIs as a part of the distribution. For other Linux or Windows distributions, you will have to install it first. For more information, read the documentation about helper scripts from AWS at https://docs.aws.amazon.com/AWSCloudFormation/latest/UserGuide/cfn-helper-scripts-reference.html.

EC2 instances support bootstrapping for initial configuration and software installation. This bootstrapping is called UserData, a simple Bash script that runs under the root user as soon as an instance is up.

How is cfn-init actually applied to UserData? It is simply added to the UserData a resource declaration. For example, we can instruct our EC2 resource to run cfn-init by adding the command and arguments as shown in the following code:

```
UserData:
  Fn::Base64: !Sub |
    #!/bin/bash -xe
    /opt/aws/bin/cfn-init -v \
    --stack ${AWS::StackName} \
    --resource Lc --configsets InstallAndRun \
    --region ${AWS::Region}
```

In the preceding code snippet, we can see that the root user will run the cfn-init command, providing the necessary arguments to it, such as the stack name, the resource to refer to, configSets, and the AWS Region.

But where is this data obtained from? Looking at the arguments, we might notice that cfn-init is attempting to talk to a stack.

You might remember that in *Chapter 2, Advanced Template Development*, we looked at stack or resource **metadata**. Metadata contains specific details about our resources or the entire stack. The metadata has specific keys, and one such key that we are going to work with is called AWS::CloudFormation::Init.

This AWS::CloudFormation::Init (for simplicity, I'm going to call it just init) metadata can be included only in EC2 resources, such as instance, launch configuration, or a launch template.

Init is a simplified configuration management system that can carry out the following actions on the EC2 resource:

- Run commands

- Write files to disk (for example, configuration files)

- Create groups

- Create users

- Install packages

- Start, enable, and stop services

- Download data from various sources (GitHub or S3)

Let's say that we want to install and run an Apache web server on an EC2 instance. To set this up, our init metadata should look like the following:

```
Web server:
  Type: AWS::EC2::Instance
  Metadata:
    AWS::CloudFormation::Init:
      configSets:
      - «Deploy"
      Deploy:
        InstallAndRun:
          packages:
            yum:
              httpd: []
          services:
          # this is a key for init metadata.
          # cfn-init will use init.d or systemd if necessary
            sysvinit:
              httpd:
                enabled: «true"
                ensureRunning: "true"
```

Here, we declare `init` in the resource's metadata and use two keys for `init`: `packages` and `services`. These keys (for example, the actions to be done) are declared under the `InstallAndRun` configuration set. Now all we need to do is add `cfn-init` to the `UserData` block:

```
Webserver:
  Type: AWS::EC2::Instance
  # Metadata block…
  Properties:
  # some properties…
    UserData:
      Fn::Base64: !Sub
        #!/bin/bash -xe
        /opt/aws/bin/cfn-init -v \
        --stack ${AWS::StackName} \
        --resource Webserver \
        --configsets Deploy \
        --region ${AWS::Region}
```

This block will make our instance talk to CloudFormation's API to obtain its metadata and run all the necessary configurations.

> **Important note**
>
> You've probably noticed that we specify the Region (because, by default, the underlying **Operating System (OS)** doesn't know which Region it belongs to), but we don't provide any API key/secret or IAM role ARN. The `cfn-init` tool doesn't need an IAM role to talk to CloudFormation's resource metadata because it authenticates CloudFormation again by checking that this *physical* resource is actually a member of this CloudFormation stack.

We've covered the basics of `cfn-init`, but there is a lot more that CloudFormation's helper scripts can do. Let's learn about them by going through some examples.

Deploying your application to EC2 during stack creation

In this section, we will get hands-on experience with `cfn-init` by using it to bootstrap an application on EC2 instances.

We will begin with a simple "Hello, World!" example.

Creating a "Hello, World!" application

We'll start by implementing a basic "Hello, World!" application, which is going to be deployed in an `AutoScaling` group. This is going to be an application based on Flask—a lightweight Python web framework:

1. Let's develop our app:

```
// hello-world-flask.py
#!/usr/bin/env python3
from flask import Flask
app = Flask(__name__)
@app.route("/")
def hello():
    return «Hello, World, from AWS!"
if __name__ == "__main__":
    app.run(host="0.0.0.0", port=80)
```

Nothing really serious. We will store this application on S3 and use `cfn-init` to install Python and Flask, pull the code from S3, create a systemd unit, and start a service that will serve our application.

2. Let's develop our templates. We'll need a preparation template (an S3 bucket and network) to store the Python script and have the network configured:

```
// hello-world-prep.yaml
AWSTemplateFormatVersion: "2010-09-09"
Description: HelloWorld prep template
Parameters:
  VpcCidr:
    Type: String
    AllowedPattern: '(\d{1,3})\.(\d{1,3})\.(\d{1,3})\.(\d{1,3})/
(\d{1,2})'
Resources:
  SourceBucket: # …
  Vpc: # …
  Igw: # …
  IgwAttachment: # …
  Subnet1: # …
  Subnet2: # …
  PublicRouteTable: # …
  PublicRoute: # …
  PublicRtAssoc1: # …
  PublicRtAssoc2: # …
Outputs:
```

```
VpcId: #...
Subnet1Id: #...
Subnet2Id: #...
```

Here, we declare our required resources with properties and necessary exports that we'll use in the next template. Let's deploy this template to the stack:

```
$ aws cloudformation deploy \
    --stack-name hello-world-prep \
    --template-file hello-world-prep.yaml
```

Now, we need to develop our application resources template. We've already done this a couple of times, so I'm going to show only the important bits in the following steps.

To run our application, we'll need an **Elastic Load Balancing** (**ELB**) load balancer, launch configuration, an AutoScaling group, an IAM role, and a few security groups.

3. We will start with the IAM role. We already know that cfn-init can access CloudFormation to retrieve metadata, but we need an instance to be able to pull the source code of our app from S3, and that's why we add this role:

```
// hello-world-app.yaml
AppRole:
  Type: AWS::IAM::Role
  Properties:
    AssumeRolePolicyDocument:
      Version: «2012-10-17»
      Statement:
        - Effect: Allow
          Action: «sts:AssumeRole"
          Principal:
            Service: «ec2.amazonaws.com"
    Policies:
      - PolicyName: S3
        PolicyDocument:
          Version: «2012-10-17»
          Statement:
            - Effect: Allow
              Action: «s3:*»
              Resource: «*»
```

4. Next, we store two metadata keys for our launch configuration. The first one is AWS::CloudFormation::Authentication:

```
// hello-world-app.yaml
AWS::CloudFormation::Authentication:
  role:
```

```
type: «S3»
buckets:
  - !ImportValue S3Bucket
roleName: !Ref AppRole
```

This block declares that `cfn-init` will use the IAM role to authenticate against S3. The second metadata key is `AWS::CloudFormation::Init`. It contains several elements:

```
// hello-world-app.yaml
AWS::CloudFormation::Init:
  configSets:
    InstallAndRun:
      - «Configure"
  Configure:
    # …
```

Here, we declare `configSets`, the configuration blocks (only one in this case) that will be applied by `cfn-init`. The `InstallAndRun` configuration set has only one configuration item, which is called `Configure`.

It contains the actions that need to be taken, which we will look at in the following steps.

5. The first action will be to install packages:

```
// hello-world-app.yaml
packages:
  yum:
    python3: []
    python3-pip: []
```

Here, we declare which packages we want to install. Since our application is based on Python 3 and requires an external dependency to be installed (Flask), we install `python3` and `python3-pip`, since they are not included in the base distribution.

6. Next, we add the actual application files:

```
// hello-world-app.yaml
files:
  /opt/helloworld.py:
    owner: root
    group: root
    mode: 755
    source: !Sub
      - "https://${bucket}.s3.${AWS::Region}.${AWS::URLSuffix}/
hello-world-flask.py"
      - bucket: !ImportValue S3Bucket
    authentification: "role"
  /etc/systemd/system/helloworld.service:
```

```
owner: root
group: root
mode: 755
content: |
  [Unit]
  Description=HelloWorld service
  After=network.target
  [Service]
  Type=simple
  User=root
  ExecStart=/opt/helloworld.py
  Restart=on-abort
  [Install]
  WantedBy=multi-user.target
```

There are two files that we will create. The first one (/opt/helloworld.py) is the source code of our application and is retrieved from S3. Here, we supply the authentication element called "role". This will instruct cfn-init to assume our IAM role in order to obtain the object from S3.

The second one is the systemd unit, which is added to the systemd directory to register a service.

7. Lastly, we add the commands section with the commands and services in order to install Flask, reload systemd, and start our application as a service:

```
commands:
  installflask:
    # This command runs installation
    command: «pip3 install flask"
    # This command runs BEFORE command above
    # and checks if pip3 is present on system
    # if return code is not 0 cfn-init stops
    test: «which pip3»
  reloadsystemd:
    command: «systemctl daemon-reload"
services:
  sysvinit:
    helloworld:
      enabled: «true"
      ensureRunning: "true"
```

8. Now, we are ready to deploy our application stack but, before we do this, we need to upload the source to S3:

```
$ aws s3 ls
2020-01-13 16:26:31 hello-world-prep-sourcebucket-1615b2vvpr5js
```

```
$ aws s3 cp hello-world-flask.py s3://hello-world-prep-
sourcebucket-1615b2vvpr5js
upload: ./hello-world-flask.py to s3://hello-world-prep-
sourcebucket-1615b2vvpr5js/hello-world-flask.py
$ aws cloudformation deploy \
       --stack-name helloworld \
       --template-file hello-world-app.yaml \
       --capabilities CAPABILITY_IAM
```

Once the stack is deployed, we can send an HTTP request to the ELB load balancer:

Figure 6.1 – AWS EC2 ELB console

We can check the code by running `curl` against our ELB DNS name:

```
$ curl  hello-w-Elb-1OPBMY2QEK0K-1470028701.us-east-1.elb.amazonaws.
com
Hello, World, from AWS!
```

We're all set! Now, let's try to build something bigger than just a small web app. How about a **Linux, NGINX, MySQL, PHP (LNMP)** stack?

Creating an LNMP stack

Since most LNMP stacks are single-node installations, we will install a single EC2 instance and declare all of its configuration in the metadata. We will use AWS's provided demo PHP app to check that our LNMP stack is operational.

By going through the following steps, we will have an LNMP stack running with a sample application:

1. We will start by declaring an EC2 instance. It will look like this:

    ```
    // lnmp.yaml
    Resources:
      Lnmp:
        Type: AWS::EC2::Instance
        Properties:
          ImageId: !Ref ImageId
          InstanceType: t2.micro
          KeyName: !Ref KeyName
          UserData:
            Fn::Base64:
              Fn::Sub: |
                #!/bin/bash -xe
                /opt/aws/bin/cfn-init -v \
                --stack ${AWS::StackName} \
                --resource Lnmp \
                --configsets Configure \
                --region ${AWS::Region}
    ```

    Since we need to perform more actions and configurations this time, we'll use multiple configuration items. Configuring the config set will consist of setting up MySQL, PHP, and NGINX. So, our metadata skeleton should look like this:

    ```
    Metadata:
      AWS::CloudFomration:Init:
        configSets:
          Configure:
            - «Mysql"
            - «DbSetup"
            - «Php"
            - «Nginx»
    ```

2. Let's start with the MySQL installation and database setup. We'll install the necessary packages, run the service, and create the user and database. The setup process is similar to what we did before, so I'd like to point to a few new things here:

    ```
    // lnmp.yaml
    files:
      #...
      /etc/cfn/cfn-hup.conf:
        content: !Sub |
          [main]
          stack=${AWS::StackId}
    ```

```
    region=${AWS::Region}
  mode: 400
  owner: root
  group: root
/etc/cfn/hooks.d/cfn-auto-reloader.conf:
  content: !Sub |
    [cfn-auto-reloader-hook]
    triggers=post.update
    path=Resources.Lnmp.Metadata.AWS::CloudFormation::Init
    action=#...
    runas=root
```

Let me introduce you to `cfn-hup`, which is the `cfn-init` tool's little helper! The `cfn-init` tool is declarative, so each time we update the metadata, we need to recreate the resource, which can be achieved *within* the `AutoScaling` group and update policies, but it is troublesome to do this with stateful systems.

The `cfn-hup` tool has its own configuration file, which dictates the stack that we store the information in and the Region that we should look into, and it has specific hooks. Hooks are used to look into the changes in the resource's metadata (as we pointed out in the preceding template) and run a specific action. An action is a Bash command, so we can implement automation. In our case, we will rerun `cfn-init`. The `cfn-hup` phrase has to run as a service, so we must not forget to include it in the `services` section!

3. Another important thing to note is the following code fragment, where we add numbers before the command steps:

```
// lnmp.yaml
commands:
  01_set_mysql_root_pw:
    command: #...
  02_create_database:
    command: #...
    test: #...
```

So, why add numbering to the commands? The trick is that commands in the `commands` section run *not* in the declaration order, but in *alphabetical* order! That's why we need to add numbers at the start of each command step if one command needs to run after another.

4. We also ensure that both MySQL and `cfn-hup` are running:

```
// lnmp.yaml
services:
  sysvinit:
    mariadb:
      enabled: True
```

```
      ensureRunning: True
  cfn-hup:
    enabled: True
    ensureRunning: True
    files:
      - «/etc/cfn/cfn-hup.conf"
      - "/etc/cfn/hooks.d/cfn-auto-reloader.conf"
```

We will also make sure that cfn-hup *watches* its own files and restarts if there is a change in them.

5. The PHP and NGINX setups are going to be similar, but we will run them separately. The reason why we want to separate these configurations is that NGINX is our actual frontend. Before starting the frontend, we want to have the backend (MySQL) and middleware operational:

```
// lnmp.yaml
Php:
  packages:
    yum:
      php: []
      php-mysql: []
      php-fpm: []
  files:
    /var/www/html/index.php:
      content: !Sub |
        # a lot of PHP and HTML here…
      mode: 644
      owner: root
      group: root
  services:
    sysvinit:
      php-fpm:
        enabled: True
        ensureRunning: True
```

6. The next and the last bit is our web server. We will add configuration files to NGINX and make sure that the NGINX service is running:

```
// lnmp.yaml
Nginx:
  packages:
    yum:
      nginx: []
  files:
    /etc/nginx/nginx.conf:
```

```
        content: !Sub |
          # ...
    /etc/nginx/conf.d/default.conf:
        content: !Sub |
          # ...
  services:
    sysvinit:
      nginx:
        enabled: True
        ensureRunning: True
```

7. Once it's done, we can deploy our stack:

```
$ aws cloudformation deploy \
                --stack-name lnmp \
                --template-file lnmp.yaml \
                --parameter-overrides \
                DBName=foo \
                DBUsername=bar \
                DBPassword=foobar123 \
                DBRootPassword=barfoo321
```

8. Then, we send an HTTP request to our web server:

```
$ aws cloudformation describe-stacks --stack-name lnmp --profile
personal | jq .[][].Outputs[].OutputValue
"http://ec2-18-194-210-115.eu-central-1.compute.amazonaws.com"
$ curl http://ec2-18-194-210-115.eu-central-1.compute.amazonaws.
com
# super lengthy response...
```

And that's it! We have fully configured our LNMP stack, which listens to the changes in the CloudFormation stack's metadata and will rerun `cfn-init` if there are any. There is one last thing we need to learn about before finishing this chapter.

Using cfn-signal to inform CloudFormation about resource readiness

CloudFormation reports resource readiness as soon as it retrieves a response from AWS's API that the resource is created. By this, we understand that if we create a **Relational Database Service (RDS)** instance and CloudFormation tells us that it's created, then we can connect to it right away.

While this is applicable for most of the managed services at AWS, it doesn't work on services that we run based on EC2. You see, CloudFormation is *not aware* that EC2 has a job to run and reports Done once the instance is in a Running state.

For small development environments, this might be fine, but imagine running a web application on an `AutoScaling` group. While the instance takes time to install packages and start services, `AutoScaling` reports that the instance is unhealthy and terminates it. A new one starts, time passes, and then it gets terminated. The worst thing here is that CloudFormation will tell you that your `AutoScaling` group is ready while your applications are still down.

In order to report EC2 resource readiness, there is a helper script called `cfn-signal`. This script (as it states in its name) sends a signal message to CloudFormation reporting whether a resource has been created or has failed to be created.

Let's try this with our LNMP stack. We'll need to add two additional blocks:

1. We start by adding `CreationPolicy` to the EC2 instance:

    ```
    // lnmp-signal.yaml
    Lnmp:
      Type: AWS::EC2::Instance
      CreationPolicy:
        ResourceSignal:
          Count: 1
          Timeout: PT5M
      Properties: #...
      Metadata: #...
    ```

    For individual instances, `CreationPolicy` doesn't have many attributes—only `Count` and `Timeout`.

    `Timeout` is declared using the ISO 8601 standard duration format—for example, 2023-06-15 12:34:56.123 (YYYY-MM-DD HH:MM:SS.SSS, see more at `https://www.iso.org/iso-8601-date-and-time-format.html`)—and in the preceding example, this is 5 minutes. If CloudFormation doesn't receive any signal from an instance, it will report failure because of timeout and will roll back.

    But that's only for a declaration in CloudFormation. We also need to instruct our instance to report readiness.

2. The `cfn-signal` script is already preinstalled on the machine, so we need to invoke it from `UserData`:

    ```
    // lnmp-signal.yaml
    Lnmp:
      Type: AWS::EC2::Instance
      CreationPolicy: #...
      Properties:
        ImageId: !Ref ImageId
        InstanceType: t2.micro
        KeyName: !Ref KeyName
    ```

```
    UserData:
      Fn::Base64:
        Fn::Sub: |
          #!/bin/bash -xe
          /opt/aws/bin/cfn-init -v \
          --stack ${AWS::StackName} \
          --resource Lnmp \
          --configsets Configure \
          --region ${AWS::Region}
          # signal creation
          /opt/aws/bin/cfn-signal -e $? \
          --stack ${AWS::StackName} \
          --resource Lnmp \
          --region ${AWS::Region}
```

Here, we supply CloudFormation with an exit code (the -e argument), the value of which equals the exit code of cfn-init. If cfn-init fails (if the exit code is not 0), then cfn-signal will send a different value to CloudFormation, and CloudFormation will know that something went wrong and it should roll back.

Both cfn-signal and CreationPolicy are widely used with AutoScaling groups, since we can also specify MinSuccessfulInstancesPercent, thereby performing rolling updates.

See the following, for example:

```
MyAsg:
  Type: AWS::AutoScaling::AutoScalingGroup
  CreationPolicy:
    AutoScalingCreationPolicy:
      MinSuccessfulInstancePercent: 50
```

This declaration will instruct the AutoScaling group to confirm its readiness only if at least half of the group's members send success signals; otherwise, the AutoScaling group will report as having failed to be created.

Summary

In this chapter, we learned how to perform an initial bootstrap configuration in a more human-friendly way. We learned about cfn-init, CloudFormation's native configuration management tool. We used it to deploy a "Hello, World!" application and we even launched our own LNMP stack and instructed it to report its creation status to us.

Using cfn-init allows template developers to use CloudFormation as a centralized tool to both provision resources and underlying configurations and deploy them. The cfn-init tool can also be used to install and update software as part of the stack operations.

This is the last chapter in *Part 2, Provisioning and Deployment at Scale*, and we've done a lot of work here. We are now capable of building production-ready infrastructures with CloudFormation, we can test and validate our stacks, we can apply continuous delivery, and we can deploy our stacks in multiple Regions and accounts using StackSets.

We did a lot of work, mostly utilizing core CloudFormation features, but CloudFormation is also capable of extension using powerful tools such as custom resources and template macros. In the next few chapters, we will learn how to use these.

Moreover, we will also dive into the potential successors of CloudFormation: the AWS **Serverless Application Model (SAM)** and AWS **Cloud Development Kit (CDK)**.

In the next chapter, we will look at CloudFormation's custom resources extension that allows us to declare and create resources *outside* of AWS. We will learn about custom resources and how and when to use them.

Questions

1. If the configuration set has multiple configuration items, in which order are they executed?
2. Is it possible to have multiple configuration sets?
3. Does `cfn-init` require the IAM policy to reach resource metadata?
4. Is it possible to create a directory with `cfn-init`?
5. What is `WaitCondition`?

Further reading

- LAMP stack on EC2: `https://docs.aws.amazon.com/AWSCloudFormation/latest/UserGuide/deploying.applications.html#deployment-walkthrough-basic-server`
- *Best practices for deploying applications on CloudFormation stacks*: `https://aws.amazon.com/blogs/devops/best-practices-for-deploying-applications-on-aws-cloudformation-stacks/`

Part 3:
Extending CloudFormation

CloudFormation has its limits. In this final part, we will teach it to do more than just provision resources in AWS. We will start with custom resources, template macros, nested stacks, and modules as our first step in CloudFormation customization. Once we're done with this, we will briefly touch on its possible successor, AWS CDK, and a new way of provisioning serverless applications called SAM.

The following chapters will be covered in this part:

7
Creating Resources Outside AWS Using Custom Resources

CloudFormation is usually the first **Infrastructure as Code** (**IaC**) instrument to start supporting new AWS services; however, sometimes we need to communicate to services that don't support CloudFormation. Sometimes we even need to create resources outside of AWS.

At the moment of this writing, CloudFormation added support for extensions. A private registry, which is one such extension, allows developers to build their own resource types, and we will cover this in depth in *Chapter 8, Creating Your Own Resource Registry for CloudFormation.*

Before, developers would use a **Custom Resource** (**CR**)—a CloudFormation resource type that uses AWS Lambda as a resource provisioner. If you are working in a greenfield environment, I encourage you to adopt private registries. However, some mature companies and shops may still use CRs that need to be maintained.

In this chapter, we will create external resources using CRs—a legacy way to create your own resources outside of AWS.

We will learn what they are and what are their use cases and program our very first CR using AWS Lambda.

In this chapter, we will cover the following topics:

- Understanding CRs
- The internals of the underlying Lambda function
- Writing and managing your own CRs
- Handling updates, deletions, and failures of CRs

Technical requirements

The code used in this chapter can be found in the book's GitHub repository at `https://github.com/PacktPublishing/Mastering-AWS-CloudFormation-Second-Edition/tree/main/Chapter07`.

Check out the following video to see the code in action:

`https://packt.link/3lR9k`

Understanding CRs

When we declare a resource in a CloudFormation template, we provide a `Type` attribute. This attribute declares a service and a resource that is going to be created—this means that CloudFormation *understands* where to go, what to do, and which API calls to make. `AWS` is a main namespace (e.g., resource provider), and what comes after `AWS` is another namespace, declaring the service. If it's EC2, then CloudFormation will send calls to EC2's API. If it's RDS, then it sends calls to RDS's API. The last block is the actual resource we want to create.

CRs are resources that don't fall under the native support of CloudFormation. These can be external providers, internal or self-hosted systems, or even services that don't support CloudFormation yet. The creation of CRs is usually a contract with three counteragents—the template developer, CR provider, and CloudFormation. While the template developer is responsible for resource declaration and the CR provider needs to develop a handler, CloudFormation acts as a broker, explicitly declaring the way that both parties will communicate when a resource is created, updated, or deleted.

CRs can be declared in a long form (`AWS::CloudFormation::CustomResource`) or a short form (`Custom::MyResourceName`). Nonetheless, during stack operations, CloudFormation will send a specific payload to the endpoint, which we define in the resource properties.

The declaration of a CR contains the type and the properties, which will form a payload. For example, let's say we declare a CR as shown in the following code snippet:

```
Cr:
  Type: Custom::MyResource
  Properties:
    ServiceToken: "..."
    Key1: Value1
    Key2:
      - list_element1
      - list_element2
```

CloudFormation will generate the following payload:

```
{
    «RequestType":"Create/Update/Delete",
    «ResponseURL":"http://...",
    «StackId":"...",
    «RequestId":"uniqueId for this request",
    «ResourceType":"Custom::MyResource",
    «LogicalResourceId":"Cr",
    «ResourceProperties":{
        «Key1»:»Value1»,
        «Key2»:[
            «list_element1",
            «list_element2"
        ]
    }
}
```

This payload is then sent to the endpoint. It contains fields from the resource declaration, the stack ID, the request type (`Create` resource, `Update` resource, or `Delete` resource), and the URL to which the Lambda function must send the response object.

Two endpoints can receive this kind of payload: AWS Lambda and SNS.

SNS is mostly used to program the provisioning logic processed by the backend running on EC2, ECS, or even on-premise. This is not the most efficient way to provision or process CR logic, since the backend will have to be subscribed to the SNS topic and run 24/7, but SNS-backed CRs increase the variety of provisioners.

In most cases, AWS engineers prefer using Lambda because of its cost efficiency, simplicity, and ease of management; however, we must always remember Lambda's limits and capabilities.

In this chapter, we will focus on developing CRs backed by AWS Lambda.

The internals of the underlying Lambda function

A Lambda function is code that is triggered by an event. Once run, it receives `event` and `context` objects and runs internal code that will process these objects.

While the `context` object is just metadata of the Lambda function's execution and can be used for self-maintenance and graceful shutdown, the `event` object contains the payload that we want to focus on.

In the case of CRs, we will need to parse the stack's information, run our logic, and respond to CloudFormation. The response should contain the following fields:

- Status (either SUCCESS/FAILED).

- Physical resource ID (since it is custom, we need to come up with our own resource ID).

- Stack ID (the same as from the CR request).

- Request ID (the same as from the CR request).

- Logical resource ID (the same as from the CR request).

- Data (may or may not be unnecessary, used for the intrinsic Fn::GetAtt function).

- After processing and running provisioning, the CR function must send a response to the ResponseURL instance from the original request. This response must be in the JSON format (even if the template was written in YAML).

- In the case of a successful execution, the response would look like this:

```
{
    «Status":"SUCCESS",
    «RequestId":"...",
    «LogicalResourceId":"...",
    «StackId":"...",
    «PhysicalResourceId»:»MyResourceUniqueId1234»,
    «Data»:{
        «Attr1»:»foo»,
        «Attr2»:»bar»
    }
}
```

- In the case of a failure, we don't need to provide data, but we want to provide a status and reason, so our response object will be different:

```
{
    «Status":"FAILED",
    «Reason":"This failed because of reasons",
    «RequestId":"...",
    «LogicalResourceId":"...",
    «StackId":"...",
    «PhysicalResourceId»:»MyResourceUniqueId1234»
}
```

The reason is what we will then see in the **Events** section on the CloudFormation console, so it is wise to provide explanatory reasons as to why the resource failed to create.

Let's take a quick look at the flow of a Lambda-backed CR:

Figure 7.1 – CR flow

The preceding diagram is explained in the following steps:

1. The user runs a stack operation. At this point, CloudFormation will run a stack operation that can be the creation of the stack, its update, or deletion.

2. The stack operation affects the CR. CloudFormation generates a payload containing the stack's and resource's metadata.

3. CloudFormation invokes the Lambda function, providing it with a payload.

4. The Lambda function runs provisioning logic and returns the response to CloudFormation.

Another thing that we want to know about is the cfn-response module.

cfn-response is a wrapper that generates a response object and sends it back to CloudFormation. This module already contains the necessary attributes and methods and makes responding to CloudFormation way easier.

For example, the pseudocode using cfn-response would look like this:

```
import cfnresponse
def handler(event, context):
    in = event[<ResourceProperties'] ['foo']
    # do some magic
    out = generate_id(event['ResourceType'])
    cfnresponse.send(event,
                    context,
                    cfnresponse.SUCCESS,
                    «»,
                    physicalResourceId=out
```

In the preceding code, we parse the event, run custom provisioning logic, and send the response to CloudFormation.

`cfn-response` already has the necessary functionality, so we only need to focus on provisioning logic.

> **Important note**
> The `cfn-response` module can only be imported if you upload the Lambda code using `zipfile`. If you use S3 for sources, you will have to program the logic on your own. The source code of `cfn-response` is available in AWS's documentation at https://docs.aws.amazon.com/AWSCloudFormation/latest/UserGuide/cfn-lambda-function-code-cfnresponsemodule.html#w2ab1c20c25c14b9c15.

All this theory makes no sense without practice. Let's get some hands-on experience!

Writing and managing your own CRs

Let's start with a simple task. Let's say that we have a *shared* RDS instance and we need to create databases in it. Since CloudFormation doesn't support that out of the box, we will have to develop our CR.

Creating databases in RDS using CRs

We are going to create a CR that will connect to the RDS instance and perform SQL operations on it to create a database, user, password, and necessary privileges in the following steps:

1. Let's define our CR, like so:

    ```
    // customdb.yaml
    CustomDb:
      Type: Custom::DB
      Properties:
        ServiceToken: # ARN of Lambda-backed CR
        DBName:       # the name of our DB
        DBUser:       # the username for our DB
        DBPassword:   # the password for our DB's user
        RDSEndpoint:  # the endpoint of RDS instance
        RDSUser:      # the admin user with RDS access
        RDSPassword:  # the password of admin user
    ```

    These fields should be enough to start with. Some of the properties are required (RDS endpoint, user, password, database name, and so on), but we will develop provisioning logic in Lambda.

2. Let's start with a skeleton:

```python
// customdb.py
import cfnresponse

class CustomResourceException(Exception):
    pass

def handler(event, context):
    physicalResourceId = ""
    cfnresponse.send(event,
                    context,
                    cfnresponse.SUCCESS,
                    physicalResourceId=physicalResourceId,
                    responseData="")
```

With this code, we configure the parameters that we want to make mandatory so that the process fails if one of them is not provided.

3. Let's create a simple filter check to *fail* Lambda if some of the properties are missing:

```python
// customdb.py
def handler(event, context):
    # ...
    input_props = event["ResourceProperties"]
    required_props = ["DBName", "RDSEndpoint", "RDSUser",
"RDSPassword"]
    missing_props = [prop for prop in required_props if prop not
in input_props]
    if missing_props:
        cfnresponse.send(event,
                        context,
                        cfnresponse.FAILED,
                        physicalResourceId="",
                        responseData="")
        raise CustomResourceException(f"Required properties are
missing: {missing_props}"))
    # ...
```

Error handling is done at this stage. We check the keys of the `event` object while adding missing properties to the error message. The `cfn-response` module doesn't support adding the status reason out of the box. Instead, it instructs the program to look at the CloudWatch logs, so we send our error message to `stdout`.

4. Now, we need to start developing our provisioning logic. Our flow will consist of the following:

    A. Connection to the RDS instance

    B. Creation of the user

    C. Creation of the database

    D. Granting privileges to the created user on the new database

    But what if the user doesn't provide credentials for the new database? We didn't make these properties mandatory, but Lambda won't be able to create an empty user and password. We could enforce these properties, but instead, we will assign them the value of DBName. We also need to assign the values of other properties, as follows:

```
// customdb.py
def handler(event, context):
    # ...
    db_name = input_props['DBName']
    rds_endpoint = input_props['RDSEndpoint']
    rds_user = input_props['RDSUser']
    rds_password = input_props['RDSPassword']
    if not «DBUser" in input_props or len(input_props["DBUser"])
== 0:
        db_user = db_name
    else:
        db_user = input_props['DBUser']
    if not «DBPassword" in input_props or len(input_
props["DBPassword"]) == 0:
        db_password = db_name
    else:
        db_password = input_props['DBPassword']
    # ...
```

    Here, we check whether the property exists and is not empty and store the value.

5. Now, we need to develop our provisioning logic. To keep the handler clean, let's create a separate function to clean it:

```
// customdb.py
import pymysql
def create_or_update_db(dbname, dbuser, dbpassword, rdsendpoint,
rdsuser, rdspassword):
    create_db_query = f"CREATE DATABASE {dbname};"
    create_user_query = f"CREATE USER '{dbuser}'@'%' IDENTIFIED
BY '{dbpassword}';"
    grant_query = f"GRANT ALL PRIVILEGES ON {dbname}.* TO
{dbuser}@'%'; FLUSH PRIVILEGES;"
    try:
```

```
                conn = pymysql.connect(host=rdsendpoint,
                                user=rdsuser,
                                password=rdspassword)
            cursor = conn.cursor()
            cursor.execute(create_db_query)
            cursor.execute(create_user_query)
            # ...
        except Exception as err:
            raise CustomResourceException(err)
```

This function (`create_or_update_db()`) connects to the database, runs queries, and returns an error message if, for some reason, the creation or updates to the database have failed. Don't worry about updates yet! We will cover them a bit later.

6. Let's call this function in our handler:

```
// customdb.py
def handler(event, context):
    try:
        if event["RequestType"] == "Create":
            create_or_update_db(db_name, db_user, db_password,
rds_endpoint, rds_user, rds_password)
    except CustomResourceException as err:
        send(event, context, FAILED, physicalResourceId="",
responseData={})
        sys.exit(1)
    # ...
```

All good, right?

However, there is a potential problem in our Lambda. We introduced **PyMySQL**, a pure Python MySQL client (this client doesn't require external MySQL libraries to be installed, so it's a perfect module for Lambda), which is an external package and has to be installed using `pip`. If we install an external dependency, we have to package our source code and upload it to S3. If we upload it to S3, we can't import `cfn-response` (remember the preceding note?).

7. In order to solve this, we will have to copy the code of `cfn-response` from the CloudFormation documentation (`https://docs.aws.amazon.com/AWSCloudFormation/latest/UserGuide/cfn-lambda-function-code-cfnresponsemodule.html`). So, our code will look a bit different and more Pythonic, as we can see here:

```
// customdb.py
import requests
import json
import pymysql
```

```
SUCCESS = "SUCCESS"
FAILED = "FAILED"

class CustomResourceException(Exception):
    pass

def create_or_update_db(#...):
    # ...
def handler(event, context):
    # ...
# And the "send" function from cfn-response module...
def send(#...):
    # ...
```

8. We will introduce an improvement for the `cfn-response.send` function in the next section. For now, let's create our CR function (you might have to come up with your S3 bucket name), as follows:

```
$ aws s3 mb s3://masteringcloudformation
$ pip3 install -t custom-db/ \
                -r custom-db/requirements.txt
$ cd custom-db && zip -r lambda-cr.zip *
$ aws s3 cp lambda-cr.zip s3://masteringcloudformation
$ cd .. && aws cloudformation deploy \
                --stack-name cr \
                --template-file cr.yaml \
                --capabilities CAPABILITY_IAM
```

9. Now, we need to deploy our stack with an RDS instance (MySQL). Replace `$VPCID` with the ID of the VPC you have in your account:

```
$ aws cloudformation deploy --stack-name rds \
                            --template-file rds.yaml \
                            --parameter-overrides \
                            VpcId=$VPCID
```

10. Once this is done, we can deploy our CR stack, like so:

```
$ aws cloudformation deploy \
                --stack-name customdb \
                --template-file customdb.yaml
```

11. Once the resource is created, we can evaluate the created database by connecting to it. Here's how to do that:

```
$ mysql -u mydbuser -pfoobar1234 -h $RDS_INSTANCE mydb
```

And that's it! Our CR function is capable of creating the new resource; however, it is far from perfect and will definitely fail when we want to update or delete this resource from CloudFormation's state.

In the next section, we will focus on how to manage updates and deletions and how to work with stack operation errors.

Handling updates, deletions, and failures of CRs

Our CR can create a database for us. But try to guess what will happen if you attempt to delete this resource or stack from CloudFormation.

It will fail to delete. Why? Because our CR function runs only one function, `create_db`, it doesn't matter which *request type* is received by CloudFormation. Exactly the same will happen if we try to update our database.

We need to add support for *updates* and *deletes* for our Lambda instance. We will start with the delete functionality because what we will do is make our CR immutable.

This means that whenever we change our custom database, the old one will always be deleted. Sounds scary? Unfortunately, this is the default behavior for CRs. Moreover, some AWS resources are also *replaced* (for example, a new resource is created while the old one is being deleted), even if nothing major is being changed.

Deleting resources

We will cover the delete operation in the following steps:

1. We will create an extra function in our Lambda script and call it `delete_db`:

    ```
    // customdb.py
    def delete_db(dbname, dbuser, rdsendpoint, rdsuser,
    rdspassword):
        return None
    ```

    We have the skeleton of our function. It has arguments similar to `create_db`, except `dbpassword`; we don't need to know the user's password to delete it from the database.

2. Now, let's add the actual deletion logic. First, we need the queries to run on the database:

    ```
    // customdb.py
    def delete_db(dbname, dbuser, rdsendpoint, rdsuser,
    rdspassword):
        delete_db_query = f"DROP DATABASE {dbname}"
        delete_user_query = f"DROP USER '{dbuser}'"
    ```

3. Next, we need a `try-except` block with a database connection and query execution:

```
// customdb.py
def delete_db(dbname, dbuser, rdsendpoint, rdsuser,
rdspassword):
    delete_db_query = f"DROP DATABASE {dbname}"
    delete_user_query = f"DROP USER '{dbuser}'"
    try:
        conn = pymysql.connect(host=rdsendpoint,
                                user=rdsuser,
                                password=rdspassword)
        cursor = conn.cursor()
        cursor.execute(delete_db_query)
        cursor.execute(delete_user_query)
        cursor.close()
        conn.commit()
        conn.close()
    except Exception as err:
        raise CustomResourceException(err)
```

What we do here is connect to the same RDS instance, run queries, and close the connection. If anything goes wrong, we raise a custom exception, which we will handle in the `handler` method. Otherwise, `None` is returned (an empty Python object).

4. Now, we need to parse the incoming event and obtain the request type. We will do this in the `handler` function:

```
// customdb.py
import ...
# ...
def handler(event, context):
# ...
    try:
        if event["RequestType"] == "Delete":
            delete_db(db_name, db_user, rds_endpoint, rds_user,
rds_password)
        elif event["RequestType"] =="Create":
            create_or_update_db(db_name, db_user, db_password,
rds_endpoint, rds_user, rds_password)
    except CustomResourceException as err:
        # ...
# ...
```

What we've changed is the actual function that runs during the stack operation. If CloudFormation sends a `Delete` request, then we go to the RDS instance and drop the database and user. If it sends `Create`, then we create a database.

5. We need to update the source code. Since we already have all the stacks in place, let's do it manually:

```
$ cd custom-db/
$ zip -r lambda-cr.zip *
$ aws s3 cp lambda-cr.zip s3://masteringcloudformation
$ aws cloudformation list-stack-resources \
      --stack-name cr \
      --query \
      '.StackResourceSummaries[0].PhysicalResourceId'\
      --output text
cr-CrFunction-EX3NB14PJARD
$ aws lambda update-function-code \
      --function-name cr-CrFunction-EX3NB14PJARD \
      --s3-bucket masteringcloudformation \
      --s3-key lambda-cr.zip
# long output from Lambda...
```

6. Now, let's delete the stack:

```
$ aws cloudformation delete-stack \
      --stack-name customdb
$ aws cloudformation list-stacks \
      --stack-status-filter DELETE_COMPLETE
{
    "StackSummaries": [
    # ....
        {
            # ...
            "StackName": "customdb",
            # ...
            "StackStatus": "DELETE_COMPLETE",
            # ...
        },
    # ...
}
```

7. Now, let's check that the database really doesn't exist:

```
$ mysql -u rdsuser -pbarfoo12344321 -h $RDSENDPOINT
mysql > show databases;
+--------------------+
| Database           |
+--------------------+
| information_schema |
| innodb             |
```

```
| mysql              |
| performance_schema |
| sys                |
+--------------------+
5 rows in set (0.02 sec)
```

This confirms that the `Delete` operation works as expected.

Let's add support for updates so that we can change databases, users, and so on within our CR.

Updating resources

Our resource is immutable. If it's changed, then the old one is deleted and a new one is created. CloudFormation sends an `Update` request to create a new resource. Once it is done, during `UPDATE_COMPLETE_CLEANUP_IN_PROGRESS` CloudFormation will send a `Delete` request with the properties of the resource that was created during the previous stack operation. We'll now proceed as follows:

1. Since we already support create and delete operations, all we need to do is change the filtering to support both `Create` and `Update` in the `handler` function:

    ```
    // customdb.py
    import ...
    # ...
    def handler(event, context):
    # ...
        if event[<RequestType'] == "Delete":
            delete_db(db_name, db_user, rds_endpoint, rds_user, rds_
    password)
        elif event['RequestType'] in ("Create", "Update"):
            create_or_update_db(db_name, db_user, db_password, rds_
    endpoint, rds_user, rds_password)
    # ...
    ```

2. We are going to repackage our function, upload it to S3, and update the Lambda function's code (the same way we did in the previous section). Since we deleted the custom database stack, we need to recreate and then update it, like so:

    ```
    $ aws cloudformation deploy \
          --stack-name customdb \
          --template-file customdb.yaml
    $ aws cloudformation deploy \
          --stack-name customdb \
          --template-file customdb.yaml \
          --parameter-overrides \
          DBName=mynewdb DBUser=mynewuser
    ```

3. When the deployment is finished, we can check the database again by running the following command:

```
$ mysql -u rdsuser -pbarfoo12344321 -h $RDSENDPOINT
mysql> show databases;
+--------------------+
| Database           |
+--------------------+
| information_schema |
| innodb             |
| mysql              |
| mynewdb            |
| performance_schema |
| sys                |
+--------------------+
6 rows in set (0.02 sec)
```

All good! Our CR now fully supports creation, updating, and deletion! Now, we are going to teach our CR function a few more tricks.

Extra features for the custom database function

Our CR performs as expected, but there is always room for improvement. In this section, we will make our CR nicer and more self-explanatory in case of failures.

Custom status reasons

Until now, if we had an error, it was returned as an invitation to read the Lambda logs. This is because `cfn-response.send` has the following line:

```
responseBody["Reason"] = f"See the details in CloudWatch Log Stream:
{context.log_stream_name}"
```

This `Reason` string is sent to CloudFormation and is mandatory when the status is `FAILED`. The preceding string generation is hardcoded into `cfn-response`; however, since we copied the code, we have control over it.

We are going to add support for custom status reasons by going through the following steps:

1. Let's make a few changes to the `send()` function:

```
// customdb.py
def send(event, context, response_status, response_data,
response_reason="", physical_resource_id=None, no_echo=False):
    # ...
```

```
        response_body = {}
        response_body["Status"] = response_status
        response_body["Reason"] = response_reason
    # ...
```

Here, we add the non-mandatory response_reason argument and use it as a value for response_body["Reason"]. This will give us the ability to send our own custom messages to CloudFormation.

2. Now, we are going to make our provisioning handler logic to send these reasons. Let's start with our required properties check:

```
// customdb.py
# ...
def handler(event, context):
    input_props = event["ResourceProperties"]
    required_props = ["DBName", "RDSEndpoint", "RDSUser",
"RDSPassword"]
    missing_props = [prop for prop in required_props if prop not
in input_props]
    if missing_props:
        reason = f"Required properties are missing: {missing_
props}"
        send(event, context, FAILED, response_reason=reason,
response_data={})
        raise CustomResourceException(reason)
    # ...
```

3. Let's check this error handling by creating a stack with one of the missing properties (*don't forget to update the function code!*):

```
$ aws cloudformation deploy \
    --stack-name broken-custom \
    --template-file customdb_missing_property.yaml
```

We will see some very interesting behavior:

Logical ID	Status	Status reason
customdb -broken	⊗ ROLLBACK_FAILED	The following resource(s) failed to delete: [CustomDb].
CustomDb	⊗ DELETE_FAILED	Failed to delete resource. Required properties are missing: ['DBName']
CustomDb	ⓘ DELETE_IN_PROGRESS	-
customdb -broken	⊗ ROLLBACK_IN_PROGRESS	The following resource(s) failed to create: [CustomDb]. . Rollback requested by user.
CustomDb	⊗ CREATE_FAILED	Failed to create resource. Required properties are missing: ['DBName']
CustomDb	ⓘ CREATE_IN_PROGRESS	Resource creation Initiated
CustomDb	ⓘ CREATE_IN_PROGRESS	-

Figure 7.2 – CloudFormation console

This is because our check is applied to any request type. When creation fails, CloudFormation still considers the resource to be created and wants to clean it up. The database doesn't exist, so CloudFormation will get stuck in a loop until at some point it gives up and says DELETE_FAILED.

In order to make our CR more error-free, we need to apply a few changes to the Lambda function.

Sending a success message upon the deletion of nothing

CloudFormation insists there is a resource. We know there isn't. If we try to delete a database or user that doesn't exist, our script will definitely fail, and so will the stack operation in CloudFormation.

To make our CR more redundant, we will make our CR function able to handle this properly, as follows:

1. Let's add a few lines to our function, where we check if some properties are missing:

```
// customdb.py
def handler(event, context):
# ...
    if missing_props:
        if event[<RequestType'] == "Delete":
            send(event, context, SUCCESS, response_data={})
            sys.exit(0)
        reason = f"Required properties are missing: {missing_props}"
        send(event, context, FAILED, response_reason=reason,
responseData={})
        raise CustomResourceException(reason)
    # ...
```

Here, we check whether CloudFormation is performing a deletion. If it is and no props are provided, then that means it is a dry cleanup. All we need to do is to report to CloudFormation that everything was successful.

2. We'll upload the new code and rerun stack creation:

```
$ aws cloudformation delete-stack \
    --stack-name broken-custom
$ aws cloudformation deploy \
    --stack-name broken-custom \
    --template-file customdb_missing_property.yaml
```

The result will be different this time:

Logical ID	Status	Status reason
customdb-broken	⊗ ROLLBACK_COMPLETE	-
CustomDb	⊘ DELETE_COMPLETE	-
CustomDb	ⓘ DELETE_IN_PROGRESS	-
customdb-broken	⊗ ROLLBACK_IN_PROGRESS	The following resource(s) failed to create: [CustomDb]. . Rollback requested by user.
CustomDb	⊗ CREATE_FAILED	Failed to create resource. Required properties are missing: ['DBName']

Figure 7.3 – CloudFormation console

But there is one more thing that we want to add. What if the database that is to be deleted doesn't exist anymore (for example, it was deleted manually)?

3. Let's also handle that eventuality by setting up the following code:

```
// customdb.py
def delete_db(dbname, dbuser, rdsendpoint, rdsuser,
rdspassword):
# ...
    db_exists_query = f"SHOW DATABASES LIKE '{dbname}'"
    user_exists_query = f"SELECT user FROM mysql.user where
user='{dbuser}'"
    try:
        # ...
        if cursor.execute(db_exists_query):
            cursor.execute(delete_db_query)
        if cursor.execute(user_exists_query):
            cursor.execute(delete_user_query)
```

```
# ...
except Exception as err:
    raise CustomResourceException(err)
```

What we do is check whether both the database and the user exist in the database. If not, we skip the deletion query to avoid getting `Database doesn't exist` or `Operation DROP USER failed for` errors.

That being said, we've added custom status reasons to our CR function and made it more error-resistant.

Summary

In this chapter, we learned about CRs, the most universal way to extend CloudFormation. We created our own CR backed by AWS Lambda, made it stable and secure, and also made it able to handle updates, deletions, and errors.

CRs are widely used to either create resources in AWS that are not yet supported by CloudFormation or create resources outside of AWS, whether they are other cloud platforms or your own platforms and systems running on EC2.

We covered CRs and provisioning logic and understood what actually happens under the hood. To get real hands-on experience with CRs, we developed our own CR, made it error-resistant, and added support for custom reason messages.

In the next chapter, we will learn about another and more modern way to manage resources outside CloudFormation, called private registries and resource types.

Questions

1. What are the possible request types for CRs?
2. Is it possible to use `cfnresponse` if we package the Lambda function with external dependencies?
3. Which AWS services are used for CR processing?
4. Which CR response object has to be used to specify the reason for failed resource changes?
5. What are `event` and `context` in Lambda?

Further reading

-   Alex DeBrie's blog on CRs: `https://www.alexdebrie.com/posts/cloudformation-custom-resources/`

-   GitHub repository with sample CRs: `https://github.com/aws-samples/aws-cfn-custom-resource-examples`

8

Creating Your Own Resource Registry for CloudFormation

In the previous chapter, we managed non-AWS resources using CloudFormation's custom resource. For a very long time, this was the only way to manage external resources and services, and CloudFormation was in a difficult place compared to its main competitor, Terraform.

The notion of **provisioners** allows Terraform to implement infrastructure on any cloud or service provider that has an API. The extensibility of Terraform was one of the strongest arguments in favor of Terraform versus CloudFormation.

To stay competitive, AWS developed the CloudFormation registry, a centralized place where CloudFormation users can store their own resource types, modules, and hooks.

In this chapter, we will set up CloudFormation to use third-party public extensions through our AWS account. Later, we will develop our own private registry that implements a capability to create custom databases in the RDS instance using CloudFormation, just like we did in the last chapter with custom resource type.

In this chapter, we will cover the following topics:

- Understanding the CloudFormation registry
- Activating and using public extensions
- Creating and using private extensions

Technical requirements

The code used in this chapter can be found in the book's GitHub repository at: `https://github.com/PacktPublishing/Mastering-AWS-CloudFormation-Second-Edition/tree/main/Chapter08`

Check out the following video to see the Code in Action: `https://packt.link/juP2x`

Understanding the CloudFormation registry

The journey of the CloudFormation registry began in 2019, when the private registry was announced and released (along with other major and important updates; for more details, see `https://aws.amazon.com/blogs/aws/cloudformation-update-cli-third-party-resource-support-registry/`). This update introduced a centralized approach to modeling, building, and maintaining custom resources.

The first and main reason was to enable AWS service teams to onboard newly developed services faster. Previously, this was the responsibility of the CloudFormation team itself, and handing service onboarding tasks over to the service teams with the right tool in place improved the speed of onboarding to CloudFormation. Another good use was to centrally maintain custom resources in a single place.

Two years later, AWS released the public registry – a registry for resource types developed by various software vendors, such as MongoDB, Atlassian, DataDog, and others (`https://aws.amazon.com/blogs/aws/introducing-a-public-registry-for-aws-cloudformation/`). This allowed users to apply Infrastructure-as-Code practices for things external to AWS using the well-known CloudFormation syntax.

Custom resource types are not the only thing supported by the CloudFormation registry. It also supports **modules** – yet another way to scale stacks and templates – and **hooks** – which allow for server-driven resource validation.

In addition, the registry takes over resource-provision handling. In the previous chapter, we created our own Lambda function to handle the provisioning logic that we developed. Now, the registry takes over the hosting aspects, while requiring two important things from the extension creator:

- All handling logic must comply with the extension specification and be well tested
- Any resource types used must comply with the resource-provider definition schema (`https://docs.aws.amazon.com/cloudformation-cli/latest/userguide/resource-type-schema.html`)

Right now, the registry consists of public and private parts. The public registry contains public extensions, e.g., public resource types, such as MongoDB Atlas Cluster or even a DynamoDB Item resource type! The private registry contains private extensions: the ones that we developed ourselves and activated public extensions. The latter seems confusing (*how can a private extension have a public extension?!*), so let's wait no longer and jump right into using extensions.

Activating and using public extensions

Let's reiterate what we did in the previous chapter one more time. We built a Lambda function that receives an API call from CloudFormation and runs SQL queries against our provisioned RDS cluster.

Now, imagine that we want to publish our custom resource handler and let anyone use it. Since Lambda is hosted on our AWS account, the user of the RDS instance would need to make it accessible from the outside world, thus introducing a security risk. If we were to use Aurora Serverless V1, we could enable the Data API, but we would still need to provide access to it using an IAM role, which introduces the following two-sided security risk:

- We, as the Lambda owner, have to expose our AWS account ID
- We create an IAM role that grants the user with access to the Data API

Even if we ignore the security risks resulting from the above, there are still other risks such as costs and reliability. We host the Lambda function, which means we own it, and thus we have to pay for it. In the event of an influx of requests, our function may get throttled, introducing service quality degradation for users, and if it does manage to handle the load effectively, we will get an unpleasantly high AWS bill. Handling abusive callers will require us to suspend them and build rails such as rate limiting.

So, what is the best way to publish a custom resource publicly and let anyone use it? Extension developers who want their resource types to be available on the public registry follow this publishing workflow:

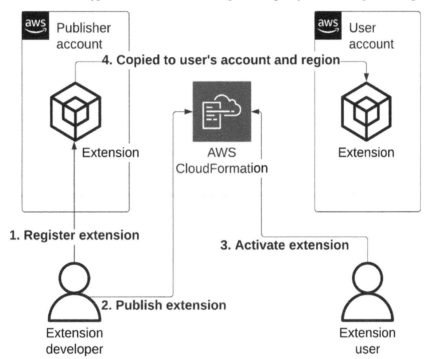

Figure 8.1 – Extension publishing process

The following are the mandatory steps for developers to enable their extensions for public use:

1. First and foremost, the publisher ensures they are verified by having an account on AWS Marketplace, Bitbucket, or GitHub, as well as an AWS account that is used for publishing. The publisher registers this AWS account as a publisher of a public extension in the registry. Later, the publisher ensures that the extension is tested against the registry's contract, stores the resource type extension handler in an open-source repository, such as GitHub, and assigns a SemVer version number to the extension.

2. The publisher submits the extension to the registry. Once submitted, the extension is available for use.

3. The customer then uses the AWS CLI or console to activate the extension.

4. Upon activation, the provisioning handler bundler is copied from the publisher's registry to our own.

To activate an extension, we need an IAM Role and a CloudWatch Log Group that will be used by CloudFormation to use the extension, for example, to provision a resource.

In the next section, we will activate a public extension that maintains DynamoDB items.

Managing DynamoDB items with CloudFormation

Using CloudFormation to maintain DynamoDB items may indeed look weird, but there are some valid cases for it – for instance, if we have a DynamoDB table that stores configuration items, and we want to use DynamoDB because it's cheaper than SSM Parameter Store.

In that case, we want an iterative, reliable, and atomic way to update items in the table. Luckily for us, such a resource type already exists and has been published by the AWS community (`https://github.com/aws-cloudformation/community-registry-extensions/tree/main/resources/DynamoDB_Item`), so we only need to activate and use it.

In the following exercise, we will set up and add a custom resource type extension for DynamoDB items:

1. Let's begin with setting up our account. We provision the necessary resources using CloudFormation, beginning with an IAM role that the extension will assume:

```
// prerequisite.yaml
ExtensionIamRole:
  Type: "AWS::IAM::Role"
  Properties:
    AssumeRolePolicyDocument:
      Version: "2012-10-17"
      Statement:
        - Sid: "AllowAssumeRole"
          Effect: "Allow"
```

```
      Principal:
        Service:
          - "resources.cloudformation.amazonaws.com"
      Action: "sts:AssumeRole"
```

2. Note a few things here. The principal is `resources.cloudformation.amazonaws.com`, which indicates that the **Resources Type** extension is going to be used, as opposed to **hooks** or **modules**.

3. Next, we provision the DynamoDB table to store configuration items:

```
Table:
  Type: "AWS::DynamoDB::Table"
  Properties:
    BillingMode: "PAY_PER_REQUEST"
    AttributeDefinitions:
        - AttributeName: "configItem"
          AttributeType: "S"
    KeySchema:
      -
        AttributeName: "configItem"
        KeyType: "HASH"
```

For this table, we will use a simple primary key. If you have not worked with DynamoDB, it supports two kinds of primary keys: simple and composite. The simple primary key contains a single attribute known as a partition key.

4. The extension code calls the DynamoDB API, so we need a policy to allow reading from and writing to the table. Following the least-privilege principle, we are not going to allow any calls to DynamoDB and will limit the resources given to the table we create:

```
DynamoDbPolicy:
  Type: "AWS::IAM::Policy"
  Properties:
    PolicyName: "ExtensionDynamoDBPolicy"
    PolicyDocument:
      Version: "2012-10-17"
      Statement:
        - Sid: "AllowExtensionAccessToDynamoDBTable"
          Effect: "Allow"
          Action:
            - "dynamodb:*Item"
          Resource:
            - !GetAtt Table.Arn
    Roles:
      - !Ref ExtensionIamRole
```

In this policy, we allow any call related to the item, such as `GetItem`, `PutItem`, `UpdateItem`, or `DeleteItem` (note the wildcard in the `Action` block), and we attach this policy to the role.

5. For the extension to properly report any issue, we need a CloudWatch log group, so let's declare that as well:

```yaml
ExtensionLogGroup:
  Type: "AWS::Logs::LogGroup"
  Properties:
    RetentionInDays: 7
```

Note that if you were doing this in production, you may want to add a name to the log group, but for this demonstration setup it is not necessary.

6. And of course we need a logging policy:

```yaml
LogPolicy:
  Type: "AWS::IAM::Policy"
  Properties:
    PolicyName: "ExtensionLogPolicy"
    PolicyDocument:
      Version: "2012-10-17"
      Statement:
        - Sid: "AllowExtensionLogging"
          Effect: "Allow"
          Action:
            - "logs:CreateLogStream"
            - "logs:PutLogEvents"
          Resource:
            - !GetAtt ExtensionLogGroup.Arn
            - !Sub "${ExtensionLogGroup.Arn}:log-stream:*"
    Roles:
      - !Ref ExtensionIamRole
```

Here we need to allow the handler to create log streams in a group and then put logs in it. Finally, we attach the policy to the same role.

7. Let's include the role's ARN, log group, and the table's name in the output, as we will need these in the following steps:

```yaml
Outputs:
  RoleArn:
    Value: !GetAtt ExtensionIamRole.Arn
  LogGroup:
    Value: !Ref ExtensionLogGroup
  DynamoDbTable:
    Value: !Ref Table
```

8. Now we can provision our stack and assign the required output to the environment variables:

```
$ aws cloudformation deploy \
      --stack-name extension-dynamo-item \
      --template-file prerequisite.yaml \
      --capabilities CAPABILITY_IAM
```

We don't want to manually copy resource names and ARNs, so instead we check the order of the stack outputs. Knowing this order is necessary to work out how to assign each output value to the environment variable:

```
$ aws cloudformation describe-stacks \
      --stack-name extension-dynamo-item \
      --query 'Stacks[0].Outputs[]'
```

In this command, I am using a filtering query to list only the outputs. In my case, the outputs look like this:

```
[
    {
        "OutputKey": "LogGroup",
        "OutputValue": "extension-dynamo-item-ExtensionLogGroup-
psK6elzmNFhv"
    },
    {
        "OutputKey": "DynamoDbTable",
        "OutputValue": "extension-dynamo-item-Table-
855RIGY14OJP"
    },
    {
        "OutputKey": "RoleArn",
        "OutputValue": "arn:aws:iam::ACCOUNTID:role/extension-
dynamo-item-ExtensionIamRole-BISPEKHXKE8F"
    }
]
```

So, the log group name goes first in the list, followed by the table name, and then ending with the extension role ARN. This order helps us construct the proper command for assigning the stack output to each environment variable:

```
$ LOGGROUP=$(aws cloudformation describe-stacks \
    --stack-name extension-dynamo-item \
    --query 'Stacks[0].Outputs[0].OutputValue' \
    --output text)
```

Note the list index number in `Outputs` that we use for the log group. Similarly, we craft the commands for the role and table as follows:

```
$ TABLE=$(aws cloudformation describe-stacks \
    --stack-name extension-dynamo-item \
    --query 'Stacks[0].Outputs[1].OutputValue' \
    --output text)
$ ROLE=$(aws cloudformation describe-stacks \
    --stack-name extension-dynamo-item \
    --query 'Stacks[0].Outputs[2].OutputValue' \
    --output text)
```

9. We're good to activate the extension!

```
$ aws cloudformation activate-type \
    --type RESOURCE \
    --type-name AwsCommunity::DynamoDB::Item \
    --execution-role-arn $ROLE \
    --logging-config \
    LogRoleArn=$ROLE,LogGroupName=$LOGGROUP \
    --publisher-id \
    # AWSCommunity Publisher Id
    c830e97710da0c9954d80ba8df021e5439e7134b
```

That's it! If we navigate to the AWS console, we will find the activated extension in the list of third-party extensions.

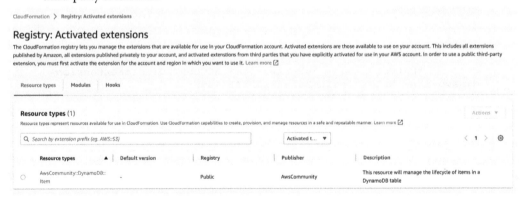

Figure 8.2 – CloudFormation console – Registry: Activated extensions

Now we can manage DynamoDB items using CloudFormation!

The following are the steps to use the custom resource type extension in a CloudFormation template:

1. We will create a new template that uses the extension we just activated. In this template, we will declare an item that defines a configuration for the log level of the app:

```
// item.yaml
Parameters:
  TableName:
    Type: String
Resources:
  LogLevel:
    Type: "AWSCommunity::DynamoDB::Item"
    Properties:
      TableName: !Ref TableName
      Item:
        LogLevel:
          S: "DEBUG"
      Keys:
        - AttributeName: "configurationItem"
          AttributeType: "S"
          AttributeValue: "ApplicationLogLevel"
```

The `Key` block represents the partition key to which we will assign a value. In the `Item` section, we list each item attribute with a corresponding DynamoDB type. Type `S` stands for *string* data type.

2. Let's deploy the stack right away! Previously, we assigned the table name output to the environment variable. We did this so we don't have to manually paste the table name in the command line:

```
$ aws cloudformation deploy \
      --stack-name configuration-items \
      --template-file item.yaml \
      --parameter-overrides TableName=$TABLE
Waiting for changeset to be created..
Waiting for stack create/update to complete
Successfully created/updated stack - configuration-items
```

What we could do differently is to not just add the table name to the output, but export the value and reuse it in the template with `Fn::ImportValue`. In such a case, we would need to add an additional policy to the role that allows listing exports (`cloudformation:ListExports`).

3. Let's check out the results. Go to the DynamoDB console and click on our table and then on **Explore Items**:

Items returned (1)		
configItem ▽	**LogLevel**	▽
ApplicationLogLevel	DEBUG	

Figure 8.3 – DynamoDB console – Table – Explore table items

4. Voila! Let's add one more item to the template. This time, let's use a Zookeeper server:

```
ZookeeperNodes:
  Type: "AwsCommunity::DynamoDB::Item"
  Properties:
    TableName: !Ref TableName
    Item:
      Nodes:
        L:
            - S: "10.0.0.10"
            - S: "10.0.0.20"
            - S: "10.0.0.30"
      Keys:
          - AttributeName: "configItem"
            AttributeType: "S"
            AttributeValue: "ZookeeperNodes"
```

Here we use a type of *list* (L) that contains IP addresses formatted in a type of *string* (S).

5. Let's roll it out:

```
$ aws cloudformation deploy \
      --stack-name configuration-items \
      --template-file item.yaml \
      --parameter-overrides TableName=$TABLE
```

6. Once the stack update is complete, we can observe the table items again:

Items returned (2)		
configItem ▽	LogLevel ▽	Nodes ▽
ZookeeperNodes		[{ "S" : "10.0.0.10" }, { "S" : "10.0.0.20" }, { "S" : "10.0.0.30" }]
ApplicationLogLevel	DEBUG	

Figure 8.4 – DynamoDB console – Table – Explore table items

There are dozens of different public resource types, that are now available on the registry. For example, you can create a MongoDB Atlas cluster (`https://www.mongodb.com/blog/post/deploy-manage-mongodb-atlas-aws-cloud-formation`), manage a CloudFlare CDN instance (`https://github.com/aws-ia/cloudformation-cloudflare-resource-providers.git`), and even set up Atlassian Opsgenie or DataDog monitoring!

However, we can also make great use of the registry by creating our own resource types and using them. So, let's refactor our database custom resource on the RDS in the next section.

Creating and using private extensions

To enable the registry, we first need to understand the limits and nuances of registry resource handlers. In the previous chapter, we had our Lambda function run in a public network and connect to the RDS instance, also hosted on the public network, via a native Python MySQL driver.

In this chapter, we will follow a similar path.

Preparing database infrastructure

We will provision the same stack as used in the previous chapter. If you still have it running, feel free to skip this step:

```
$ aws cloudformation deploy \
    --stack-name rds \
    --template-file rds.yaml
```

When the RDS instance is provisioned and ready for use, we can leave it and move on to modeling our resource type.

Modeling resource types for the CloudFormation registry

CloudFormation requires extension developers to properly model the resource types. This is crucial for provisioning reliability and troubleshooting, as well as the testability of the extension, so let's cover this first.

Sneak peek into the schema

This model is defined in a schema provided by AWS itself and can be viewed at `https://docs.aws.amazon.com/cloudformation-cli/latest/userguide/resource-type-schema.html`. The schema is very rich and extensible, but in this chapter, we will cover only a few important sections for our exercise:

- For example, the schema has a property called `replacementStrategy` (`https://docs.aws.amazon.com/cloudformation-cli/latest/userguide/resource-type-schema.html#schema-properties-replacementstrategy`), which defines how CloudFormation behaves when we make an update to the resource that requires it to be completely replaced. The replacement strategy has two possible values that speak for themselves: `create_then_delete` and `delete_then_create`. This applies to resource properties that do not support in-place modifications, such as Standard and FIFO SQS queues that are defined only on creation and cannot be changed later.

  When we declare a resource in a template and do not specify its name, during replacement, CloudFormation will create a new instance of that resource, point the stack's logical name to a new physical ID, and then delete the old resource.

  For our database case, where we expect the user to enter the database name, this is not easily handled as MySQL does not allow the creation of two databases with the same name. Hence our replacement strategy is *delete and then create*.

- Another noteworthy field is `properties` (`https://docs.aws.amazon.com/cloudformation-cli/latest/userguide/resource-type-schema.html#schema-properties-properties`). This field is an array of the properties that we identify for the custom resource type among with a data type, regex pattern, and min/max length.

- The `required` field contains a list of required properties, that is, the ones that we don't want to offload to CloudFormation to generate and explicitly want a user to define.

- Lastly, the `handlers` field (`https://docs.aws.amazon.com/cloudformation-cli/latest/userguide/resource-type-schema.html#schema-properties-handlers`) has a set of IAM permissions for each handler (create, read, update, and delete).

We will dive deeper into the necessary sections of the schema in just a moment. For now, let's bootstrap the code for our resource type.

Bootstrapping the project

We are going to install a new piece of AWS software and use it to bootstrap the extension development code:

1. To work with extensions, we need the CloudFormation CLI (this is different from the AWS CLI!) and the AWS SAM CLI (which we will cover in depth in *Chapter 11, Deploying Serverless Applications Using AWS SAM*). Let's install them as follows:

```
# Linux / Windows / MacOS
$ pip install cloudformation-cli aws-sam-cli
# MacOS installation with brew
$ brew update
$ brew install cloudformation-cli aws-sam-cli
```

2. To develop the resource type handler, we also need the Python plugin for the CloudFormation CLI. Let's install that too:

```
$ pip install cloudformation-cli-python-plugin
```

> **Important note**
> While we choose to develop the resource type in Python, it can also be developed in other languages, such as Java, Go, and Typescript. The CloudFormation CLI has its own plugins for each supported language.

3. Now we can bootstrap the code base with an interactive menu:

```
$ cfn init
```

4. We are going to build a custom resource type, so the answer to this first question is clear:

```
Initializing new project
Do you want to develop a new resource(r) or a module(m) or a
hook(h)?.
>> r
```

5. For the resource type name, we must follow the conventional naming syntax. The first part represents the wider org, such as our company; the second part refers to a service or a scope, and the last is the actual resource. In this example, I am going to go with some straightforward names for each part:

```
What's the name of your resource type?
(Organization::Service::Resource)
>> Org::Storage::Database
```

6.   Next, we have the language. Let's choose the latest supported Python version:

```
Select a language for code generation:
[1] go
[2] java
[3] python36
[4] python37
[5] python38
[6] python39
(enter an integer):
>> 6
```

7.   Use Docker for packaging to avoid platform issues:

```
Use docker for platform-independent packaging (Y/n)?
This is highly recommended unless you are experienced
with cross-platform Python packaging.
>> Y
```

8.   After all these steps, we will see a notification reporting that the project was bootstrapped successfully:

```
Initialized a new project in ~/projects/aws/demo
```

9.   If we run `tree` in the directory we will see the project structure as follows:

```
$ tree
.
├── README.md
├── docs
│   ├── README.md
│   ├── memo.md
│   └── tag.md
├── example_inputs
│   ├── inputs_1_create.json
│   ├── inputs_1_invalid.json
│   └── inputs_1_update.json
├── org-storage-database.json
├── requirements.txt
├── resource-role.yaml
├── rpdk.log
├── src
│   └── org_storage_database
│       ├── __init__.py
│       ├── handlers.py
│       └── models.py
└── template.yml
```

Note that these files are prefilled with dummy code and fields, so we need to change them. For now, let's focus on the schema file (the one with the name `org-storage-database.json`).

10. When we open the file, we are presented with a lot of prefilled data and some fields missing altogether. We will change the description of the resource type and add our replacement strategy as follows:

```
// org-storage-database.json
{
    "typeName": "Org::Storage::Database",
    "description": "Manage a MySQL database on a shared RDS
instance",
    "sourceUrl": "https://github.com/aws-cloudformation/
aws-cloudformation-rpdk.git",
    "replacementStrategy": "delete_then_create",
}
```

11. The next thing we have to handle is the properties. Here, we will reuse the same properties we had in the custom resource:

```
// org-storage-database.json
{
    "properties": {
        "DatabaseName": {
            "type": "string",
            "pattern": "^[A-Za-z0-9]+$"
        },
        "DatabaseUser": {
            "type": "string",
            "pattern": "^[A-Za-z0-9]+$"
        },
        "DatabasePassword": {
            "type": "string",
            "pattern": "^[A-Za-z0-9]+$",
            "minLength": 8
        },
    // and so on...
    }
}
```

12. All these properties are required, so let's mark them as such:

```
// org-storage-database.json
{
    "required": [
        "DatabaseName",
```

```
            "DatabaseUser",
            "DatabasePassword",
            "RdsHost",
            "RdsUser",
            "RdsPassword"
        ],
    }
```

13. All CloudFormation resources have a physical ID. For EC2 instances it's the instance ID, whereas for S3 buckets it's a bucket name. For our database, we can use a database name, as it must be unique:

```
// org-storage-database.json
{
    "primaryIdentifier": [
        "/properties/DatabaseName"
    ],
}
```

14. Lastly, we need to set the permissions that the handler needs to communicate with external services. In our case, it is empty:

```
// org-storage-database.json
{
    "handlers": {
        "create": {
            "permissions":[]
        },
        "read": {
            "permissions": []
        },
        // and so on...
    }
}
```

You will have noticed that we put in quite a bit of effort there to edit just one file, and it'll take a hundred more pages to do the same for the rest of the project. Luckily, AWS can take care of this for us. As soon as we have completed editing the schema, we simply ask the CloudFormation CLI to generate a project for us:

```
$ cfn generate
Resource schema is valid.
Generated files for Org::Storage::Database
```

Some of the code will be generated immediately. For example, check what the Python model code looks like now:

```
// models.py
class ResourceModel(BaseModel):
    DatabaseName: Optional[str]
    DatabaseUser: Optional[str]
    DatabasePassword: Optional[str]
    RdsHost: Optional[str]
    RdsUser: Optional[str]
    RdsPassword: Optional[str]
```

The project also has a template that provisions the necessary IAM role and policies for the use of the extension:

```
// resource-role.yaml
Resources:
  ExecutionRole:
    Type: AWS::IAM::Role
    Properties:
      Policies:
        - PolicyName: ResourceTypePolicy
          PolicyDocument:
            Statement:
              - Effect: Deny
                Action:
                - "*"
                Resource: "*"
```

If we needed to call the AWS resources and mention IAM actions, this policy section is where we would put them. But because we are using a native database driver, this block denies all API calls to the role.

Additionally, let's take a good look at the `AssumeRole` policy document as it has a few notable conditions:

```
// resource-role.yaml
Resources:
  ExecutionRole:
    Type: AWS::IAM::Role
    Properties:
      AssumeRolePolicyDocument:
        Version: '2012-10-17'
        Statement:
          - Effect: Allow
            Principal:
              Service: resources.cloudformation.amazonaws.com
```

```
                    Action: sts:AssumeRole
                  Condition:
                    StringEquals:
                      aws:SourceAccount: !Ref AWS::AccountId
                    StringLike:
                      aws:SourceArn:
                        Fn::Sub: arn:${AWS::Partition}:cloudformation:$
{AWS::Region}:${AWS::AccountId}:type/resource/Org-Storage-Database/*
```

The source account makes perfect sense – we don't want to allow anyone to abuse our cloud, but the source ARN mentions AWS::Region. This likely means that this role will be used only by a given resource type in a given Region. We will dive deeper into extension accessibility within Regions a bit later.

Some of the project was not updated, such as the example inputs. We will fill in the inputs when we are ready to test our code.

Now, let's get our hands dirty!

Editing the handlers

The CloudFormation resource type handler code has everything we need. It has the model code, the serializers and deserializers, exception handling, and so on. All we need to do is to build the actual provisioning logic!

1. Let's add a separate file that contains the code that interacts with the database. We will build a class that takes the database host, login, and password and initializes a database connection and a cursor:

    ```
    // dbclient.py
    class DbClient():
        def __init__(self, endpoint, user, password):
            self.con = pymysql.connect(
                        host=endpoint,
                        user=user,
                        password=password
                    )
            self.cursor = self.con.cursor()
    ```

2. Let's add some query templates as static fields as well:

    ```
    class DbClient():
        CREATE_DB = "CREATE DATABASE {};"
        CREATE_USER = "CREATE USER '{}'@'%' IDENTIFIED BY '{}';"
        GRANT = "GRANT ALL PRIVILEGES ON {}.* TO '{}'@'%';"
        FLUSH = "FLUSH PRIVILEGES;"
        DELETE_DB = "DROP DATABASE {}"
    ```

```
DELETE_USER = "DROP USER '{}'"
DB_EXISTS = "SHOW DATABASES LIKE '{}'"
USER_EXISTS = "SELECT user FROM mysql.user where user='{}'"
```

Later, we will call this variable with `str.format()` to render an actual SQL query.

3. We're good to go with the provisioning logic. Some of the methods should be familiar to you:

```
def db_exists(self, db):
    if self.cursor.execute(self.DB_EXISTS.format(db)):
        return True


def user_exists(self, user):
    if self.cursor.execute(
            self.USER_EXISTS.format(user)
    ):
        return True
```

These methods call our wrappers with the database name and user respectively, and return `True` if they exist in the RDS instance.

4. The deletion code is also trivial:

```
def delete_db(self, db):
    self.cursor.execute(self.DELETE_DB.format(db))


def delete_user(self, user):
    self.cursor.execute(self.DELETE_USER.format(user))


def delete(self, db, user):
    if self.db_exists(db):
        self.delete_db(db)
    if self.user_exists(user):
        self.delete_user(user)
```

5. We reuse the method that creates or updates the resource:

```
def create_or_update(self, db, user, pw):
    if self.db_exists(db):
        self.delete_db(db)
     if self.user_exists(user):
        self.delete_user(user)
    self.cursor.execute(
        self.CREATE_USER.format(user,pw)
    )
    self.cursor.execute(self.CREATE_DB.format(db))
```

```
        self.cursor.execute(self.GRANT.format(db, user))
        self.cursor.execute(self.FLUSH)
```

6. In the previous chapter, we discussed how updating a database resource will push us to delete an old database and create a new one. The schema and provisioning logic also assumes that any property change will trigger database re-creation. What is undesired – and we should have covered it in the previous chapter – is to delete the database when we simply want to change a user's password. Let's handle this in a more targeted way, by providing one more query template and a separate method:

```
CHANGE_PASSWORD = "ALTER USER '{}'@'%' IDENTIFIED BY '{}'"

def change_user_password(self, u, pw):
    if not self.user_exists(u):
        raise ValueError(f'User {u} does not exist!')
    self.cursor.execute(
        self.CHANGE_USER_PASSWORD.format(user, pw)
    )
```

> **Important note**
>
> The password is not the only thing that is mutable in our resource. For example, we can also change a database user without needing to recreate the database or refresh the credentials with RDS.
>
> When you finish this chapter, try to build some logic that handles these cases properly as a side activity.

We have done a fine job with the low-level provisioning logic, and introduced helper functions, wrappers, and provisioners for in-place and replace changes. It is time to embody this into some generated handler code!

The CloudFormation CLI has generated a lot of code, so for the sake of saving space in this book, I will show you the skeleton function and then the code containing the implementation that emits the function arguments and returns.

The skeleton code for create handler looks as follows:

```
// handlers.py
@resource.handler(Action.CREATE)
def create_handler(
    session: Optional[SessionProxy],
    request: ResourceHandlerRequest,
    callback_context: MutableMapping[str, Any],
) -> ProgressEvent:
```

```
    model = request.desiredResourceState
    progress: ProgressEvent = ProgressEvent(
        status=OperationStatus.IN_PROGRESS,
        resourceModel=model,
    )
    return read_handler(session, request, callback_context)
```

The difference between the create, update, read, and delete handler functions is the decorator that passes the action type. Note that in the preceding update handler, the decorator looks slightly different:

```
@resource.handler(Action.UPDATE)
def update_handler():
    return
```

Next, let's introduce two more wrappers to keep the handler methods clean:

```
def get_db_connection_parameters(request: ResourceHandlerRequest) ->
(str, str, str):
    return (
        request.desiredResourceState.RdsHost,
        request.desiredResourceState.RdsUser,
        request.desiredResourceState.RdsPassword
    )
def get_db_properties(request: ResourceHandlerRequest) -> (str, str,
str):
    return (
        request.desiredResourceState.DatabaseName,
        request.desiredResourceState.DatabaseUser,
        request.desiredResourceState.DatabasePassword,
    )
```

The first method gets the connection settings from the resource request and the second takes the database parameters. We need to initialize the database client every time we make calls, so we want as little code repetition as possible. Using these helper methods will save us some space and time.

To this end, the easiest change to make in the handler is of course the create handler. What it should do is just the following:

1. Check whether the database and users exist, then return an error if they do.

2. Run SQL and return a response.

Therefore, the create handler looks like this (you can refer to the full version of the code in the repo):

```
@resource.handler(Action.CREATE)
def create_handler():
    host, rds_user, rds_pw = get_db_connection_parameters(request)
```

```
        db, user, pw = get_db_properties(request)
        client = DbClient(host, rds_user, rds_pw)
        if (client.user_exists(user) or
            client.db_exists(db)):
            return ProgressEvent.failed(
                HandlerErrorCode.AlreadyExists,
            )
        try:
            client.create_or_update(db, user, pw)
            progress.status = OperationStatus.SUCCESS
        except Exception as e:
            return ProgressEvent.failed(
                HandlerErrorCode.HandlerInternalFailure
            )
        return read_handler(session, request, callback_context)
```

The preceding code first checks whether the database and users exist. If they do, we should immediately return an error, as the handler is not supposed to create a given resource when one already exists. With AWS CloudFormation resources, we handle this using resource imports, and it is a good idea to have the same behavior for custom resource types.

Another important bit here is what the method returns: either a built-in error (`AlreadyExists` or `HandlerInternalFailure`) or the read handler call. We will enforce the return of a proper response type with the contract test that we will run before submitting the resource type to the private registry.

The update handler is similar, while naturally skipping the check for whether the resource exists already, as updating an existing resource is exactly the desired behavior – but the delete and read handlers must check if the resource exists. What's even more interesting, these handlers *must return an error if it does not*! This behavior is also pushed by the contract:

```
@resource.handler(Action.DELETE)
def delete_handler():
    h, rds_u, rds_p = get_db_connection_parameters(request)
    db, user, _ = get_db_properties(request)
    client = DbClient(h, rds_u, rds_p)
    if not (client.db_exists(db) or
            client.user_exists(user)):
        return ProgressEvent.failed(
                HandlerErrorCode.NotFound,
                f'Database or user do not exist'
            )
    try:
        client.delete(db, u)
```

```
        progress.status = OperationStatus.SUCCESS
    except Exception as e:
        return ProgressEvent.failed(
            HandlerErrorCode.HandlerInternalFailure,
            f'Failed to delete resource. Reason: {e}')
    return progress
```

The preceding code covers only the delete method, but the read handler is similar, just lacking the delete calls.

Another method worth mentioning here is `list_handler`. This method is used to return all resources of the same type. Therefore, if a resource exists, it returns its properties, otherwise it returns a None object:

```
@resource.handler(Action.LIST)
def list_handler():
    model = request.desiredResourceState
    h, rds_u, rds_p = get_db_connection_parameters(request)
    db, user, _ = get_db_properties(request)
    client = DbClient(h, rds_u, rds_p)

    models = []
    if client.db_exists(db) and client.user_exists(user):
        models.append(model)

    return ProgressEvent(
        status=OperationStatus.SUCCESS,
        resourceModels=models,
    )
```

That's pretty much it with the handler. If you consult the full code in the repository, you will notice that the methods are much larger. As mentioned before, some parts of the code were emitted to save space, as most of the code is generated by the CLI.

The next thing to do is to add some sample input data so we can run contract tests against our handler. By default, the CloudFormation CLI will run tests generating random properties based on its type (`https://docs.aws.amazon.com/cloudformation-cli/latest/userguide/resource-type-test.html#resource-type-test-input-data`), and that does not work for us, as we need the cluster and credentials ARN. Hence, we need to provide the input ourselves.

In the project folder, we will add a directory named `input` and store several files for create and update calls, and invalid call respectively:

```
// inputs_1_create.json
{
```

```
        "DatabaseName": "myDatabase",
        "DatabaseUser": "MyDatabaseUser",
        "DatabasePassword": "SuperUser12",
        "RdsHost": "db_identifier.us-east-1.rds.amazonaws.com",
        "RdsUser": "rdsuser",
        "RdsPassword": "barfoo12344321"
    }
```

Replace the `RdsHost` field with a value from the stack you created at the beginning of this section.

For the update input functionality, you can just change the database password, and we can simply leave the invalid input field empty:

```
// inputs_1_invalid.json
{
    "DatabaseName": "myDb",
    "DatabaseUser": "MyDbUser",
    "DatabasePassword": "",
    // ...
}
```

Now we are good to go! The next sequence of actions will finalize and roll out our resource type:

1. We need to compile the resource type provisioner into a package that we will test. We can do that by running `submit` in a dry run – this will store the build artifact locally. When running this command, wait for it to complete:

   ```
   $ cfn submit --dry-run
   ```

2. In a separate tab, start the local Lambda that will serve provisioners:

   ```
   $ sam local start-lambda
   ```

3. In the previous terminal, run the tests:

   ```
   $ cfn test
   ```

4. You will see requests incoming to locally running Lambda functions and the tests passing. When all of this is complete, we are safe to submit the resource type:

   ```
   $ cfn submit -v --region us-east-1
   ```

   You will see a lengthy response, and after a while, a JSON string will appear. Wait a bit and then check your brand-new private resource type in the CloudFormation console:

Resource types (1)

Resource types represent resources available for use in CloudFormation. Use CloudFormation capabilities to create, provision, and manage resources in a safe and repeatable manner. Learn more ⃞

Actions ▼

🔍 Search by extension prefix (eg. AWS::S3)

Filter extension type

Privately registered ▼

‹ 1 › ⚙

Resource types	▲	Default version	Registry
Org::Storage::Database		1	Private

Figure 8.5 – CloudFormation registry – Activated extensions

5. Let's draft a quick template for a new resource type:

```
// database.yaml
AWSTemplateFormatVersion: "2010-09-09"
Description: Custom DB
Parameters:
// parameters...
Resources:
  Database:
    Type: Org::Storage::Database
    Properties:
      DatabaseName: !Ref DBName
      DatabaseUser: !Ref DBUser
      DatabasePassword: !Ref DBPassword
      RdsHost: !ImportValue RdsEndpoint
      RdsUser: !Ref RdsUser
      RdsPassword: !Ref RdsPassword
```

6. Then deploy it as follows:

```
$ aws cloudformation deploy \
      --stack-name mydatabase \
      --template-file database.yaml
Waiting for changeset to be created..
Waiting for stack create/update to complete
Successfully created/updated stack - mydatabase
```

Awesome! This concludes our theory and practice with private resource types. When we are done playing around, we can clean up our cloud and private resources as follows:

```
$ aws cloudformation delete-stack \
     --stack-name mydatabase
$ aws cloudformation delete-stack \
     --stack-name rds
```

If you want to keep your account clean and deregister the private extension, run the following command:

> **Important note**
> Delete custom resources before deregistering the extension! Otherwise, you will not be able to delete the custom stack at all.

```
$ aws cloudformation deregister-type \
     --type RESOURCE \
     --type-name 'Org::Storage::Database'
```

Well done! This marks the end of our experimentation with the CloudFormation registry and private resource types.

Summary

In this chapter, we learned about one of the biggest features of CloudFormation for managing custom resource types. We managed not only to activate and use public resource types, but also to develop our own.

Resource types were built for third-party services such as those from other cloud service providers, but they also allow us to build powerful automations for our internal tools.

And that is what we did! We generated our own resource schema, built some code that communicates with our database, and adopted it to work with the CloudFormation native handler. Before submitting the resource type, we ensured it matches the contract by running an acceptance test.

Deployments using publicly accessible databases are not, however, a secure option. Think, how could you harden it and make it more secure? Would you try using IAM authentication or some secure endpoint such as RDS Proxy?

I leave these answers to you. Try out answering the following questions to test your knowledge before we dive into the next chapter, where we will learn about extending our templates even further with macros and modules.

Questions

1. What is the difference between public and private extensions?

2. What extensions are available in the registry?

3. What are the required actions in the resource type handler?

4. Which command-line tools can we use to register and deregister a private extension?

5. Which command generates resource code based on a schema?

Further reading

- Public AWS community extensions: `https://github.com/aws-cloudformation/community-registry-extensions/tree/main`

- Learnings from building custom resource types from Cloudsoft: `https://cloudsoft.io/blog/what-we-learned-from-building-60-third-party-resources-for-aws-cloudformation`

9

Scale Your Templates Using Macros, Nested Stacks, and Modules

Sometimes, when we work with templates, we want to dynamically assign values to resources or alter the template quickly during stack operations. Sometimes, we want to have a modular structure for our stacks and enhance reusability.

One of the most well-known template macros is the **Serverless Application Model** (**SAM**), which is a simplified CloudFormation template for serverless applications (we will cover SAM in the next few chapters). Another well-known macro is `AWS::Include`, which allows us to append the CloudFormation template with boilerplate snippets. When it comes to reusability and modularity, we can use nested stacks or register CloudFormation module extensions.

In this chapter, we will learn about template macros and their use cases, and we will develop our own macros. Later, we will take a quick look at nested stacks, examining why they are used way less than before and why modules have succeeded them. Finally, we will create our own module and deploy a stack using the SAM CLI.

In this chapter, we will cover the following topics:

- Understanding the use cases of template macros
- Introducing the template macro
- Writing your own macros
- Learning about the history of nested stacks
- Building and using your own CloudFormation modules

Technical requirements

The code used in this chapter can be found in the book's GitHub repository at https://github.com/PacktPublishing/Mastering-AWS-CloudFormation-Second-Edition/tree/main/Chapter09.

Check out the following video to see the code in action:

https://packt.link/2tkJD

Understanding the use cases of the template macro

Before we dive into the internals of macros, we need to know what we can solve with them. Let's look at a few cases and examples.

Auto-filling resource property values

Imagine having a launch template where you need to define an **Amazon Machine Image** (**AMI**) ID. For Amazon Linux AMI, you could use AWS's Parameter Store:

```
Parameters:
  ImageId:
    Type: AWS::SSM::Parameter::Value<AWS::EC2::Image::Id>
    Default: </aws/service/ami-amazon-linux-latest/amzn2-ami-hvm-
x86_64-gp2'
Resources:
  LaunchTemplate:
    Type: «AWS::EC2::LaunchTemplate»
    Properties:
      LaunchTemplateData:
        ImageId: !Ref ImageId
```

However, what if we don't use Amazon Linux, but Ubuntu? We'd have to manually specify the AMI IDs and use mappings:

```
Mappings:
  RegionMap:
    us-east-1: "ami-123"
    us-west-1: "ami-456"
    # and so on...
Resources:
  Inst:
    Type: "AWS::EC2::Instance"
    Properties:
      ImageId: !FindInMap [RegionMap, !Ref AWS::Region]
```

Alternatively, we can build a macro that looks the AMI ID up for us and use it in our template.

The following template is an example of how to fill in an AMI ID using a macro:

```
Resources:
  LaunchTemplate:
    Type: «AWS::EC2::LaunchTemplate»
    Properties:
      LaunchTemplateData:
        ImageId:
          Fn::Transform:
            Name: FindAmi
            Parameters:
              OSFamily: "ubuntu"
```

As you can see in the preceding example, the macro name is supplied after the intrinsic function, `Fn::Transform`, followed by its parameters. During the stack operation, the macro will store the necessary AMI ID. Let's look at another example.

Adding extra resources

Let's say we have some sort of resource that is the same for every stack, but it has to be part of each one individually – for example, CloudWatch rules and alerts for applications. We could copy and paste the same resource declaration over and over again, which is considered to be code duplication and is bad practice.

For cases like this, there is a CloudFormation macro called `AWS::Include`. The `AWS::Include` macro looks for a template on S3 and appends the current template with an extra one. The `AWS::Include` macro is not a *global* macro, so it has to be declared in the `Resources` section, as shown in the following code:

```
Resources:
  # ... some of our resources...
  «Fn::Transform»:
    Name: «AWS::Include»
    Parameters:
      Location: «s3://mybucket/my_set_of_resources.yaml»
```

Although it is a common macro, we should avoid using duplicated resources, following the **Don't Repeat Yourself (DRY)** pattern, and organize our stack properly.

Making resource declaration easier for developers

We have a standard way of developing applications. Let's say that each application is an **Elastic Container Service (ECS)** task running on Fargate. It may or may not have additional resources, and it will always run on the same ECS cluster as the others. We can make a huge template with conditional elements and ask developers to provide a lot of parameters, or we can make a nice and easy-to-use template for them with the help of a macro.

The following example template shows how this *standard* application will look:

```
Transform: StandardApplication
Resources:
  Application:
    Properties:
      TaskCount: 1
      Memory: 512
      CPU: 256
      RDS: "postgresql"
      RDSSize: "db.t2.micro"
      # and so on...
```

During transformation, the macro will evaluate the properties and render a new template, such as the following:

```
Resources:
  EcsTaskDefinition:
    Type: # ...
    Properties:
      Cpu: 256
      Memory: 512
      # ...
  EcsService:
    Type: #...
    Propeties:
      DesiredCount: 1
      # ...
# and so on...
```

Developers will always have control over their application's infrastructure and resources, yet they will not have to dive deep into CloudFormation and AWS.

This all sounds good, but how do we make this happen? Let's look at what exactly a template macro is.

Introducing the template macro

First of all, macros are an optional part of CloudFormation. AWS already provides us with its own macros (AWS::Serverless and AWS::Include) – they are a part of CloudFormation and are executed whenever we use a Transform block in a template or resource.

Custom macros (that is, macros created by us) are also part of the CloudFormation and are created as a resource with an AWS::CloudFormation::Macro type. Each macro in particular is a Lambda function, which is similar to a custom resource, as it receives an event from CloudFormation and needs to return a response.

This Lambda function will receive a part of the template (or the full template), run custom processing, and return a transformed template.

The request from CloudFormation will look like the following:

```
{
    «region»: «...»,
    «accountId»: «...»,
    «fragment»: {...},
    «transformId»: «...»,
    «params»: {...},
    «requestId»: «...»,
    «templateParameterValues»: {...}
}
```

Here are the key code terms and their description:

- fragment: Either a partial or full template
- params: A list of parameters, if the macro function is invoked using the intrinsic function, Fn::Transform
- templateParameterValues: Template parameters

templateParameterValues, unlike params, are values that are evaluated before processing (during the template validation step).

After processing, our Lambda should return a response. This response should contain a request identifier (exactly the same as in the original request), response status, and processed content. All in all, it will look like the following:

```
{
    «requestId»: «...»,
    «status»: «...»,
```

```
      «fragment»: {...}
}
```

Before we create our own macro, we need to know about a few limitations that we might face.

Considerations

Macros bring plenty of benefits to ease the development of CloudFormation templates, but there are many things that we need to keep in mind when writing them.

Mainly, we need to know the following facts:

- Macros will only work in the regions where AWS Lambda is available

- Processed templates must pass the validation check

- Macros don't support iteration – we can't include a macro in a macro

- Macros don't support `Fn::ImportValue`

- Macros are not supported in `StackSets`

> **Important note**
> For the full list of considerations, please read CloudFormation's documentation (`https://docs.aws.amazon.com/AWSCloudFormation/latest/UserGuide/template-macros.html`).

These are the main things that we need to bear in mind. Now, let's build macros for a few of the cases that were mentioned at the beginning of this chapter.

Writing your own macro

In this section, we will develop macros to solve the cases introduced in the first section of this chapter, the *Understanding the use cases of template macros* section. This will help us to get some hands-on experience and practice partial and full template processing.

Let's start with the AMI ID filler!

AMI ID filler

Let's start with a simple task and create a macro that will automatically find the AMI ID for EC2. By the end of this section, we will have a macro that automatically puts a correct AMI in the resource properties.

As you might remember, our main template will look like the following:

```
Resources:
  LaunchTemplate:
    Type: «AWS::EC2::LaunchTemplate»
    Properties:
      LaunchTemplateData:
        # This is a replacement for the field ImageId:
          Fn::Transform:
            Name: AMIFiller
            Parameters:
              OSFamily: "ubuntu"
```

This means that CloudFormation will send the request with the following payload:

```
{
    «region»: «...», # region name, where the stack is
    «accountId»: «...», # AWS account ID
    «fragment»: {...}, # the fragment of the template
    «transformId»: «...», # unique ID of transformation
    «params»: {«OSFamily»: «ubuntu»},
    «requestId»: «...», # request ID for Lambda
    «templateParameterValues»: {...} # template parameters
}
```

So, all we need to do is return the string that contains the AMI ID that we need. The response body would look like the following:

```
{
    «requestId»: "...", # same as in original request
    «status»: «...», # SUCCESS or FAILURE
    «fragment»: {«ImageId»: «ami-123454321»}
}
```

Let's begin by developing a Lambda function so that our macro can find a proper AMI:

1. We will start with an actual function that will invoke EC2's API in order to retrieve the AMI ID:

```
// amifinder.py
image_names = {
    'amazonlinux': 'al2023-ami-2023.1.20230809.0-kernel-
6.1-x86_64',
    'ubuntu': 'ubuntu/images/hvm-ssd/ubuntu-jammy-22.04-amd64-
server-20230516',
    'rhel': 'RHEL-9.2.0_HVM-20230503-x86_64-41-Hourly2-GP2',
    'sles': 'suse-sles-15-sp5-v20230620-hvm-ssd-x86_64'
}
def get_image(img_name):
    client = boto3.client('ec2')
    resp = client.describe_images(
        Filters=[{'Name': 'name',
                  'Values': [img_name]}])
    return resp[<Images>][0][<ImageId>]
```

Since AWS has plenty of AMIs (both new and older versions), it is hard to find the necessary image with a single word (such as `"ubuntu"` or `"rhel"`), so we will create a dictionary that will contain the exact AMI name.

Then, we use a function that will connect to the API and request the AMI ID for that name.

2. Now, we need our handler function:

```
// amifinder.py
def lambda_handler(event, context):
    response = {}
    response[<requestId>] = event[<requestId>]
    response[<fragment>] = {'ImageId': ''}
    response['status'] = 'SUCCESS'
    osfamily = event[<params>][<OSFamily>]
    if osfamily not in image_names.keys():
        response[<status>] = 'FAILURE'
        return response
    image_id = get_image(image_names[osfamily])
    response[<fragment>]['ImageId'] = image_id
    return response
```

This function will parse the event from CloudFormation. If the supplied parameter, OSFamily, doesn't equal ubuntu, amazonlinux2, rhel, or sles, it will immediately return FAILURE with an empty body, signaling to CloudFormation that the macro has failed; otherwise, it will invoke the get_image() function and form a proper response.

3. Now, we need to create a macro stack (thereby registering the macro function):

```
$ aws cloudformation deploy
    --stack-name amimacro \
    --template-file macro.yaml \
    --capabilities CAPABILITY_IAM
```

4. Our macro is in place. Let's create a template to test it out. Our testing template is small and simple; all we need to do is check that the macro performs its function:

```
// lt.yaml
Resources:
  Lt:
    Type: "AWS::EC2::LaunchTemplate"
    Properties:
      LaunchTemplateData:
        Fn::Transform:
            Name: AMIFiller
            Parameters:
              OSFamily: «ubuntu»
```

5. We will create a stack from this template:

```
$ aws cloudformation deploy
    --stack-name lt \
    --template-file lt.yaml
```

6. After a while, we will see our stack created. Let's check the template on the CloudFormation console:

Figure 9.1 – The CloudFormation console – an unprocessed template

There is an interesting trigger. Let's click on it and see what happens!

```
⬤ View processed template

{
  "AWSTemplateFormatVersion": "2010-09-09",
  "Resources": {
    "Lt": {
      "Properties": {
        "LaunchTemplateData": {
          "ImageId": "ami-053b0d53c279acc90"
        }
      },
      "Type": "AWS::EC2::LaunchTemplate"
    }
  }
}
```

Figure 9.2 – The CloudFormation console – a processed template

So, what actually happened is that the macro ran a transformation, changing the block where we call Fn::Transform to an image ID. Exactly what we wanted!

Now, let's simulate an error. We will change the OSFamily parameter from ubuntu to something that is not in our macro's dictionary and rerun the stack deployment:

```
// lt.yaml
Resources:
  Lt:
    Type: "AWS::EC2::LaunchTemplate"
    Properties:
      LaunchTemplateData:
        Fn::Transform:
          Name: AMIFiller
          Parameters:
            OSFamily: «yolo»
```

7. Now, let's deploy the stack:

```
$ aws cloudformation deploy --stack-name lt --template-file
lt.yaml
Waiting for changeset to be created..
Failed to create the changeset: Waiter ChangeSetCreateComplete
failed: Waiter encountered a terminal failure state Status:
FAILED. Reason: Transform ACCT_ID::AMIFiller failed without an
error message.
```

> **Important note**
>
> Note that the stack update failed *before* the execution of the changeset. This is because CloudFormation runs template validation before *and* after macro processing, and since our function returned FAILED, CloudFormation couldn't continue.

With this in mind, let's create a more powerful template macro that will render the whole application template from just a bunch of input data.

Rendering the application template from a short declaration

In this section, we will develop a macro that will create a full CloudFormation stack by transforming a shortened version of it – the *standard application* declaration.

> **Important note**
>
> Don't forget to check the repository for the full version of the macro!

So, we have the following kind of template for our so-called standard application:

```
// app.yaml
Transform: StandardApplication
Resources:
  Application:
    Properties:
      ApplicationImage: «»
      ApplicationPort: 0
      TaskCount: 0
      Memory: 0
      CPU: 0
      RDS: «»
      RDSSize: «»
      RDSMultiAz: False
      NeedsBalancer: False
      PubliclyAvailable: False
```

This application may or may not have the following resources:

- A **Relational Database Service (RDS)** instance

- **Elastic Load Balancer (ELS)**

- An **Elastic Container Service (ECS)** service

Imagine a case where developers, who are mainly focused on solving business cases, don't care about the underlying infrastructure, so we as cloud engineers have to take care of it. The only requirement for the developers is that they must supply a valid Docker image.

Transformation is applied to a template as a whole – this means that we need stricter and more complex processing logic. With these inputs from the template, we will understand which resources to create and which properties to assign to them.

Let's first build our skeleton for the macro:

```
// standard_app.py
def render_ecs(input):
    ecs_definition = {}
    return ecs_definition
def render_rds(input):
    rds_definition = {}
    return rds_definition
def render_elb(input):
    elb_definition = {}
    return elb_definition
def lambda_handler(event, context):
    response = {}
    response[<requestId>] = event[<requestId>]
    response[<status>] = 'SUCCESS'
    response[<fragment>] = {}

    return response
```

What we do here is create three additional functions, each of which is responsible for processing the input data (for example, properties), and then create the necessary resource declarations.

These functions are as follows:

- `render_ecs()`
- `render_rds()`
- `render_elb()`

However, before that, we will parse the incoming payload in the Lambda handler function.

Parsing properties

Before we render the final template, we need to make a decision based on which resources we will create. We do this by parsing the input properties. According to our template, a fragment of CloudFormation's request will look like the following:

```
«fragment» : {
  «Resources»: {
    «Application»: {
      «Properties»: {
        «ApplicationImage»: «»,
        «ApplicationPort»: 0,
        «TaskCount»: 0,
        «Memory»: 0,
        «CPU»: 0,
        «RDSEngine»: «»,
        «RDSSize»: «»,
        «RDSMultiAz»: «»,
        «NeedsBalancer»: false,
        «PublciclyAvailable»: false
      }
    }
  }
}
```

At least four of the properties are mandatory – the image, network port, count, memory, and CPU; otherwise, we have nothing to declare for our ECS task. Let's add a check in our Lambda handler:

```python
// standard_app.py
def lambda_handler(event, context):
    # ...
    required_properties = ['ApplicationImage', 'ApplicationPort',
'TaskCount', 'Memory', 'CPU']
    properties = event[<fragment>][<Resources'] ['Application']
['Properties']
    for req in required_properties:
        if req not in properties.keys() or not properties[req]:
            response[<status>] = 'FAILED'
            return response
    # ...
```

If at least one of the properties is not set or set to `null`, the Lambda function will respond with `FAILED`.

In addition to the required properties, we have optional ones. Those are declared if we need additional resources (such as an RDS instance or ELB) depending on what are the properties of these resources.

The `RDSEngine`, `RDSSize`, and `RDSMultiAz` properties provide information on the RDS instance that we will provision. If `RDSEngine` is not specified, we assume that no database is required. For `RDSSize`, we have a default value of `db.t2.micro`, and for `RDSMultiAz`, we have `false`. Let's add these to our handler:

```
// standard_app.py
def lambda_handler(event, context):
    # ...
    rds_props = {}
    rds_props[<RDSEngine>] = ''
    rds_props[<RDSSize>] = 'db.t2.micro'
    rds_props[<RDSMultiAz>] = 'false'
    for key in rds_props.keys():
        if key in properties.keys() and properties[key]:
            rds_props[key] = properties[key]
    # ...
```

What we do here is set the default values to RDS properties and the `null` value to `RDSEngine`. If they are provided in the CloudFormation request, we overwrite them.

We will do the same with the ELB properties:

```
// standard_app.py
def lambda_handler(event, context):
    # ...
    elb_props = {}
    elb_props[<NeedBalancer>] = False
    elb_props[<PubliclyAvailable>] = False
    for key in elb_props.keys():
        if key in properties.keys() and properties[key]:
            elb_props[key] = properties[key]
    # ...
```

Now, when we have all our properties sorted, we can start developing our provisioning logic.

Declaring resources from a macro

Since the macro must return a valid JSON template, this is the first (and hopefully the last) time that we write templates in the JSON format.

We will improve the `render_ecs()` function so that it returns a valid declaration. We already know that we receive the application image, its port, CPU share settings, task count, and memory settings properties.

Simultaneously, we know that we need to provision CloudWatch logs and the ECS task definition and its service, both of which are compatible with ECS Fargate.

Let's build a skeleton for the ECS task definition. We will follow the same formatting as we did for the CloudFormation JSON template (you can find the full version on GitHub):

```python
// standard_app.py
def render_ecs(input):
    # ...
    ecs_task_definition = {
    # ...
      'Family': '',  # placeholder
    # ...
      'Name': '',  # placeholder
      'Image': '',  # placeholder
    # ...
      'ContainerPort': '',  # placeholder
    # ...
      'awslogs-stream-prefix': ''  # placeholder
    # ...
      'Cpu': '',  # placeholder
      'Memory': '',  # placeholder
    # ...
}
```

Our ECS task definition is now a dictionary object. We need to fill those placeholders with the values from the input:

```python
// standard_app.py
def render_ecs(input):
    # ...
    application_image = input[<ApplicationImage>]
    application_name = application_image.strip(':')
    ecs_task_definition_properties = ecs_task_
definition[<TaskDefinition>][<Properties>]
    ecs_task_definition_properties[<Family>] = application_name
    ecs_task_definition_properties[<ContainerDefinitions>][0][<Name>]
= application_name
    ecs_task_definition_properties['ContainerDefinitions'][0]['Image']
= application_image
    # and so on...
```

Once the task definition has all the values, we can continue with the ECS and CloudWatch logs.

Ultimately, our function will look like the following:

```
// standard_app.py
def render_ecs(input):
    ecs_definition = {}
    ecs_task_definition = {...}
    # generation of ecs_task_definition...
    ecs_service_definition = {...}
    # generation of ecs_service_definition...
    ecs_definition[<Logs>] = {...}
    ecs_definition[<Sg>] = {...}
    # generation of the rest...
    ecs_definition.update(ecs_task_definition)
    ecs_definition.update(ecs_service_definition)

    return ecs_definition
```

Finally, we will retrieve a set of CloudFormation resources required for our application, such as the ECS task definition, service, CloudWatch logs, and EC2 security.

The generation of additional resources (ELB and the RDS instance) is similar, so let's not focus on that and jump to the deployment of our macro.

Deploying a standard app

By performing the following steps, we will deploy a macro and test it out:

1. Since our application needs to have a foundation (an ECS cluster, network, and so on), we first need to provision those (you will find them in the repository):

    ```
    $ aws cloudformation deploy
          --stack-name core \
          --template-file core.yaml \
          --capabilities CAPABILITY_IAM
    ```

2. Once the stack is deployed, we can provision our macro. Our code is too big to fit in a CloudFormation template, so we will have to upload it manually to S3:

```
$ aws s3 mb s3://masteringcfn # your bucket name may differ
$ zip lambda-macro.zip standard-app.py
$ aws cloudformation deploy
      --stack-name standard-app-macro \
      --template-file macro.yaml \
      --capabilities CAPABILITY_IAM
```

3. We are all set. We can proceed with our application:

```
$ aws cloudformation deploy
      --stack-name app \
      --template-file app.yaml
```

4. Let's look at the CloudFormation console. We are interested in what our template will look like after processing:

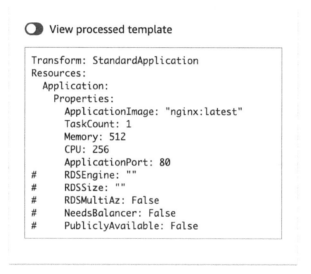

Figure 9.3 – The CloudFormation console – an unprocessed template

However, we are interested in the processed template:

⬤ View processed template

```json
{
  "Resources": {
    "Logs": {
      "Type": "AWS::Logs::LogGroup",
      "Properties": {
        "LogGroupName": "nginx",
        "RetentionInDays": 1
      }
    },
    "Sg": {
      "Type": "AWS::EC2::SecurityGroup",
      "Properties": {
        "GroupDescription": "Security Group",
        "VpcId": {
          "Fn::ImportValue": "VpcId"
        }
      }
    },
    "TaskDefinition": {
      "Type": "AWS::ECS::TaskDefinition",
      "Properties": {
        "Family": "nginx",
        "RequiresCompatibilities": [
          "FARGATE"
        ],
        "ContainerDefinitions": [
          {
            "Name": "nginx",
            "Image": "nginx:latest",
            "PortMappings": [
              {
                "ContainerPort": 80,
                "Protocol": "tcp"
              }
            ]
```

Figure 9.4 – The CloudFormation console – a processed template

That's it! We have successfully created our first macro, which processes the whole template! With this knowledge, we can tweak and extend the CloudFormation templates in the way that we need to.

Let's move on to modularity with nested stacks and CloudFormation modules.

Learning about the past of nested stacks

As infrastructure scales, engineers face the challenge of maintaining an increased load with a reasonable amount of effort. For example, a team may need to deploy the same application across multiple AWS regions or accounts. For that, they can use **StackSets** and manage the same infrastructure using granular rollouts and rollbacks.

Another example of scale is the stack itself. While provisioned in a single stack, a template can grow in size and turn into a multi-thousand-line YAML or JSON file, thus becoming hard to maintain.

One example of maintaining scale is the `Transform` macro, which we explored in the previous section, but this macro requires engineering effort to maintain an AWS Lambda function and, at some point, will become backwards-incompatible. Therefore, we need sustainable ways to introduce modularity to the template and allow independent updates for each part of the stack.

The CloudFormation development team built two features that facilitate such modularity – nested stacks and, later, modules (as a part of CloudFormation's extensions registry).

In this section, we will learn about the history of nested stacks, what their intentions were, and why it is hard to maintain them.

CloudFormation stack resource

The CloudFormation stack is a collection of resources that are declared in the template. The resources belong to various services – instances belong to EC2, tables belong to DynamoDB, topics and subscriptions belong to SNS, and so on.

CloudFormation is also a service; hence, it has resources, such as stacks and StackSets. And since CloudFormation is also supported by CloudFormation, we can use CloudFormation to maintain CloudFormation resources!

This sounds strange and silly, right? Let me give you an example:

```
Resources:
  SomeStack:
    Type: AWS::CloudFormation::Stack
    Properties:
      TemplateURL: "https://s3.amazonaws.com/bckt/tpl.yaml"
      Parameters:
        SomeParameter: "SomeValue"
        OtherParameter: "OtherValue"
```

What you see in the preceding code is a dummy declaration of a CloudFormation stack resource in a template. Such a configuration is called a **nested stack**, which means we declare a stack in another stack. Nested stacks take a template S3 URL as a required property and pass parameters if the downstream template needs it.

To provide a more practical example, imagine the following template:

```
Parameters:
  InstanceType:
    Type: String
  VolumeSize:
    Type: String
Resources:
  Ec2:
    Type: "AWS::EC2::Instance"
    Properties:
      ImageId: "ami-123456abcd" # hardcoded AMI!
      KeyName: "key_name" # harcoded key name!
      InstanceType: !Ref InstanceType
      BlockDeviceMappings:
      - DeviceName: "/dev/sda"
        Ebs:
          VolumeType: "gpt4"
          VolumeSize: !Ref VolumeSize
```

The preceding template has almost all the properties hardcoded and takes only the instance type and EBS volume size as parameters. If we were to upload this template file to S3, we could use it as a nested stack:

```
Resources:
  Instance:
    Type: "AWS::CloudFormation::Stack"
    Properties:
      TemplateURL: "https://s3.amazonaws.com/bkt/ec2.yaml"
      Parameters:
        InstanceType: "t3.large"
        VolumeSize: 100
```

Such an approach is useful to abstract protected properties – in our case, AMI and key names – from end users.

Nested stacks also support nested outputs that can be used between other nested stacks. Imagine a setup where you have an AWS Lambda function that uses an IAM role. This role has a policy to make DynamoDB calls to a certain table. Assuming the function and the table are deployed in separate stacks, the table template would look as follows:

```
// table.yaml
Resources:
  Table:
    Type: "AWS::DynamoDB::Table"
```

```
      Properties: # ...
  Outputs:
    TableArn:
      Value: !GetAtt Table.Arn
```

And the function template would look like this:

```
// function.yaml
Parameters:
  TableArn:
    Type: String
Resources:
  Function:
    Type: "AWS::Lambda::Function"
    Properties: # ...
  FunctionRole:
    Type: "AWS::IAM::Role"
    Properties: # ...
  FunctionPolicy:
    Types: "AWS::IAM::RolePolicy"
    Properties:
      PolicyDocument:
        Version: "2012-10-17"
        Statement:
          - Effect: "Allow"
            Action: "dynamodb:*"
            Resource: !Ref TableArn
      RoleName: !Ref FunctionRole
```

In this case, we can pass the table ARN output as a parameter value to the function template. This is done by referring to the output name from the table template:

```
Resources:
  Table:
    Type: "AWS::CloudFormation::Stack"
    Properties:
      TemplateURL: "https://s3url/templates/table.yaml"
  Function:
    Type: "AWS::CloudFormation::Stack"
    Properties:
      TemplateURL: "https://s3url/templates/function.yaml"
      Parameters:
        TableArn: !GetAtt [Table, Outputs.TableArn]
```

In the preceding code, we use the intrinsic function, `Fn::GetAtt`, and pass the stack's logical and output names as a value to the function template parameter.

This way, we can visualize nested stacks – various pieces of the parent stack – as a graph.

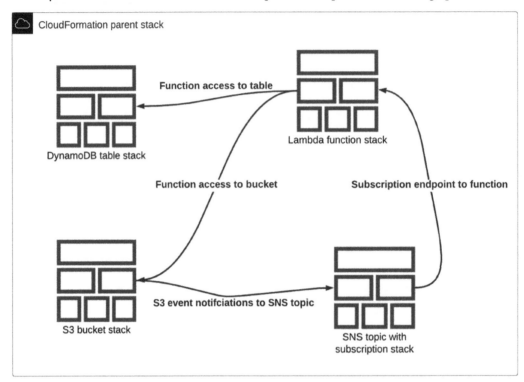

Figure 9.5 – A CloudFormation nested stack graph with dependencies

The graph in the preceding figure is another example of a modular stack structure:

1. We have an S3 bucket that generates events when an object is put or removed from it. The notifications are sent to an SNS topic, declared in another stack.

2. The SNS subscription points to Lambda function in its own stack.

3. Lambda reads resources ARNs from the S3 and Dynamo stacks to add them to its function IAM policy.

The observant among you will see the risk of having a so-called *circular dependency*, and you may be right! S3 depends on SNS, SNS depends on Lambda, Lambda depends on S3, S3 depends on SNS...

Note also that the code present in this section is purely for observation purposes. This is because I believe that every CloudFormation user should be aware of nested stacks – ultimately, you may end up working with them in a large engineering organization that has used AWS for a while – but I discourage you from using them unless you really must.

In the following section, we will cover the caveats of nested stacks. I believe that will build a strong case against using nested stacks if you ever have this discussion at work or an AWS community gathering.

The caveats of nested stacks

Nested stacks have plenty of history and have been around since at least 2013. Their rich history also has some pain points that we should cover, allowing you to decide whether to use them or not.

Nested stacks do not support versioning

When we declare nested stacks, we provide a URL for a template. When updating the stack, CloudFormation will resolve the latest template object version from S3 and update the underlying stack accordingly. The template URL does not support specifying the version of an object; therefore, it always refers to the latest one. If there is a bug in a template, we will have to revert the object using S3 features and run the update again, which leads us to the following topic.

Nested stacks rolling back and forward take plenty of time

Nested stacks are rolled in parallel unless there is a dependency. If there is a problem in one of the nested stacks, the whole parent stack will be rolled back. We will have then to find an individual nested stack that failed, make a fix, and then deploy the change again. CloudFormation changes are atomic; we cannot say, *"Deploy these stacks and keep them even if this one fails."* In worst-case scenarios, where resources have deletion protection, CloudFormation will block the rollback, and the parent stack will persist in a failed state.

Nested stacks are hard to maintain

Even if everything goes well, the lack of versioning makes it harder to maintain the parent stack. If we want to introduce a breaking change in the nested stack that impacts dependent nested stacks (let's say they refer to the output), we need to make sure that other nested stacks adopt the change before we push it forward. Not knowing which parent stacks use our template makes it hard to find the dependencies. However, this is not to say that inevitably large graphs built from nested stacks become *spaghetti code* that no one wants to own.

As we can see, nested stacks allow us to reuse existing CloudFormation features with poor maintainability as a trade-off. In the following section, we will look into a modern way of implementing modularity using the CloudFormation modules registry.

Building and using your own CloudFormation modules

If you come from the Terraform realm, you will have likely heard about modules before. Hence, I think it's fair to do a quick comparison between Terraform and CloudFormation module functionality.

Comparing Terraform and CloudFormation modules

A Terraform module is a generic configuration stored in a local directory or repository. Consider the following Terraform files:

```
// instance.tf
resource "aws_instance" "instance" {
  # some resource properties
  instance_type = var.type
}
// variables.tf
variable "type" {}
```

We can refer to this module via a directory, similar to how we would refer to templates in nested stacks:

```
// main.tf
module "my_instance" {
  source = "path/to/module/"
  type = "t3.nano"
}
```

The module is being referred to in a `source` property, followed by module variables.

Terraform modules support versioning if you use a Terraform registry (`https://developer.hashicorp.com/terraform/language/modules/syntax#version`). As a trade-off, if a module developer wants to host modules locally, they will not have version capability.

Conversely, CloudFormation modules are uploaded to a registry and can be published (i.e., become publicly available) if needed. AWS does not charge for storing any extension in the registry, which allows a developer to use known tools to apply modularity to CloudFormation stacks.

The module itself is a common template with all its features built in, including macros. The reference to the CloudFormation modules is done by creating a resource with a module type:

```
Resources:
  ModuleResource:
    Type: "MyOrg::Namespace::ModuleName::MODULE"
    Properties:
      ModuleParameter: "SomeValue"
```

In the preceding code above, the `Type` attribute refers to a module name that is used when uploading a module to a registry. We will cover this more in depth in the following section.

As you can see, the semantics of Terraform and CloudFormation modules are similar. Now, let's build our own module.

Building CloudFormation modules

In this section, we will rewrite the `Transform` macro from the beginning of this chapter in the form of a module. We will still deploy a standardized app, providing it with the necessary conditions and parameters for each resource.

We will begin by bootstrapping the module code:

1. Let's run `cfn init` to generate a project skeleton:

    ```
    $ cfn init
    Initializing new project
    ```

2. In the selection menu, we choose `module` or m:

    ```
    Do you want to develop a new resource(r) or a module(m) or a
    hook(h)?.
    >> m
    ```

3. Choose a nice name for our module:

    ```
    What's the name of your module type?
    (<Organization>::<Service>::<Name>::MODULE)
    >> Org::Apps::StandardApp::MODULE
    ```

    Note that the module name always ends with MODULE.

4. Ultimately, we will see that the module was successfully initialized:

    ```
    Directory   /path/to/my/module/fragments   Created
    Initialized a new project in /path/to/my/module
    ```

5. In the `fragments` directory, we will find a file called `sample.json`. Let's delete this example file and create our own template:

    ```
    $ rm fragments/sample.json
    $ touch fragments/template.yaml
    ```

Now, we are ready to build our module. Unlike macros, where we defined resource properties using a Lambda function, here we need to leverage the CloudFormation language entirely.

The template is very huge, so let's look at the crucial parts. The module inputs consist of a resource property and conditional parameters:

```yaml
// template.yaml
Parameters:
    ApplicationName:
      Type: String
    ApplicationImage:
      Type: String
    TaskCount:
      Type: Number
    NeedsDatabase:
      Type: String
      AllowedValues: [True, False]
    PubliclyAvailable:
      Type: String
      AllowedValues: [True, False]
```

Some properties will have default values:

```yaml
Parameters:
    RDSEngine:
      Type: String
      Default: MySQL
    RDSSize:
      Type: String
      Default: db.t3.small
    RDSMultiAz:
      Type: String
      AllowedValues: [True, False]
      Default: False
    RDSStorage:
      Type: Number
      Default: 10
```

This is because the template expects parameters to be defined if they are referred to in the resource, even if the resource is not created due to a condition. These default values protect the module user from getting errors about not setting an RDS instance type, while they explicitly set that they do not need a database.

Conditional parameters are used to define conditions:

```yaml
// template.yaml
Conditions:
  NeedsBalancer: !Equals [!Ref NeedsBalancer, True]
  NeedsDatabase: !Equals [!Ref NeedsDatabase, True]
  PubliclyAvailable: !Equals [!Ref PubliclyAvailable, True]
```

For example, when we expect our application to be behind a load balancer, we need to create a few ELB resources, such as a security group:

```yaml
// template.yaml
Resources:
  LbSg:
    Condition: NeedsBalancer
    Type: "AWS::EC2::SecurityGroup"
    Properties:
      GroupDescription: "LB Security Group"
      VpcId: !Ref VpcId
```

If we were to create a module with `NeedsBalancer` equal to `False`, this security group would be skipped.

Elsewhere, the `PubliclyAvailable` condition is used to define the scheme of the load balancer:

```yaml
// template.yaml
Resources:
  Lb:
    Condition: NeedsBalancer
    Type: "AWS::ElasticLoadBalancingV2::LoadBalancer"
    Properties:
      Scheme:
        !If:
          - PubliclyAvailable,
          - "internet-facing"
          - "internal"
      SecurityGroups:
        - !Ref LbSg
      Subnets: !Ref PublicSubnets
```

You might have noticed that this template does not use stack exports and `Fn::ImportValue`. This is because CloudFormation modules are expected to be transparent and universal, and the usage of `Transform` macros and stack exports is not possible. Modules also cannot consist of nested stacks and have tags. These limits may change in the future, so for a complete, up-to-date list of constraints, please check the AWS documentation (https://docs.aws.amazon.com/cloudformation-cli/latest/userguide/modules-structure.html#modules-template-fragment).

6.   Once the module is ready, we can validate it:

```
$ cfn validate
Module fragment is valid.
```

7.   Then, we submit it to the registry:

```
$ cfn submit --region REGION # pick your favorite
Module fragment is valid.
Successfully submitted type. Waiting for registration with token
 'a9e0a24b-ccee-4ae2-a892-f843cc556bcf' to complete.
Registration complete.
```

And we're done! By logging in to the AWS Management Console and navigating to the registry, we can examine what the uploaded module extension looks like.

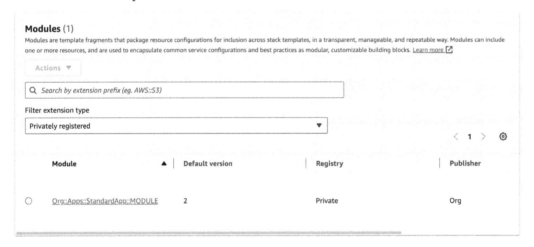

Figure 9.6 – The CloudFormation registry – modules

Note that the default version is set to **2**. This is because I run the submission twice, and each submission creates a new version of the module.

If we click on the module, we will see its content, just like we did with the resource type extensions. While the schema is not the most interesting part of the module, there are two noticeable things in the web interface.

First, the module page shows which resources can be created in the scope of the module:

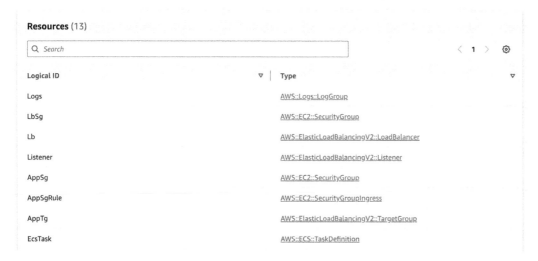

Figure 9.7 – The CloudFormation registry – module resources

Another tab has input parameters:

Figure 9.8 – The CloudFormation registry – module parameters

This tab also indicates whether the input parameters are required and have value or not. The fields here are a bit misleading – CloudFormation parameters do not have the **Required** attribute. **Required** is defined by the usage of the parameters in the template and whether it has a default value. Moreover, the default values that we defined in the template are not present here, so the need for a **Value** tab is unclear too. Perhaps the CloudFormation team plans to introduce parameter constraints in the future – who knows?

The final interesting part is an example template:

Example template   📋 **Copy template**

```json
{
    "Resources": {
        "MyModule": {
            "Type": "Org::Apps::StandardApp::MODULE",
            "Properties": {
                "ApplicationName": "ApplicationName",
                "ApplicationImage": "ApplicationImage",
                "TaskCount": "TaskCount",
                "Memory": "Memory",
                "CPU": "CPU",
                "ApplicationPort": "ApplicationPort",
                "NeedsDatabase": "NeedsDatabase",
                "RDSEngine": "RDSEngine",
                "RDSSize": "RDSSize",
                "RDSMultiAz": "RDSMultiAz",
                "RDSStorage": "RDSStorage",
                "NeedsBalancer": "NeedsBalancer",
                "PubliclyAvailable": "PubliclyAvailable",
                "VpcId": "VpcId",
                "PublicSubnets": "PublicSubnets",
                "AppSubnets": "AppSubnets",
                "ExecRoleArn": "ExecRoleArn",
                "EcsCluster": "EcsCluster",
                "DbSubnetGroup": "DbSubnetGroup"
            }
        }
    }
}
```

Figure 9.9 – The CloudFormation registry – a module example template

If we want to start using this module right away, we can copy a template and fill in the parameter values. The only downside here is that, at the time of writing, an example template is present only in the JSON format.

We are good to go with this module! In the following section, we will deploy a standard app stack using it.

Deploying modular stacks

In this section, we will create a standard app stack using the module from the previous section:

1. Let's begin by creating a prerequisites stack that deploys the network and container infrastructure:

    ```
    $ aws cloudformation deploy
        --stack-name core
        --template-file core.yaml
    ```

2. Now, let's check out our standard app skeleton:

    ```
    // standard_app.yaml
    Resources:
      StandardApp:
        Type: "Org::Apps::StandardApp::MODULE"
        Properties:
          ApplicationName: nginx
          ApplicationImage: nginx:latest
          TaskCount: 1
          Memory: 512
          CPU: 512
          ApplicationPort: 80
          NeedsDatabase: False
          NeedsBalancer: False
          PubliclyAvailable: False
    ```

We will define the preceding properties ourselves. We will declare the container properties as well if the app needs the database of the load balancer.

The latter properties are taken from stack exports:

```
//standard_app.yaml
VpcId: !ImportValue VpcId
DbSubnetGroup: !ImportValue DbSubnetGroup
ExecRoleArn: !ImportValue ExecRole
EcsCluster: !ImportValue EcsCluster
PublicSubnets: !Split [",",!ImportValue PublicSubnets]
AppSubnets: !Split [",",!ImportValue AppSubnets]
```

Modules do not support importing stack exports, but we still can do it in the high-level template.

3. Let's deploy the template:

```
$ aws cloudformation deploy \
    --stack-name app \
    --template-file standard_app.yaml
```

4. When the deployment is complete, we can take a look at the created resources in the console.

Figure 9.10 – The CloudFormation console – the stack resources

5. Now, suppose that the application needs a load balancer. Let's update the template:

```
Resources:
  StandardApp:
    Type: "Org::Apps::StandardApp::MODULE"
    Properties:
      # ...
      NeedsBalancer: True
      PubliclyAvailable: True
      # ...
```

6. Then, we deploy the stack again:

```
$ aws cloudformation deploy \
    --stack-name app \
    --template-file standard_app.yaml
```

When that is done, we will see the load balancer appear in the **Resources** tab:

Logical ID	Physical ID	Type	Status	Module
StandardAppLogs	nginx ☑	AWS::Logs::LogGroup	⊘ CREATE_COMPLETE	StandardApp
StandardAppAppTg	arn:aws:elasticloadbalancing:us-east-1: target group/nginx/dea3192eb 3e3d85e ☑	AWS::ElasticLoadBalanci ngV2::TargetGroup	⊘ CREATE_COMPLETE	StandardApp
StandardAppLb	arn:aws:elasticloadbalancing:us-east-1: :loadba lancer/app/app-Standar-13APV2FR01I6T/41764b 831064444f ☑	AWS::ElasticLoadBalanci ngV2::LoadBalancer	⊘ CREATE_COMPLETE	StandardApp
StandardAppListener	arn:aws:elasticloadbalancing:us-east-1: :listene r/app/app-Standar-13APV2FR01I6T/41764b 831064444f/11eae0613 4ab2e5d ☑	AWS::ElasticLoadBalanci ngV2::Listener	⊘ CREATE_COMPLETE	StandardApp

Figure 9.11 – The CloudFormation console – the stack resources

We can achieve the same behavior with the RDS by providing RDS parameters and setting `NeedsDatabase` to `True`.

And that's it! As you can see, it is much easier to build and use CloudFormation modules compared to nested stacks.

To clean up, let's remove the stack resources:

```
$ aws cloudformation delete-stack --stack-name app
$ aws cloudformation delete-stack --stack-name core
```

When the stacks are deleted, we can deregister the module extension:

```
$ aws cloudformation deregister-type
      --type MODULE
      --type-name Org::Apps::StandardApp::MODULE
```

This marks the end of this exercise. If you want to practice more with a module or add your own features to it, feel free to keep it in the registry for a while, and don't worry about the costs! As mentioned previously, module extensions are not charged separately.

Summary

In this chapter, we learned about the macro, a tool that allows us to transform templates. We learned that AWS has its own macros – AWS::Serverless and AWS::Include – and what macros consist of.

To learn about macro processing, we also developed our own macros. Now, we know how and when we can use them.

Macros allow AWS engineers to avoid complexity in templates by moving this complexity to Lambda functions that process the template. The best example of how macros can make templates simple to write and read is the AWS SAM, and we will cover this in more detail in *Chapter 11, Deploying Serverless Applications Using AWS SAM*.

Later, we reviewed other ways to scale CloudFormation templates by implementing modularity. We explored nested stacks, how they work, and what their downsides are. Later, we explored CloudFormation modules and compared them with Terraform, built our own modules, and deployed the same standard app using modules instead of `Transform` macros.

In the following chapter, we will learn about AWS **Cloud Development Kit** (**CDK**). CDK introduces a completely different way of creating and managing CloudFormation stacks, allowing AWS engineers to *programmatically* declare infrastructure.

See you in the next chapter!

Questions

1. When a macro processes a template, in which format is it returned?
2. What is a *fragment* in CloudFormation's transform request?
3. What happens if the macro function returns a status other than `SUCCESS`?
4. Can you use multiple macros in a single template?
5. Can we use CloudFormation language extensions in modules?

Further reading

- Alex DeBrie's blog on CloudFormation macros: `https://www.alexdebrie.com/posts/cloudformation-macros/`
- The GitHub repository with macro examples: `https://github.com/aws-cloudformation/aws-cloudformation-macros`
- The AWS re:Invent 2021 talk about using modules: `https://youtu.be/LDJiq5kTDlg`

10

Generating CloudFormation Templates Using AWS CDK

In this chapter, we are going to learn about one of the latest developments from AWS – **Cloud Development Kit**, or **CDK**. CDK is not meant to be a replacement for CloudFormation. Instead, it was developed to add additional functionality to CloudFormation.

CDK is a framework that supports multiple programming languages and allows AWS engineers to declare infrastructure as code, thereby increasing the speed of AWS development. By the end of this chapter, you will have a running infrastructure generated by CDK.

In this chapter, we will cover the following topics:

- Introducing AWS CDK
- Facilitating template development with AWS CDK
- Writing your first template using AWS CDK and Python

Technical requirements

The code that's used in this chapter can be found in this book's GitHub repository at `https://github.com/PacktPublishing/Mastering-AWS-CloudFormation-Second-Edition/tree/main/Chapter10`.

Check out the following video to see the Code in Action: `https://packt.link/AJzpA`.

Introducing AWS CDK

CDK is not the first attempt to generate CloudFormation templates with high-level programming languages. Since writing complex CloudFormation templates can be a long-running task with many repetitive actions, developers were interested in finding a different way of generating templates.

One of those ways was a Python framework called **Troposphere**, developed by the Cloudtools team and released in 2013 (`https://github.com/cloudtools/troposphere`). Another attempt was made by AWS Labs in 2017 when they released a similar library named **GoFormation**, written in Golang (`https://github.com/awslabs/goformation`).

In the end, AWS came up with a framework that not only provided a full **Infrastructure as Code (IaC)** experience but also supported multiple programming languages. This framework was called AWS CDK.

CDK supports the following programming languages:

- TypeScript
- JavaScript
- Python
- C#
- Java

CDK's team promises to add more languages to this list, but in the meantime, any company that is willing to integrate CDK into their development workflow should use the language that they feel most comfortable with.

CDK as a framework consists of *constructs*, which represent the building blocks of infrastructure that need to be provisioned. These constructs can be any of the following:

- **CloudFormation resources**: Examples include S3 buckets, DynamoDB tables, and EC2 instances.
- **Apps**: These act as logical groupings of resources for a single purpose and result in one or more stacks.
- **Stacks**: Units of deployment, similar to CloudFormation stacks.
- **Environments**: Targets of deployments; these can be different regions and/or accounts.
- **Assets**: Local files or Docker images that are bundled with the app. They can be a handler code for a Lambda function or a Docker image for an ECS task.

When the template developer starts working with CDK, they need to define each resource as a variable – for example, the definition of the S3 bucket would look like this (don't worry if you don't understand the following code yet! We are going to cover it a bit later):

```
from aws_cdk import Stack, App
from constructs import Construct
import aws_cdk.aws_s3 as s3
class BucketStack(Stack):
    def __init__(self, scope: Construct, construct_id: str, **kwargs)
-> None:
        super().__init__(scope, id, **kwargs)
```

```
        bucket = s3.Bucket(self, 'myBucket')
app = App()
BucketStack(app, 'bucket')
app.synth()
```

In this code, the stack is a Python *class* (`BucketStack`), with necessary construct attributes. We declare a `bucket` variable, which is an object of the `s3.Bucket` type, where `s3` is an imported library, `aws_cdk.aws_s3`. The stack is assigned in a membership of the application, `App`. We also specify the account to which we are going to deploy, but we'll cover this in the next few sections.

> **Important note**
>
> If you have read *Mastering CloudFormation – First Edition*, you will find that the code is different in this edition. *Second Edition*, which you hold now, uses CDK v2, which is slightly different from v1. Experience-wise, these changes are minor, although experienced CDK users will know otherwise, and migrating CDK v1 stacks to v2 may be challenging.
>
> However, CDK deserves its own book and in this chapter, we will focus on the basics of it.

We will acquire more in-depth knowledge of CDK once we build our own template, but first, let's see how CDK can make our template development life easier.

Facilitating template development with AWS CDK

Why would we choose CDK if we already have extensive experience with CloudFormation? While CloudFormation has a lot of powerful features and deep integration with AWS, its declarative nature may be a burden for those who have just started practicing IaC and AWS.

CloudFormation is simple when you need to create a sample set or resources and want to set most of the properties to the default values. But let's take a look at the full declaration of an S3 bucket:

```
Type: AWS::S3::Bucket
Properties:
  AccelerateConfiguration: ...
  AccessControl: ...
  AnalyticsConfigurations: [ ... ]
  BucketEncryption: ...
  BucketName: ...
  CorsConfiguration: ...
  InventoryConfigurations: [ ... ]
  LifecycleConfiguration: ...
  LoggingConfiguration: ...
  MetricsConfigurations: [ ... ]
  NotificationConfiguration: [ ... ]
  # And counting!..
```

Most of the properties aren't even string or Boolean; those are separate key-value sections that need to be filled. This is not the hardest task to do, but it requires time to find the proper declaration section and not mess up with YAML or JSON formatting. Adding property blocks or even additional resources may be simpler.

Let's say that we want to have a subnet in a VPC associated with a route table, which has a route to the internet.

When using CloudFormation, the following resources will be included:

```
Vpc:
  Type: AWS::EC2::VPC
  Properties: ...
Igw:
  Type: AWS::EC2::InternetGateway
IgwAttach:
  Type: AWS::EC2::VPCGatewayAttachment
  Properties: ...
Subnet:
  Type: AWS::EC2::Subnet
  Properties: ...
RouteTable:
  Type: AWS::EC2::RouteTable
  Properties: ...
PublicRoute:
  Type: AWS::EC2::Route
  Properties: ...
PublicRouteTableAssoc:
  Type: AWS::EC2::SubnetRouteTableAssociation
  Properties: ...
```

Again, this is the minimum number of resource declarations that we have to do.

Doing this in CDK is simpler because of its programmatic nature:

```
CIDR = '10.0.0.0/16'
vpc = ec2.Vpc(self,
              'Vpc',
              ip_addresses=ec2.IpAddresses.cidr(CIDR),
              subnet_configuration=[
                    ec2.SubnetConfiguration(name='Public', subnet_
type=ec2.SubnetType.PUBLIC, cidr_mask=24),
                    ec2.SubnetConfiguration(name='Private', subnet_
type=ec2.SubnetType.PRIVATE_WITH_EGRESS, cidr_mask=24)
              ])
```

Because CDK has a lot of abstraction inside it, we don't need to explicitly define resources one by one – CDK will do this for us.

Another beneficial feature is that we can use all the abilities of the programming language, such as iterations and conditions.

For example, let's say we want to deploy our stack in multiple regions. We can instruct CDK to create a stack by initializing the `Stack` class:

```
MyStack(app, 'StackName;)
```

Then, we can declare the AWS `regions` and run stack creation, as shown in the following code snippet:

```
regions = ['us-east-1', 'eu-west-1', 'us-west-1']
for i in range(len(regions)):
    MyStack(app, f'stack-{i}', env=cdk.Environment(region=regions[i]))
```

This will create multiple stacks called `stack-0`, `stack-1`, and `stack-2`, all set to be deployed in a single account, but in multiple regions.

Here comes another benefit of CDK: we don't need to use `awscli` to deploy stacks generated by CDK. CDK comes with a set of features and aims to be an all-in-one IaC instrument. We can define our major infrastructure as an application and declare the stacks that will form parts of this application. Once developed and tested, we can deploy all the stacks with a simple command:

```
$ cdk deploy
```

This will deploy the stacks to a target region and account.

Overall, these are the reasons why we could choose to use CDK:

- High-level abstractions create necessary resources for us
- No need to run additional tools such as `awscli`
- We can develop infrastructure in Python or any other programming language that allows us to test software

Let's develop our very first template with CDK.

Writing your first template using AWS CDK and Python

We will begin by installing the prerequisites for CDK. Even though we are going to write our code in Python, we still need to install Node.js. Once this is done, we can install CDK:

```
$ npm install -g aws-cdk
```

After this, we need to check whether everything is correct by printing out the version of CDK that's been installed:

```
$ cdk --version
```

Then, we need to initialize the environment and CDK Python library:

```
$ mkdir app && cd app
$ cdk init app --language=python
$ source .env/bin/activate
$ pip install -r requirements.txt
```

The cdk init phrase will create all the files, so we can start developing our infrastructure right away.

Preparing constructs

We will build the same infrastructure that we built in *Chapter 2, Advanced Template Development*. Our infrastructure will consist of the following stacks:

- Core (network, security, and so on)
- Web tier
- Storage tier

We will start by building the core stack, as many resources will be inherited from it.

After running cdk init, we will have created several files and directories.

The main file that will handle generation and deployment is called app.py and looks like this:

```
// app.py
import aws_cdk as cdk
from app.app_stack import AppStack
app = core.App()
AppStack(app, 'app')
app.synth()
```

This script initializes the *construct*, app, and AppStack class and, in the end, runs the synth() method, which generates the CloudFormation template.

In addition, we have another file that contains the AppStack class:

```
app/app_stack.py
from aws_cdk import Stack
from constructs import construct
class AppStack(Stack):
    def __init__(self, scope: Construct, construct_id: str, **kwargs)
```

```
-> None:
        super().__init__(scope, id, **kwargs)
        # The code that defines your stack goes here
```

This is the class in which we must declare our resources.

> **Important note**
>
> The naming of the files and objects created by CDK might look strange. When we run cdk
> init, it will create an app.py file (app here is the main building block in CDK) and a
> directory, X, where X is the name of the current working directory where you run cdk init.
> In this new directory, cdk init will create an X_stack.py file and an XStack() class.
> For ease of development and transparency, you should spend time renaming the files and
> objects accordingly.

CDK created a stack class, but the naming is not what we need here (moreover, we will need multiple classes). So, let's rename app_stack.py to core_stack.py and AppStack to CoreStack:

```
app/core_stack.py
from aws_cdk import Stack
class CoreStack(Stack):
    # ...
```

We will also make a few changes to app.py so that importing works correctly:

```
app.py
import aws_cdk as cdk
from app.core_stack import CoreStack
app = cdk.App()
CoreStack(app, 'CoreStack')
app.synth()
```

We've also made a change in the class initialization call, where we've changed "app" to "core":

```
CoreStack(app, "core")
```

The string in quotes stands for Id, a unique identifier for a stack inside CDK. During deployment, this ID will be a stack name, but we made this change now to keep things clearer for us.

With that, we have completed all our preparations. Now, let's begin with the core template.

Rendering core resources

As you may recall, we need the following resources in a core stack:

- 1x VPC
- 3x public subnets
- 3x private subnets
- 1x internet gateway
- 1x NAT gateway
- 1x public route table
- 1x private route table
- 2x IAM roles (for administrators and developers)

The CDK library comes with built-in service libraries, so we can import them right away:

```
// app/core_stack.py
from aws_cdk import Stack, Fn
from constructs import Construct
import aws_cdk.aws_ec2 as ec2
import aws_cdk.aws_iam as iam
```

By performing the following steps, we will declare the core stack using CDK:

1. Let's start with IAM roles. We create them by declaring variables in a stack class:

    ```
    // app/core_stack.py
    class CoreStack(Stack):
        def __init__(self, scope: Construct, construct_id: str,
    **kwargs) -> None:
            super().__init__(scope, id, **kwargs)
            admin_role = iam.Role(self,
                                  'admin',
                                  assumed_by=iam.
    AccountPrincipal(Fn.ref('AWS::AccountId')))
            dev_role = iam.Role(self,
                                'developer',
                                assumed_by=iam.AccountPrincipal(Fn.
    ref('AWS::AccountId')))
    ```

    Again, we have less code to write because the `iam.Role` object has an `assumed_by` attribute. This will automatically transform into `AssumeRolePolicyDocument`.

2. To check that everything has been generated as expected, we can run `cdk synth`:

```
$ cdk synth
Resources:
  admin81D8EBF0:
    Type: AWS::IAM::Role
    Properties:
      AssumeRolePolicyDocument:
        Statement:
          - Action: sts:AssumeRole
            Effect: Allow
            Principal:
              AWS:
                Fn::Join:
                  - ""
                  - - "arn:"
                    - Ref: AWS::Partition
                    - ":iam::"
                    - Ref: AWS::AccountId
                    - :root
        Version: "2012-10-17"
# the rest of the output...
```

3. The template looks valid, so we can continue by adding policies to our roles:

```
// app/core_stack.py
class CoreStack(core.Stack):
    def __init__(self, scope: core.Construct, id: str, **kwargs)
-> None:
        # ...
        admin_role.add_managed_policy(iam.ManagedPolicy.from_
aws_managed_policy_name('AdministratorAccess'))
        dev_role.add_managed_policy(iam.ManagedPolicy.from_aws_
managed_policy_name('ReadOnlyAccess'))
```

We only need to add managed policies, so we will use the `add_managed_policy()` method.

4. We can now start building up our network. We will need one public and several private subnets:

```
class CoreStack(core.Stack):
        # VPC section
        self.vpc = ec2.Vpc(self,
            'vpc', cidr='10.0.0.0/16',
            enable_dns_hostnames=True,
            enable_dns_support=True,
            max_azs=3, nat_gateways=1,
            subnet_configuration=[
```

```
        ec2.SubnetConfiguration(name=»Public», subnet_
type=ec2.SubnetType.PUBLIC, cidr_mask=24),
        ec2.SubnetConfiguration(name=»Private», subnet_
type=ec2.SubnetType.PRIVATE_WITH_EGRESS, cidr_mask=24)])
```

There are a few things that we can tweak here. We set `max_azs` to 3 so that we can make sure that our stack can support almost every region (most of the regions have three **availability zones (AZs)**). If this number is higher than the number of AZs in a region, then the creation of the stack will fail. We also set `nat_gateways` to 1 so that there will only be a single NAT gateway in a VPC, just to avoid extra costs when we practice using CDK in our account (best practice is for there to be one NAT gateway per AZ).

Each subnet group (public, web, middleware, and storage) is a separate `SubnetConfiguration` object. By using the `PUBLIC` or `PRIVATE` subnet type, we can instruct CDK to configure a proper routing table for subnets (either via an internet gateway or NAT gateway).

The main benefit here is that we have defined a single Python `vpc` object, but CDK will generate a lot of resources on our behalf: an internet gateway, a NAT gateway, subnets, route tables with routes and associations, network ACLs with associations – almost every piece of the core infrastructure that we had to declare manually previously!

Now, we can continue with the rest of the tiers.

Rendering the web tier

The web tier is a stack that is built on top of the core stack. We are going to generate a template that references another stack that we have in mind.

In the web tier, we expect to have the following:

- Application load balancer
- Launch configuration
- Autoscaling group
- A bunch of security groups

In the following code, we are going to generate a declaration of a web tier that uses a part of the resources from the core stack:

1. We will start by creating a new file in the same directory where the core stack resides:

    ```
    // app/web_stack.py
    from aws_cdk import Stack
    from constructs import Construct
    import aws_cdk.aws_ec2 as ec2
    ```

```
class WebStack(Stack):
    def __init__(self, scope: Construct, construct_id: str, vpc:
ec2.Vpc, **kwargs) -> None:
        super().__init__(scope, id, **kwargs)
```

We added one extra attribute to our class, `vpc`. This is because we want to inherit properties from the *core* stack (the same way we would with `Exports` and `Fn::ImportValue`).

2. Now, we can add resources:

```
// app/web_stack.py
class WebStack(Stack):
    def __init__(self, scope: Construct, construct_id: str, vpc:
ec2.Vpc, **kwargs) -> None:
        super().__init__(scope, id, **kwargs)
        self.vpc = vpc
        asg = autoscaling.AutoScalingGroup(
          self, 'WebAsg',
          instance_type=ec2.InstanceType.of(ec2.InstanceClass.
BURSTABLE2, ec2.InstanceSize.MICRO),
          machine_image=ec2.AmazonLinuxImage(),
          vpc=vpc,
          vpc_subnets=ec2.SubnetSelection(subnet_group_
name='Private'),
          min_capacity=1, max_capacity=1)
```

As we can see, some of the properties are not the ones that belong to EC2 autoscaling groups – for example, `instance_type` and `machine_image`. These properties will be used to generate the launch configuration resource.

Moreover, let's take a look at how we provide VPC and subnets for an autoscaling group. What we did was pass the resource construct attribute (`vpc`) from one class (`CoreStack`) to another (`WebStack`).

3. We can see what happens when we add the `WebStack` class to `app.py`:

```
// app.py
import aws_cdk as cdk
from app.core_stack import CoreStack
from app.web_stack import WebStack
app = cdk.App()
core = CoreStack(app, 'CoreStack')
web = WebStack(app, 'WebStack', vpc=core.vpc)
app.synth()
```

4. Let's run `cdk synth` and check how CDK will assign the resource properties:

```
$ cdk synth web
Including dependency stacks: core
Successfully synthesized to /Users/ktovmasyan/app/cdk.out
Supply a stack id (core, web) to display its template.
```

5. If we evaluate the generated template, we will see the following:

```
{
  «Resources»: {
    # some resources...
    «WebAsgASGEE4061A2»: {
      «Type»: «AWS::AutoScaling::AutoScalingGroup»,
      «Properties»: {
        # some properties...
        «VPCZoneIdentifier»: [
          {
            «Fn::ImportValue»:
«core:ExportsOutputRefvpcPrivateSubnet1Subnet934893E8236 E2271»
          },
          {
            «Fn::ImportValue»:
«core:ExportsOutputRefvpcPrivateSubnet2Subnet7031C2BA60 DCB1EE»
          }
        ]
      },
    # the rest of the resources
}
```

What CDK did was *understand* what we were going to do, create exports in the core stack, and use them with `Fn::ImportValue`.

> **Important note**
>
> The best practice with CDK is to expose class fields between stack classes; however, it only works within the same app. If you still need to export values to share between different CDK apps, then you need to use the `CfnOutput` method from `aws_cdk.core`.

6. Let's continue adding resources to our web stack. All we need to do is add an application load balancer:

```
// app/web_stack.py
class WebStack(Stack):
        alb = elbv2.ApplicationLoadBalancer(self,
            "WebLb", vpc=vpc, internet_facing=True,
```

```
                   vpc_subnets=ec2.SubnetSelection(subnet_group_
    name='Public'))
            listener = alb.add_listener(«WebListener»,
                                        port=80)
            listener.add_targets(«Target», port=80,
                                  targets=[asg])
```

We don't need to create a target group separately. When we use the `add_targets()` method, CDK will automatically declare a target group and refer to it from both the listener and autoscaling group.

7. Before we continue with a storage tier, let's deploy the web stacks (using the `cdk deploy WebStack` command) to check that our code is operational:

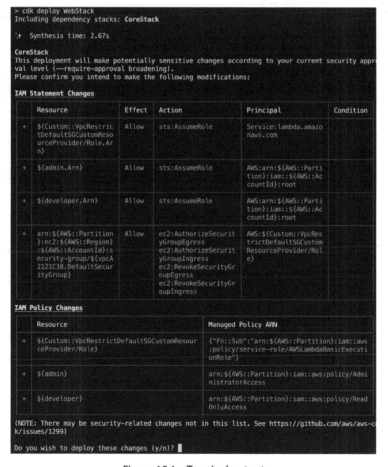

Figure 10.1 – Terminal output

We will approve deployment by typing y and hitting *Enter*.

Since the core is a dependency stack, it will be deployed first. What we are interested in is constructing a setup where CDK informs us of security-related changes, such as the IAM and security groups rule, as shown in the following code:

IAM Statement Changes

	Resource	Effect	Action	Principal	Condition
+	${WebAsg/InstanceRole.Arn}	Allow	sts:AssumeRole	Service:ec2.amazonaws.com	

Security Group Changes

	Group	Dir	Protocol	Peer
+	${WebAsg/InstanceSecurityGroup.GroupId}	In	TCP 80	${WebLb/SecurityGroup.GroupId}
+	${WebAsg/InstanceSecurityGroup.GroupId}	Out	Everything	Everyone (IPv4)
+	${WebLb/SecurityGroup.GroupId}	In	TCP 80	Everyone (IPv4)
+	${WebLb/SecurityGroup.GroupId}	Out	TCP 80	${WebAsg/InstanceSecurityGroup.GroupId}
+	${WebLb/SecurityGroup.GroupId}	Out	TCP 80	${WebServerSg.GroupId}
+	${WebServerSg.GroupId}	In	TCP 80	${WebLb/SecurityGroup.GroupId}
+	${WebServerSg.GroupId}	Out	Everything	Everyone (IPv4)

(NOTE: There may be security-related changes not in this list. See https://github.com/aws/aws-cc
k/issues/1299)

Do you wish to deploy these changes (y/n)? ▯

Figure 10.2 – Terminal output

Another interesting thing to point out is that when we associate an autoscaling group with an application load balancer, CDK will automatically add a security group rule to allow incoming traffic to a traffic port *only* from a load balancer's security group.

Let's also install some software on our launch configurations using user data.

8. We will declare `userdata` as a multiline string variable:

```
// app/web_stack.py
userdata = '''#!/bin/sh
            yum install httpd -y
            systemctl enable httpd
            systemctl start httpd
            echo «<html><head><title> Example Web Server</title></head>»  >  /var/www/html/index.html
            echo «<body>» >>  /var/www/html/index.html
            echo «<div><center><h2>Welcome AWS $(hostname -f)</h2>" >>  /var/www/html/index.html
            echo «<hr/>» >>  /var/www/html/index.html
```

```
                    curl http://169.254.169.254/latest/meta-data/
        instance-id >> /var/www/html/index.html
                    echo «</center></div></body></html>» >>  /var/www/
        html/index.html'''
```

9. Then, we will process it via CDK and pass it as an attribute to the autoscaling group:

    ```
    // app/web_stack.py
    class WebStack(Stack):
        # ...
            self.vpc = vpc
            userdata = '...'
            websrv = ec2.UserData.for_linux()
            websrv.add_commands(userdata)
            asg = autoscaling.AutoScalingGroup(
              self, # some attributes...
              user_data=websrv)
    ```

    There is one small thing that we need to add to the web tier. Since we don't want to expose our RDS instance to the public, we want it to be accessible only from the web servers.

10. To do this, we will create a security group and add it to the autoscaling group construct:

    ```
    // app/web_stack.py
    class WebStack(Stack):
        # …
            self.webserver_sg = ec2.SecurityGroup(
              self, "WebServerSg", vpc=vpc)
            asg.add_security_group(self.webserver_sg)
    ```

After this, our autoscaling group will have two security groups: one that we assigned while creating the autoscaling group (between the load balancer and the autoscaling group) and the one that we declared here.

With that, we have finished generating our web tier, which contains the application load balancer and the autoscaling group, so we can continue with the storage tier.

Rendering the storage tier

Our storage tier will be an RDS instance, created in a VPC from a core stack:

1. First, we will create a new stack class in a separate file:

    ```
    // app/rds_stack.py
    from aws_cdk import Stack, RemovalPolicy
    from constructs import Construct
    import aws_cdk.aws_ec2 as ec2
    ```

```python
import aws_cdk.aws_rds as rds
class RdsStack(Stack):
    def __init__(self, scope: Construct, construct_id: str, vpc:
ec2.Vpc, webserver_sg: ec2.SecurityGroup, **kwargs) -> None:
        super().__init__(scope, id, **kwargs)
        self.vpc = vpc
        self.webserver_sg = webserver_sg
```

We added two extra fields to a class declaration: `vpc` (we will use a VPC construct from the core stack) and `webserver_sg` (the security group construct we declared at the end of the previous section).

2. There is not much that we need to do with RDS – just create an RDS instance and add a rule to its security group:

```python
// app/rds_stack.py
class RdsStack(Stack):
    # ...
        rds_instance = rds.DatabaseInstance(
            self, "Rds",
            # Avoid using hardcoded password in
            # production! Use Secrets Manager instead
            credentials=rds.Credentials.from_generated_
secret('admin')
            database_name=»db»,
            engine=rds.DatabaseInstanceEngine.MYSQL,
            vpc=vpc,
            instance_type=ec2.InstanceType.of(
                ec2.InstanceClass.BURSTABLE2,
                ec2.InstanceSize.MICRO),
            removal_policy=core.RemovalPolicy.DESTROY,
            deletion_protection=False)
        rds_instance.connections.allow_from(
            webserver_sg,
            ec2.Port.tcp(3306))
```

This will create a set of resources – a DB subnet group and an RDS instance with a security group to which the new rule will be added. Because we refer to a field from another class (the web tier), CDK will create an export with a security group ID.

3. Lastly, we are going to add a new class to app.py:

```
// app.py
import aws_cdk as cdk
from app.core_stack import CoreStack
from app.web_stack import WebStack
from app.rds_stack import RdsStack
app = cdk.App()
core = CoreStack(app, "CoreStack")
web = WebStack(app, "WebStack", vpc=core.vpc)
rds = RdsStack(app, "RdsStack", vpc=core.vpc, webserver_sg=web.
webserver_sg)
app.synth()
```

We have added all three stacks to our application, so now, we can begin deployment.

Deploying the CDK application

We can deploy CDK applications using the cdk deploy command. This command will run synth to generate the CloudFormation template and then create and execute a change set.

If we have any security-related resources (such as security groups and IAM entities), then CDK will request our confirmation. If we want to avoid this (for example, when deployment is done as part of the CI/CD pipeline), we can use the --require approval never argument.

We can deploy stacks one by one, as shown in the following code:

```
$ cdk deploy core
$ cdk deploy web
$ cdk deploy rds
```

However, our RDS stack has a dependency on the core and web. So, if we just run deployment on this, CDK will attempt to deploy all dependencies first:

```
$ cdk deploy rds
Including dependency stacks: core, web
# the rest of the output
```

Alternatively, you can just deploy all stacks:

```
$ cdk deploy --all
```

The deployment of the CDK application has an interactive response. This means that we can continuously observe the current state of the CloudFormation deployment:

```
Do you wish to deploy these changes (y/n)? y
CoreStack: deploying... [1/3]
CoreStack: creating CloudFormation changeset...
[           .............................................] (2/28)

10:35:35 PM | CREATE_IN_PROGRESS | AWS::CloudFormation::Stack  | CoreStack
10:35:39 PM | CREATE_IN_PROGRESS | AWS::IAM::Role              | developer
10:35:39 PM | CREATE_IN_PROGRESS | AWS::IAM::Role              | admin
10:35:40 PM | CREATE_IN_PROGRESS | AWS::EC2::InternetGateway   | vpc/IGW
10:35:40 PM | CREATE_IN_PROGRESS | AWS::EC2::EIP               | vpc/PublicSubn
et1/EIP
10:35:53 PM | CREATE_IN_PROGRESS | AWS::IAM::Role              | Custom::VpcRes
tric...ourceProvider/Role
10:35:53 PM | CREATE_IN_PROGRESS | AWS::EC2::RouteTable        | vpc/PrivateSub
net2/RouteTable
10:35:53 PM | CREATE_IN_PROGRESS | AWS::EC2::RouteTable        | vpc/PrivateSub
net1/RouteTable
10:35:53 PM | CREATE_IN_PROGRESS | AWS::EC2::RouteTable        | vpc/PublicSubn
et1/RouteTable
10:35:53 PM | CREATE_IN_PROGRESS | AWS::EC2::Subnet            | vpc/PrivateSub
net1/Subnet
10:35:53 PM | CREATE_IN_PROGRESS | AWS::EC2::Subnet            | vpc/PublicSubn
et1/Subnet
10:35:53 PM | CREATE_IN_PROGRESS | AWS::EC2::Subnet            | vpc/PublicSubn
et2/Subnet
10:35:53 PM | CREATE_IN_PROGRESS | AWS::EC2::RouteTable        | vpc/PublicSubn
et2/RouteTable
10:35:53 PM | CREATE_IN_PROGRESS | AWS::EC2::Subnet            | vpc/PrivateSub
net2/Subnet
```

Figure 10.3 – Terminal output

By the end of the deployment, we will see a confirmation message stating that the stacks have been deployed. CDK will also print the stack ARN and outputs to the terminal:

Figure 10.4 – Terminal output

If we need to delete all stacks, then we simply need to run cdk destroy. Since we are going to delete multiple stacks, we need to destroy a main dependency, which is the core stack:

```
$ cdk destroy core
Including depending stacks: web, rds
Are you sure you want to delete: rds, web, core (y/n)?
```

Once we select y, CDK will destroy all the stacks in reverse order.

With that, we've covered how to deploy and delete CDK applications. Now, let's learn about another important topic – testing CDK applications.

Testing CDK applications

Until now, the only way of testing CloudFormation has been either by creating a stack and running some tests against resources or by inspecting them with cfn-lint using custom rules.

In CDK, testing is done in the same way as common software testing, but against the stack classes and their attributes. CDK supports testing construct properties and the synthesized CloudFormation template.

In the app root, there is a tests/unit directory that contains the test_app_stack.py file. We can add our tests there:

1. Let's test whether our VPC has public subnets:

    ```
    // tests/unit/test_app_stack.py
    import aws_cdk as core
    import aws_cdk.assertions as assertions
    from aws_cdk.assertions import Template, Match
    from app.core_stack import CoreStack

    def test_vpc_has_public_subnets():
        app = core.App()
        stack = CoreStack(app, 'core')
        assert len(stack.vpc.public_subnets) > 0
    ```

    What we are going to test is whether the vpc construct contains more than one public subnet. To do so, we must initialize the app object and the core construct. Once they've been initialized, we read the attributes of the vpc object and see whether it has public subnets.

2. Let's run this test:

    ```
    $ python -m pytest
    ```

3. Let's do the same for private subnets:

```
// tests/unit/test_app_stack.py
def test_vpc_has_private_subnets():
    app = core.App()
    stack = CoreStack(app, 'core')
    assert len(stack.vpc.private_subnets) > 0
```

4. Let's run it again:

```
$ python -m pytest
```

5. We could also check that our developer role doesn't have `AdministratorAccess`. This will be a bit difficult because we can't access managed policies from the role class directly, so we will have to generate a template and then parse it:

```
// tests/unit/test_app_stack.py
from aws_cdk.assertions import Template, Match

def test_dev_role_is_readonly():
    app = core.App()
    stack = CoreStack(app, 'core')
    template = Template.from_stack(stack)
    template.has_resource_properties(
      'AWS::IAM::Role', {
          'ManagedPolicyArns':
            [Match.object_like({
                "Fn::Join": ["",["arn:",{"Ref":
"AWS::Partition"},":iam::aws:policy/ReadOnlyAccess"]]
            })]
      })
```

Here, we use CDK's `assertions`, a built-in library that renders the CloudFormation template from CDK's code and then identifies matches. CDK matching works on the resource type – not the logical resource. Therefore, we looked for an IAM role resource that has attached managed policy `ReadOnlyAccess`.

6. Let's run all the tests again:

```
$ python3 -m pytest
=============== test session starts ================
platform darwin -- Python 3.11.4, pytest-6.2.5, py-1.11.0,
pluggy-1.2.0
rootdir: /Users/kartovmas/app
plugins: typeguard-2.13.3
collected 3 items
```

```
tests/unit/test_app_stack.py ...                    [100%]


================= 3 passed in 2.03s ==================
```

We are now able to run tests against our CDK code before actually deploying it. This will make our infrastructure provisioning even more secure and reliable!

In this section, we covered all the steps for working with CDK, from initializing the CDK project to writing the multitier infrastructure declaration, deploying it, and even writing the test suite for it!

Summary

CDK introduces a new way of managing AWS and allows us to create templates and run stack operations in a completely different way.

In this chapter, we learned about CDK and its capabilities. We created our applications with multiple stacks and created a test suite to make sure that our core infrastructure template was operational before deployment.

CDK is useful for those cases where the AWS engineer role is handled by developers who have good knowledge of software engineering and who want to use this knowledge together with CloudFormation automation.

In the next chapter, we will cover another extension of CloudFormation called **Serverless Application Model (SAM)**. SAM is similar to CloudFormation but offers a different approach to developing serverless applications.

See you in the next chapter!

Questions

1. What are constructs in CDK?
2. How is it possible to have multiple stacks within a single application?
3. How can we declare private and public subnets for VPC in CDK?
4. Which programming languages are currently supported by CDK?
5. Is it mandatory to add an AWS account ID in CDK?

Further reading

- AWS CDK samples: `https://github.com/aws-samples/aws-cdk-examples`
- Testing infrastructure with AWS CDK: `https://aws.amazon.com/blogs/developer/testing-infrastructure-with-the-aws-cloud-development-kit-cdk/`
- CDK constructs library: `https://constructs.dev/`

11

Deploying Serverless Applications Using AWS SAM

CloudFormation is a powerful instrument. However, as new technologies and ways of working emerge, new requirements appear for **Infrastructure-as-Code** (**IaC**) tools. After the release of Lambda and its integration with other AWS services, including S3, SNS, SQS, and DynamoDB, it appeared that most of CloudFormation's capabilities were not required for serverless development.

So, a **Serverless Application Model** (**SAM**) was developed. AWS SAM introduces a different and more simplified way of developing, building, testing, deploying, and operating serverless applications. In this chapter, we are going to learn about AWS SAM and how to use it to facilitate the development of serverless applications.

In this chapter, we will cover the following topics:

- Introducing AWS SAM
- Understanding the differences between AWS SAM and CloudFormation
- Writing your first serverless applications with AWS SAM

Technical requirements

The code used in this chapter can be found in this book's GitHub repository at `https://github.com/PacktPublishing/Mastering-AWS-CloudFormation-Second-Edition/tree/main/Chapter11`.

Check out the following video to see the Code in Action:

`https://packt.link/yucsc`

Introducing AWS SAM

Before we learn about AWS SAM, let's quickly look at what serverless is. **Serverless** is a way of developing, running, and operating applications without needing to manage their underlying infrastructure. You might wonder what the key difference is since you don't manage *any* infrastructure in AWS, and you would be right.

You don't have to manage any physical infrastructure in AWS, but if you run an EC2 instance, you need to take care of its underlying OSs, security, patches, and updates.

Then, you will need to consider AWS's managed **Relational Database Service** (**RDS**), where you don't have to worry about the underlying OS but you still have to tweak its parameters, carry out performance tuning by reorganizing queries and tables, and create database indexes.

Serverless doesn't guarantee that no operational work will be required, but there are several differences between instance-based services (such as EC2, RDS, EMR, and MSK) and serverless services (such as S3, SNS, SQS, Lambda, and DynamoDB).

With serverless services, the following points stand:

- You pay only for the service usage, for example, storage ($ per GB) and the actual compute operation (number of requests)
- You don't operate with instances, but with compute and storage units
- You work with specific entities (such as functions instead of whole runtimes or tables instead of whole databases)

These core concepts are what make serverless computing cost-efficient for many business cases.

AWS SAM was introduced to fully support the development, packaging, and deployment of serverless applications using IaC as its approach.

AWS SAM consists of two parts:

- The actual framework (the CLI that performs all the operations)
- A template, which has similar specifications to CloudFormation

Similar to CDK, AWS SAM can perform all of its operations out of the box, such as building, testing locally, and provisioning serverless stacks to AWS.

AWS SAM templates are easier to write due to their restricted abilities. For example, a DynamoDB table definition looks like the following:

```
Transform: AWS::Serverless-2016-10-31
Resources:
  DynamoDb:
```

```
    Type: "AWS::Serverless::SimpleTable"
    Properties:
      TableName: "myTable"
      PrimaryKey:
        Name: "id"
        Type: "string"
```

Does the `Transform: AWS::Serverless-2016-10-31` line look familiar?

Remember from *Chapter 9, Scale Your Templates Using Macros, Nested Stacks, and Modules*, that AWS has two internal macros: `AWS::Serverless` and `AWS::Include`. The AWS SAM template, on its own, is nothing but a macro template that will be processed during deployment by CloudFormation. The previous template will look different after transformation, as shown:

```
{
  «Resources»: {
    «DynamoDb»: {
      «Type»: AWS::DynamoDB::Table,
      «Properties»: {
        «KeySchema»: [
          {
            «KeyType»: «HASH»,
            «AttributeName»: «id»
          }
        ],
        «TableName»: «myTable»,
        «AttributeDefinitions»: [
          {
            «AttributeName»: «id»,
            «AttributeType»: «S»
          }
        ],
        «BillingMode»: «PAY_PER_REQUEST»
      }
    }
  }
}
```

`SimpleTable` in AWS SAM is the same as a DynamoDB table in CloudFormation!

We will cover more on AWS SAM when we start building our own applications, but for now, let's compare AWS SAM and CloudFormation, so we can get the most out of both.

Understanding the differences between AWS SAM and CloudFormation

First of all, an AWS SAM template is designed to be used with serverless applications and services. At the time of writing, the AWS SAM template reference supports the following resource types:

- `AWS::Serverless::API`: Creates an API gateway and related resources
- `AWS::Serverless::Application`: Creates a serverless application
- `AWS::Serverless::Function`: Creates a Lambda function and related resources
- `AWS::Serverless::HttpApi`: Creates an HTTP API gateway and related resources
- `AWS::Serverless::LayerVersion`: Creates a Lambda layer
- `AWS::Serverless::SimpleTable`: Creates a simplified DynamoDB table (only a primary key without a sort key)

It is still possible to combine CloudFormation's resources with AWS SAM's resources. For example, if we want to create an S3 bucket with `SimpleTable`, we can do so by adding the CloudFormation resource, as in the following code:

```
Transform: AWS::Serverless-2016-10-31
Resources:
  DynamoDb:
    Type: AWS::Serverless::SimpleTable
    Properties:
      TableName: "myTable"
      PrimaryKey:
        Name: "id"
        Type: "string"
  Bucket:
    Type: "AWS::S3::Bucket"
```

All we need to do is to specify the CloudFormation-specific resource types.

Secondly, you *must* have a bucket when you want to deploy an AWS SAM application via a CLI and without an interactive dialog. The reason for this is that AWS SAM applications consist of source code and a template. The AWS SAM CLI will take care of building the application, if it requires compilations, and will upload the artifact for your Lambda function to S3.

Last but not least, AWS SAM allows you to run tests locally by creating a local API gateway or running test events against your applications.

That said, let's start by building our own serverless applications with AWS SAM.

Writing your first serverless application with AWS SAM

In this section, we will create a few serverless applications to cover most of AWS SAM's capabilities. The first one—Hello, World—will be created using AWS Quick Start templates, so we can quickly get hands-on experience with AWS SAM.

The second—Party Planner—will be developed from scratch. You don't have to worry—the actual code is not in the scope of this book and the actual focus will be on creating a complex application with more than one function.

Before we begin development, let's make sure we have everything we need.

Prerequisites

In order to run the AWS SAM CLI commands, we need to install AWS SAM CLI and its dependencies first. Depending on the OS you have, the steps will be different. The following steps are for installation on macOS.

The guides on how to install AWS SAM CLI on other OSs can be found at `https://docs. aws.amazon.com/serverless-application-model/latest/developerguide/ serverless-sam-cli-install.html`.

The following steps show you how to install AWS SAM CLI:

1. Make sure you have Docker and Homebrew installed.

2. Install the AWS SAM CLI by issuing the following commands:

    ```
    $ brew tap aws/tap
    $ brew install aws-sam-cli
    ```

3. Check the installation by running the following command:

    ```
    $ sam --version
    ```

If you don't see any errors in the output, you are good to go!

We have everything installed, so let's start to build our first application.

Developing a Hello, World application

What is the best entry point if not a good old Hello, World application? By the end of this section, we will have deployed a standard AWS Quick Start application to get some hands-on experience with AWS SAM:

1. We are going to start with the project initialization:

    ```
    $ sam init
    ```

2. AWS SAM will respond with a dialog. Since it is our very first application, let's follow it. We will choose 1 - AWS Quick Start Templates this time:

    ```
    Which template source would you like to use?
            1 - AWS Quick Start Templates
            2 - Custom Template Location
    Choice: 1
    ```

3. Next, we need to choose the runtime for our application. Let's choose python3.8:

    ```
    Which runtime would you like to use?
            1 - nodejs12.x
            2 - python3.8
            3 - ruby2.5
            4 - go1.x
            5 - java11
            # the rest of the options...
    Runtime: 2
    ```

4. For the application name, simply enter hello-world:

    ```
    Project name [sam-app]: hello-world
    ```

5. AWS SAM will clone the templates from GitHub and ask us to choose a Quick Start template. We will go for Hello World Example:

    ```
    AWS quick start application templates:
            1 - Hello World Example
            2 - EventBridge Hello World
            3 - EventBridge App from scratch (100+ Event Schemas)
    Template selection: 1
    ```

6. After all the responses, AWS SAM will generate an app and inform us of the next steps:

    ```
    -----------------------
    Generating application:
    -----------------------
    Name: hello-world
    Runtime: python3.8
    Dependency Manager: pip
    Application Template: hello-world
    Output Directory: .
    Next steps can be found in the README file at ./hello-world/
    README.md
    ```

7. Let's examine the new directory:

```
$ tree .
.
├── README.md
├── __init__.py
├── events
│   └── event.json
├── hello_world
│   ├── __init__.py
│   ├── app.py
│   └── requirements.txt
├── template.yaml
└── tests
    ├── __init__.py
    └── unit
        ├── __init__.py
        └── test_handler.py
```

Looks like we have everything set! We could deploy this application right away, but first, let's examine what is in the template! There are a few things that look interesting:

```
// template.yaml
Globals:
  Function:
    Timeout: 3
```

The Globals section is used when we need to define the same properties for multiple resources. Let's say you are building a Lambda application consisting of multiple functions. All of them will use the same runtime and have the same timeout. In order to avoid duplicating the same property many times, we can just store them in Globals.

8. Let's look at our Lambda function:

```
// template.yaml
Resources:
  HelloWorldFunction:
    Type: AWS::Serverless::Function
    Properties:
      CodeUri: hello_world/
      Handler: app.lambda_handler
      Runtime: python3.8
      Events:
        HelloWorld:
          Type: Api
          Properties:
```

```
Path: /hello
Method: get
```

What we can learn from here is that the `function` definition has a `CodeUri` property, which points to the local path where our source code exists.

Secondly, take a look at the `Events` property. This property defines the event source that will trigger the function. Moreover, AWS SAM will *create* this resource when the application is deployed! In this case, it will create an API gateway.

9. Lastly, take a look at `Outputs`:

```
// template.yaml
Outputs:
  HelloWorldApi:
    Description: «API Gateway endpoint URL for Prod stage for
Hello World function»
    Value: !Sub «https://${ServerlessRestApi}.execute-
api.${AWS::Region}.amazonaws.com/Prod/hello/"
  HelloWorldFunction:
    Description: «Hello World Lambda Function ARN»
    Value: !GetAtt HelloWorldFunction.Arn
  HelloWorldFunctionIamRole:
    Description: «Implicit IAM Role created for Hello World
function"
    Value: !GetAtt HelloWorldFunctionRole.Arn
```

The API at the top is created as part of the `Events` property. However, the IAM role wasn't defined anywhere, so how can we get its attribute?

Remember that AWS SAM is a macro. This role (and many other resources) will be created along with the function, which is declared in this template.

10. Next, let's build this application and run local tests:

```
$ sam build --use-container
Starting Build inside a container
Building resource 'HelloWorldFunction'
Fetching lambci/lambda:build-python3.8 Docker container
image....
Mounting /Users/karentovmasyan/hello-world/hello_world as /tmp/
samcli/source:ro,delegated inside runtime container
Build Succeeded
Built Artifacts  : .aws-sam/build
Built Template   : .aws-sam/build/template.yaml
Commands you can use next
=========================
[*] Invoke Function: sam local invoke
```

```
[*] Deploy: sam deploy --guided
Running PythonPipBuilder:ResolveDependencies
Running PythonPipBuilder:CopySource
```

The build command, with a --use-container argument, will pull a Docker image and build the source function, thereby installing all the dependencies. The artifact will be stored in a local directory.

11. Let's invoke it:

```
$ sam local invoke
Invoking app.lambda_handler (python3.8)
Fetching lambci/lambda:python3.8 Docker container image...
Mounting /Users/karentovmasyan/hello-world/.aws-sam/build/
HelloWorldFunction as /var/task:ro,delegated inside runtime
container
START RequestId: c165be27-ff86-1ed2-f5c7-9158dce5d95b Version:
$LATEST
END RequestId: c165be27-ff86-1ed2-f5c7-9158dce5d95b
REPORT RequestId: c165be27-ff86-1ed2-f5c7-9158dce5d95b  Init
Duration: 199.95 ms        Duration: 3.57 ms        Billed
Duration: 100 ms Memory Size: 128 MB     Max Memory Used: 23 MB
{"statusCode":200,"body":"{\"message\": \"hello world\"}"}
```

We don't need to provide many arguments to a local invocation since there is only a single Lambda function and a single event. However, if we had various events and functions, we would have needed to specify them by name, as follows:

```
$ sam local invoke FunctionNameAsInTemplate \
            --event path/to/the/event.json
```

What we also get before the actual response is the duration and memory information of the Lambda execution. This comes in handy when we need to estimate the cost of a future serverless application.

There is also another way to test the function execution. Let's do the same with a call to the API gateway.

12. We will start the API:

```
$ sam local start-api
```

In the output, there will be a URL that we can invoke. We have to use a different terminal window because the current one will show the logs of the API gateway:

```
$ curl localhost:3000/hello
{"message": "hello world"}
```

While in the logs of the API gateway, we will see a similar output as when we ran a local invocation.

We've played around enough—let's now run this application in the cloud!

Running AWS SAM applications

Creating and running AWS SAM applications is a bit different from creating a CloudFormation stack.

Following the previous steps, we will launch our Hello, World application:

1. Let's deploy it using the preceding command:

```
$ sam deploy \
      --stack-name hello-world
      --resolve-s3
        Deploying with following values
        ===============================
        Stack name                    : hello-world
        Region                        : None
        Confirm changeset             : False
        Deployment s3 bucket          : None
        Capabilities                  : null
        Parameter overrides           : {}
Initiating deployment
=====================
Error: Failed to create changeset for the stack: hello-world,
Parameter validation failed:
Invalid type for parameter Capabilities, value: None, type:
<class 'NoneType'>, valid types: <class 'list'>, <class 'tuple'>
```

    The reason it failed is that AWS SAM will create an IAM role, but we haven't provided any capabilities.

2. Let's fix this by adding the necessary capabilities with a command-line argument:

```
$ sam deploy \
      --stack-name hello-world \
      --capabilities CAPABILITY_IAM
      --resolve-s3
```

    In the output, we will see something similar to the CDK deployments—the resources that SAM is going to create, the event log, and the outputs:

```
CloudFormation stack changeset
------------------------------------------------------------------------------
Operation            LogicalResourceId              ResourceType
------------------------------------------------------------------------------
+ Add                HelloWorldFunctionHelloWorldPe  AWS::Lambda::Permission
                     rmissionProd
+ Add                HelloWorldFunctionRole          AWS::IAM::Role
+ Add                HelloWorldFunction              AWS::Lambda::Function
+ Add                ServerlessRestApiDeployment47f  AWS::ApiGateway::Deployment
                     c2d5f9d
+ Add                ServerlessRestApiProdStage      AWS::ApiGateway::Stage
+ Add                ServerlessRestApi               AWS::ApiGateway::RestApi
------------------------------------------------------------------------------
```

Figure 11.1 – The terminal output (resources)

We can follow the deployment process by examining the events right from the terminal output:

```
CloudFormation events from changeset
------------------------------------------------------------------------------
ResourceStatus        ResourceType          LogicalResourceId       ResourceStatusReason
------------------------------------------------------------------------------
CREATE_IN_PROGRESS    AWS::IAM::Role        HelloWorldFunctionRole  Resource creation
                                                                    Initiated
CREATE_IN_PROGRESS    AWS::IAM::Role        HelloWorldFunctionRole  -
CREATE_COMPLETE       AWS::IAM::Role        HelloWorldFunctionRole  -
CREATE_IN_PROGRESS    AWS::Lambda::Function HelloWorldFunction      -
CREATE_IN_PROGRESS    AWS::Lambda::Function HelloWorldFunction      Resource creation
                                                                    Initiated
CREATE_COMPLETE       AWS::Lambda::Function HelloWorldFunction      -
CREATE_IN_PROGRESS    AWS::ApiGateway::RestA ServerlessRestApi      -
                      pi
CREATE_COMPLETE       AWS::ApiGateway::RestA ServerlessRestApi      -
                      pi
CREATE_IN_PROGRESS    AWS::ApiGateway::RestA ServerlessRestApi      Resource creation
                      pi                                            Initiated
CREATE_IN_PROGRESS    AWS::Lambda::Permissio HelloWorldFunctionHell -
```

Figure 11.2 – The terminal output (events)

3. Lastly, let's invoke our API to make sure that the application deployment was successful:

```
$ curl https://39llxp6wl2.execute-api.eu-central-1.amazonaws.
com/Prod/hello/ # your output will be different
{"message": "hello world"}
```

That's it! We have an application running on an AWS environment that was developed and deployed using AWS SAM.

But that's not the only thing that AWS SAM can do! In addition to building and deploying operations, it can be used to examine application logs.

Examining logs with AWS SAM

AWS SAM allows you to fetch CloudWatch logs right from the CLI. It makes debugging or tracking an application in production a bit easier.

To read the logs, we only need to provide the following arguments:

```
$ sam logs \
      -n FUNCTION_LOGICAL_NAME \
      --stack-name STACK_NAME \
      --tail
```

So, for our case, we will run the command as follows:

```
$ sam logs \
      -n HelloWorldFunction \
      --stack-name hello-world \
      --tail
```

Once we run it, we will get the exact entries from CloudWatch Logs. Since there are no print statements in our function code, the logs won't show us that much:

```
2020-02-18T14:12:54.944000 START RequestId: 4dd811f0-79a6-4806-a8cc-26d2e0da9543 Version: $LATEST
2020-02-18T14:12:54.951000 END RequestId: 4dd811f0-79a6-4806-a8cc-26d2e0da9543
2020-02-18T14:12:54.951000 REPORT RequestId: 4dd811f0-79a6-4806-a8cc-26d2e0da9543  Duration: 1.75 ms

2020-02-18T14:13:01.379000 START RequestId: cc85630f-a1f0-4d52-9d77-65248adfb102 Version: $LATEST
2020-02-18T14:13:01.382000 END RequestId: cc85630f-a1f0-4d52-9d77-65248adfb102
2020-02-18T14:13:01.382000 REPORT RequestId: cc85630f-a1f0-4d52-9d77-65248adfb102  Duration: 1.43 ms
```

Figure 11.3 – The terminal output (the AWS SAM logs)

To clean up the `hello-world` stack, we need to use `awscli`:

```
$ aws cloudformation delete-stack \
                     --stack-name hello-world
```

We're now done with playing around with the Hello, World application. Let's build something more complex—our second application.

Creating complex applications with AWS SAM

We are going to create a small party planner—an application that will process and store information about parties and guests.

Let's take a look at the design of this app:

Figure 11.4 – A serverless party planner

There are several steps in this application:

1. The **API** gateway will send a payload with the party and guest information.

2. The **Registration** function will create a new entry in a **Parties** table, if this party doesn't exist, and will store guest information (such as names and dietary restrictions).

3. The **Reporting** function will check whether there is a party in the future (the party date is not in the past).

4. The **Reporting** function (a scheduled task) will get the guest information and generate a planning report.

5. The **Reporting** function will store this report in an S3 bucket.

We know what our application looks like and what it is expected to do. Let's build it now using AWS SAM!

We will begin by creating the project structure:

```
$ mkdir registration reporting
$ touch template.yaml
```

Next, we need to define the resources for our template. We will need the following resources:

- Two Lambda functions (`Registration` and `Reporting`)

- One S3 bucket (`Reports`)

- Two DynamoDB tables (`Parties` and `Guests`)

- One API gateway

Remember that Lambda functions are defined with a different type (`AWS::Serverless::Function`). We will create the function using this type, so we can create event triggers (the API gateway, in our case) as part of this resource.

The following steps will help us to achieve the goal of this section:

1. Let's declare the `Registration` function in a template:

```yaml
// template.yaml
Resources:
  RegistrationFunction:
    Type: AWS::Serverless::Function
    Properties:
      CodeUri: registration/
      Events:
        register:
          Type: Api
          Properties:
            Path: /register
            Method: post
```

This function is similar to the one we created as part of the Hello, World application. However, there are a few extra things we need to add to it.

The AWS SAM stack will also have `RegistrationFunctionRole`, which is an IAM role with basic IAM policies for the Lambda function. We also need to have a policy that allows our function to put items in DynamoDB.

2. We will create the tables first:

```yaml
// template.yaml
Resources:
  # ...
  PartiesTable:
    Type: AWS::Serverless::SimpleTable
    Properties:
      PrimaryKey:
        Name: PartyName
        Type: String
  GuestsTable:
    Type: AWS::Serverless::SimpleTable
    Properties:
      PrimaryKey:
        Name: GuestName
        Type: String
```

3. Now, we can add an extra policy for our function to access these tables:

```
// template.yaml
Resources:
  RegistrationFunction:
    Type: AWS::Serverless::Function
    Properties:
      # ...
      Policies:
        Statement:
          - Effect: Allow
            Action:
              - dynamodb:PutItem
              - dynamodb:GetItem
            Resource:
              - !Sub
b:${AWS::Region}:${AWS::AccountId}:table/${PartiesTable}"
              - !Sub
db:${AWS::Region}:${AWS::AccountId}:table/${GuestsTable}»
```

Since `AWS::Serverless::SimpleTable` doesn't return the ARN of the DynamoDB table, we have to generate it using `Fn::Sub`.

4. We also need to create a bucket where we will store our reports:

```
// template.yaml
Resources:
# ...
  ReportsBucket:
    Type: AWS::S3::Bucket
```

Don't forget that we will use CloudFormation resource type for that since S3 is not part of AWS SAM's specification.

Lastly, we will declare a reporting function with a few differences.

5. The first difference is the policy since we require different IAM privileges for the `Reporting` function to work:

```
// template.yaml
Resources:
  # ...
  ReportingFunction:
    # ...
      Policies:
        Statement:
          - Effect: Allow
```

```
        Action:
          - dynamodb:GetItem
          - dynamodb:Scan
        Resource:
          - !Sub
b:${AWS::Region}:${AWS::AccountId}:table/${PartiesTable}»
          - !Sub
db:${AWS::Region}:${AWS::AccountId}:table/${GuestsTable}"
        - Effect: Allow
        Action:
          - s3:ListBucket
          - s3:GetBucketAcl
          - s3:PutObject
        Resource:
          - !GetAtt ReportsBucket.Arn
          - !Sub «${ReportsBucket.Arn}/*»
```

Next, we need to change the event since this function is a scheduled job. The only way to run scheduled jobs in Lambda is to use CloudWatch scheduled events.

6. We add a scheduled event by using a different type for `Events`:

```
// template.yaml
Resources:
# ...
  ReportingFunction:
    Type: AWS::Serverless::Function
    Properties:
      # ...
      Events:
        scheduled:
          Type: Schedule
          Properties:
            Schedule: «rate(1 day)"
```

This will create a scheduled event with a generated name and map it to the `Reporting` function.

The code for the application is not in the scope of this book, but the functions will work with the DynamoDB tables that are created as part of the stack. However, we don't set the names of the tables in the `Properties` resource, so they need to be generated during stack creation.

How, then, can we let our application know which table to connect to? We can do so via the environment variables in our template!

7. Let's add environment variables to the `Globals` section:

```
// template.yaml
Globals:
  Function:
    Timeout: 30
    Runtime: python3.8
    Handler: app.lambda_handler
    Environment:
      Variables:
        PARTIES_TABLE: !Ref PartiesTable
        GUESTS_TABLE: !Ref GuestsTable
        REPORTS_BUCKET: !Ref ReportsBucket
```

These properties will be inherited by both Lambda functions (`Registration` and `Reporting`), so we don't need to duplicate these in the resources' definitions.

There is one more thing we can do. We can create an event that we will use to test our deployment. We can also use it to test local invocations in the future.

8. Let's create a simple dummy event:

```
// events/event.json
{
  «PartyName»: «Birthday»,
  «PartyDate»: "2020-01-01",
  «GuestName»: «John Doe»,
  «GuestDiet»: «Vegan»
}
```

We will use this event later once we have created our application stack.

9. Let's build, package, and deploy our application:

```
$ sam build \
      --use-container
$ sam deploy \
      --stack-name party \
      --capabilities CAPABILITY_IAM
      --resolve-s3
```

10. We will check whether our function performs correctly by running a simple `curl` command:

```
curl -X POST \
    -d @events/event.json \
    -H "Content-Type: application/json" \
    # Your API URL might differ
```

```
https://tzsewdylmj.execute-api.eu-central-1.amazonaws.com/
Prod/register
```

We get nothing in response because our function only returns a 200 OK HTTP code.

To check the results, we will go to the DynamoDB console and examine the items:

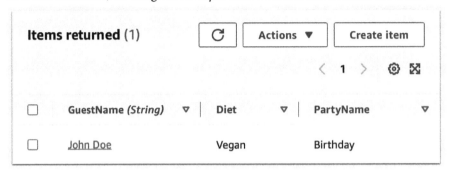

Figure 11.5 – The DynamoDB console

The new party is also added to `PartiesTable`:

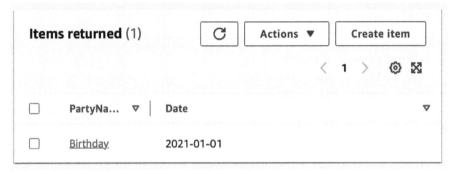

Figure 11.6 – The DynamoDB console

11. The last thing to test is running a second function. This is a scheduled task, so we will have to invoke it manually:

```
$ aws lambda invoke \
    # Your function will have a different name!
    --function-name party-ReportingFunction-17431GZNIJXPE\
    --payload '{}' \
    out.txt
{
    "StatusCode": 200,
    "ExecutedVersion": "$LATEST"
}
```

The response shows that there were no unhandled exceptions during execution, which is a good sign!

Let's examine the file, which was uploaded to S3:

```
$ aws s3 ls \
      # Your bucket name will be different!
      s3://party-reportsbucket-1usezdtprgt9z
2020-02-19 19:58:42        124 Birthday.txt
$ aws s3 cp \
      s3://party-reportsbucket-1usezdtprgt9z/Birthday.txt .
$ cat Birthday.txt
---
Party Planning Report!!!
Prepare for Birthday on 2021-01-01!
Guests list:
- John Doe who is restricted to eat Vegan
---
```

This shows the exact output of the data we've just stored on DynamoDB!

We have just successfully deployed and run a serverless application consisting of multiple Lambda functions, using AWS SAM as an all-in-one tool!

Summary

In this chapter, we learned about AWS SAM—an easy-to-use extension of CloudFormation designed specifically for serverless applications. We learned about AWS SAM, how it differs from CloudFormation, and what it consists of.

We learned about the structure of AWS SAM projects, deployment and operability options, and how to develop simple and complex serverless applications. This knowledge will help you to understand whether you want to start using AWS SAM for specific projects or applications or whether you want to stick to CloudFormation.

This is the last *technical* chapter of this book. You did a great job and I hope you've learned a lot from this book and will use this knowledge to build production-ready, scalable solutions on AWS using CloudFormation.

In the next chapter, we will sit back, relax, and find out what we can expect from CloudFormation and IaC as a whole.

Questions

1. Is it possible to create resources that are not part of an AWS SAM reference?

2. Which command starts a local API gateway?

3. Is it possible to delete an AWS SAM stack using the SAM CLI?

4. Is it possible to create a sort key in a DynamoDB table using AWS SAM?

Further reading

- *Comparing AWS SAM with the Serverless framework*: `https://sanderknape.com/2018/02/comparing-aws-sam-with-serverless-framework/`

- Example AWS SAM applications: `https://github.com/aws-samples/serverless-app-examples`

- Jeff Barr's blog post on AWS SAM: `https://aws.amazon.com/blogs/aws/aws-serverless-application-model-sam-command-line-interface-build-test-and-debug-serverless-apps-locally/`

12
What's Next?

Welcome to the last chapter of *Mastering AWS CloudFormation – Second Edition*!

In this chapter, we are going to sit back and relax since we have done a lot of hard work learning CloudFormation, its capabilities, features, and extensions. This chapter will give us an insight into what we can expect in the future for both CloudFormation and **Infrastructure as Code (IaC)**.

You might be wondering why we are finishing this book by making predictions when you are probably interested in continuing to practice using CloudFormation.

You may be right in that matter. This book is meant to help you master CloudFormation, and you have been busy doing this for 11 long chapters. But there is one thing you need to consider.

The world is continually changing, and so is IT, development, cloud providers, and AWS. We cannot be completely ready for what is going to happen, but we can try to predict it. In the end, it is not only technical skills but also erudition and mindset that make a good engineer.

What we will do is try to learn about the following topics:

- The future of infrastructure as code
- Understanding the difference between Terraform and CloudFormation
- Understanding the value of Cloud Development Kit

The future of infrastructure as code

Before we can foresee the future, we need to understand the past.

The term IaC is not new. Its roots are deep in the 90s when sysadmins used Perl and Shell scripts to automate their regular routines. Sysadmins were the same as developers but with a different focus (mostly automation and the stability of their infrastructure).

This focus started to shift as soon as **Amazon Web Services** (**AWS**) was launched in 2006, and it became a matter of a few minutes to have a fleet of virtual machines at your disposal. The increased speed of provisioning introduced the issue of scaling performance.

In addition, it was hard to develop your own infrastructure management tools using high-level programming languages. In the end, configuration-management tools started to appear: Chef, Puppet, Ansible, and others.

Later on, idempotence and declarable infrastructure became necessary requirements. Configuration-management tools *could* provide a state of the infrastructure, but scaling them from tens to hundreds to thousands of managed machines was hard, and these systems couldn't handle the load.

Engineers also wanted to combine resource provisioning and configuration management. CloudFormation was released in 2011 and was the first tool that was able to do both. It was a complex system, but it changed the way we implemented operations and infrastructure deployment. Instead of creating service requests or clicking through the AWS console, you could simply write a JSON template and provision the whole infrastructure.

Later, in 2014, HashiCorp introduced CloudFormation's competitor – *Terraform*. Terraform offered a different approach and the support of multiple cloud providers, such as GCP and Azure. Another so-called *killer feature* was its ability to create providers, as well as software programs that acted as interfaces between Terraform and service providers.

Terraform used its own **domain-specific language (DSL)** called **HashiCorp Configuration Language (HCL)**. Its syntax was similar to JSON but was simpler to read and review.

CloudFormation and Terraform followed different paths, and we will review this in the next section, but for now, we need to stick to the story.

As cloud service providers have grown and been developed, the term **infrastructure** has increasingly lost its original meaning. Infrastructure is no longer a bunch of virtual machines or databases: it is something that acts as a fundamental basis for software business and products.

Applying IaC in more and more services and integrating it with the **software development life cycle (SDLC)** introduced another set of problems.

What is a **build artifact**? Is it an end product of IaC? Is it a declaration file that instructs a service provider to launch specific resources? Is it a framework? Or is it a state of the infrastructure with necessary resources and endpoints provided?

If so, what is the *code* part of it? How do we apply common software engineering practices to it, such as unit and integration testing? How can we make sure that the change in the infrastructure doesn't break the application?

Moreover, can we integrate the application of software with infrastructure? Can we combine them as a single piece of software?

Various platforms, such as **Kubernetes**, offer the opportunity to combine the application's infrastructure (or its reference) with the source code, while the underlying infrastructure is self-managed and doesn't require that much attention.

Infrastructure has evolved from *just virtual machines* on the internet to infrastructure, platform, and software as a service. Now, you can simply order a compute, storage, or any other unit and receive an endpoint to work with. For example, instead of creating a NoSQL database, you can create a DynamoDB table and work with it immediately without thinking about the underlying infrastructure, redundancy, and performance.

At this level of abstraction, we start noticing that there is not much of a difference between an application (for example, a piece of software) and the underlying infrastructure. Could this mean we can start combining them?

Let's look at this pseudocode:

```
from infrastructure import network, database, compute
from application import Application
import source_code
# Declare infrastructure to run application on
net = network.new(cidr="10.0.0.0/16",
                  subnets=3,
                  mask=24)
db = database.new(engine="mysql",
                  cpu=2,
                  mem=2048,
                  network=net)
node_cluster = compute.vm_cluster.new(count=3,
                                      cpu=2,
                                      mem=2048,
                                      network=net)
# Declare application and attach to an infrastructure
app = Application.new()
app.use_db(db)
app.run_on(node_cluster)
app.build.from_source(source_code)
```

What this code would do (if it existed) is connect to a cloud environment, create everything we've declared it to use, and then build and deploy an application on it.

Even though we can combine an actual application and the infrastructure in the same piece of code, we still have the question of the engineering roles. Who are operations, then? Software engineers? System engineers? DevOps engineers? Site-reliability engineers?

It is certain that the classic silo model, where developers and operations worked in different responsibility zones and had different priorities, is now fading away. Nowadays, we have developers, who have a good understanding of operating systems and computer networks, and we have system engineers, who code.

The industry is shifting toward convergence and there is a high chance that IaC will simply become **code**.

But we are not there yet. And before you continue your journey in cloud automation, I want you to compare two competitors – CloudFormation and Terraform – and understand their differences. Learning this will help you make a proper decision for your particular case, current or future.

Understanding the difference between Terraform and CloudFormation

First of all, we are not evaluating CloudFormation and Terraform to find the best IaC instrument on the market. Our goal is to find a tool that fits the purpose and our use case (whatever it is going to be).

We are going to look at the following features:

- Provider support
- Declaration syntax
- Development and deployment methodologies

Let's start with provider support.

Provider support

CloudFormation, as an invention of AWS, originally supported itself as the only service provider.

Terraform was developed as a **cloud-agnostic** tool, meaning that it could communicate with various cloud and service providers, thus making it one tool to rule them all.

This concept was made available with the use of providers – specific abstractions that handle communication between a service provider and Terraform. Providers are written in the same language as Terraform (for example, Golang) and can be used locally (if you ever need to create your own provider for a specific purpose) or distributed via open source and submitted to HashiCorp via a special form.

Terraform has a wide variety of providers, both developed by vendors (`https://www.terraform.io/docs/providers/index.html`) and the community (`https://www.terraform.io/docs/providers/type/community-index.html`). HashiCorp heavily invested in building frameworks and wrappers to make provider development doable for everyone.

On the one hand, Terraform's success as a universal IaC instrument leaves no chance for its competitors from major cloud providers: AWS CloudFormation, Azure Resource Manager, and Google Cloud Deployment Manager. On the other hand, Terraform heavily relies on the speed of these providers' development – cloud providers' tools will be the first to support the newest services and API changes. In addition to that, the engineer has to take care of backward compatibility since a new version of a provider may not work with an old version of the resource declaration in the template.

However, the ability to create external resources (for example, outside of AWS) is desirable. Although **custom resources** (**CRs**) allow us to do that, it is hard to properly organize them at scale. Imagine creating CRs for GCP so that you can create resources in GCP using CloudFormation.

The CloudFormation development team came up with a centralized solution for this problem. A new feature called **CloudFormation Registry** allows us to create resource providers – in a similar manner to Terraform – using not only Go but also Java (generally available) and Python!

Let's continue our journey and look at the syntax differences.

Declaration syntax

We know that CloudFormation templates are written in JSON or YAML, depending on the developer's preference. The declaration of CloudFormation is a key-value block, where the key is a logical name of the resource and the value is its attributes, such as type and properties.

The following code shows the resource declaration of a CloudFormation resource:

```
MyResourceLogicalName:
  Type: AWS::Service::ResourceType
  Properties:
    PropertyA: some value
    PropertyB: some value
    # and so on
```

This declaration makes it easy to reference resource identifiers in the declaration using functions such as Fn::Sub, Fn::Ref, and Fn::GetAtt.

Terraform has its own DSL called HCL. HCL is a JSON-like language with a small bit of syntax sugar on top.

Let's say we want to create a VPC and a subnet in AWS using Terraform. Our template file would look like this:

```
resource "aws_vpc" "vpc" {
  cidr_block = "10.0.0.0/16"
}
resource "aws_subnet" "subnet" {
  vpc_id     = aws_vpc.vpc.id
  cidr_block = «10.0.1.0/24»
}
```

As you can see, there are huge differences.

The actual type of the resource is the first string after the keyword resource, followed by the logical name (resource "RESOURCE_TYPE" "LOGICAL_NAME" {}), while in CloudFormation, we have the logical name of the resource followed by the type in a separate field.

The second difference is that we need to provide a resource type, logical name, and attribute (aws_vpc. vpc.id) so that we can refer to it in another resource since Terraform doesn't support any default return values such as CloudFormation and Fn::Ref.

There are many other differences, such as iterations and conditions in HCL, which are used to grant the ability to provide the same features that are already supported by CloudFormation, but that's not our main focus for now.

Now, let's look at the last, but not least, thing that we should learn about – deployment and development. Let's dive in.

Development and deployment methodologies

CloudFormation is flexible for development. An AWS engineer can use nested stacks or a cross-stack resource reference using *exports* and Fn::ImportValue to manage each piece of infrastructure independently. The huge variety and agility of intrinsic functions allows AWS engineers to create reusable templates.

When it comes to deployments and stack operations, CloudFormation has it all. ChangeSets allow granular control over stack updates, yet the aws cloudformation deploy command makes it simple to create a continuous delivery pipeline for both new and existing stacks.

CloudFormation has a lot of capabilities for various cases, as shown in the following list:

- For large-scale infrastructure or products, there are StackSets
- For customization, there are template macros and custom resources
- For configuration management, there is cfn-init
- For provisioning security, there are CloudFormation service roles
- In case of failure, there is one of the most important and useful features of CloudFormation – automatic and seamless rollbacks

AWS did a great job by making CloudFormation suit any type of company, running its applications and systems on AWS.

Terraform follows a different path. It does not focus on a single cloud – instead, it tries to support as many cloud providers, third-party services, and even external systems as it can.

You can use known configuration-management systems, such as Ansible, Puppet, Chef, and SaltStack, with Terraform using provisioners, which will save a lot of time if you used them for your on-premises infrastructure and are now moving to the cloud. Terraform can retrieve information from the provider via its API using **data** – for example, it can call AWS's API to obtain the ID of an already existing VPC and use it to create subnets.

Terraform does not support rollbacks, so you have to rely on its state file backup – which is stored locally or remotely – if things go nasty.

This being said, it is up to you – the engineer – to decide whether you want to use Terraform or CloudFormation. If you feel comfortable with YAML and JSON and plan to work only with AWS, then choose CloudFormation. If you are looking for a vendor-agnostic tool with tens of services and support from the open source community, then you might want to look at Terraform.

This chapter is not only about using declarative language to define infrastructure. In the next section, we are going to look at their potential successors and what value they deliver to everybody in IT.

Understanding the value of Cloud Development Kit

DSL-based instruments, such as CloudFormation and Terraform, are still the standard of IaC. They are well known, have a huge community worldwide, and keep being developed.

However, they also have several problems that its successor, **Cloud Development Kit (CDK)**, can solve.

In this section, we are going to take a sneak peek at what changes and value CDK is bringing to the industry.

We will start by looking at its testing capabilities since this was one of the main headaches with IaC.

Testing infrastructure

To test a computer program, all we need to do is build it and then run some written test scenarios. The expected behavior of the software is known, so all you need to do is receive the proper result.

In *Chapter 4, Continuous Integration and Deployment*, we did this with CloudFormation by deploying our infrastructure and running specific infrastructure tests on it. For declarative tools, this is the only working way we have of testing them, but spinning up separate infrastructure for tests is a long and, in some cases, very expensive process. In some situations, it is even impossible.

This is mainly because the way the resources are declared in templates doesn't mean that the service provider will be able to process that information. For example, CloudFormation cannot tell whether we have supplied the correct AMI ID for the EC2 instance. Also, Kubernetes cannot tell whether a Docker image exists when we write a pod declaration.

The lack of testing support was also due to the ambiguity around what was being tested. What do we need to test? That the resource will be created? That the resource will be created *exactly* as we declared it? Why should it not?

However, what should always be tested is integration. In massive projects and infrastructures, we don't only care about a small network with a bunch of machines in it. There are hundreds and thousands of compute, storage, transport, analytics, and other resources, all of them developed and provisioned by different teams.

CDK offers a different way to create infrastructure. Instead of writing a declarative instruction on what to create, we write a computer program using the **object-oriented programming (OOP)** paradigm. Each resource is a class that has relations with other classes. VPC is a class. Subnet is a class that is related to VPC. The RDS database subnet group is a class that relates to a subnet.

These relations are declared programmatically, and the CDK is a framework for a programming language. This means that you are not writing a template – you are writing a piece of software!

This allows you to run complex testing against it, using the best practices from the software engineering world. And all this without spending even a single penny on creating tens or hundreds of resources to check this!

And testing is not the only thing we can do with the help of CDK. What about combining the application with the infrastructure?

Adding artifacts

When we use pure CloudFormation, we cannot add artifacts to it, simply because CloudFormation is a system for provisioning infrastructure and resources, something that our application will run on. Support for adding an application to the stack was partially added with `cfn-init`. With the serverless application model, it was possible to have all-in-one source code with an infrastructure template, but that only works for applications based on AWS Lambda.

CDK is not just a framework that generates CloudFormation templates – it comes with many abstractions on top of it.

One of these abstractions is **assets**, CDK constructs that are used to bundle the application artifact, whether it's a binary or a ZIP file, a directory, or a Docker image.

Imagine that you have a project structure with your source code in the `foo` directory. This directory also contains a Dockerfile, which is built and pushed to the AWS ECR repository.

In this case, we can use assets to bundle and include the image in our infrastructure, as shown in the following example:

```
import aws_cdk.aws_ecs as ecs
from aws_cdk.aws_ecr_assets import DockerImageAsset
# Declare Asset object with a path to app
asset = DockerImageAsset(self,
                         «image»,
                         directory=»/path/to/foo»)
```

```
# Declare Task Definition
td = ecs.FargateTaskDefinition(self,
                               «td»,
                               memory_limit_mib=512,
                               cpu=256)
# Add container built from the Asset image to Task Definition
td.add_container("container",image=ecs.ContainerImage.
fromEcrRepository(asset.repository,
        asset.image_uri))
```

This code builds and pushes the Docker image, along with the source code of the original application, and sends it to the ECR repository. Then, it creates an ECS task definition with a container definition that points to the ECR image URI as a source.

This abstraction allows us to mix our applications with the infrastructure, managing them as a whole! And since CDK is a multilingual project, more and more products and projects can be built with this, without forcing the developer to learn additional languages (which is still a nice skill to have and do).

CDK is only at the start of its journey, but its future is promising and game-changing. It may not replace CloudFormation (such a system simply cannot be replaced), but sooner or later, it will act as the translation mechanism between code written by developers and an actual working and serving infrastructure.

Summary

In this chapter, we learned about what we can expect in the future. First, we looked into the past and the future of infrastructure – what is changing and what these changes mean to us as AWS professionals. Then, we defined the main differences between CloudFormation and its biggest competitor, Terraform, and why these two systems follow such different paths. At the end of this chapter, we looked into the actual value that CDK brings us.

With this in mind, you should be able to understand where to go next in your journey. Will you want to keep mastering CloudFormation? After this book, the only information you will need can be found in CloudFormation's documentation. CloudFormation's development team is working hard to develop and evolve their product, so spend some time reviewing their coverage roadmap and public repository with tons of useful information.

Will you want to start practicing software development? If so, CDK is a good start for you.

I wish you all the best in this journey. Let's see where it will take us!

Further reading

- AWS's blog on CloudFormation Registry: https://aws.amazon.com/blogs/aws/cloudformation-update-cli-third-party-resource-support-registry/

- AWS CloudFormation GitHub project: https://github.com/aws-cloudformation

- AWS CloudFormation coverage roadmap: https://github.com/aws-cloudformation/aws-cloudformation-coverage-roadmap

- AWS CloudFormation awesome list: https://github.com/aws-cloudformation/awesome-cloudformation

Assessments

Chapter 1

1. `CreateStack` is invoked; CloudFormation then calls service APIs to create stack resources.

2. A CloudFormation service role is an IAM role that is assumed by CloudFormation before stack operations are performed. The policies attached to that role will then be used to perform stack operations.

3. The API credentials that are attached to the IAM entity (user or role), when we run the CloudFormation stack operations.

4. This information (physical resource ID and its metadata) is stored in CloudFormation's state.

5. If we try to create the same stack (that is, invoke the CreateStack API call), the call will fail with a `400 AlreadyExists` error.

6. If we run a stack update without any changes in a template or parameters, nothing will happen, as there are no changes. CloudFormation will not notice if the resource has been deleted manually. However, if we update the deleted resource, the operation will fail because the CloudFormation resource still exists in the state, and CloudFormation *believes* it is still there.

7. Because CloudFormation's state is immutable and cannot be managed by the end user. In order to recreate the deleted resource, we have to delete it from the state by deleting it from the template, and then add it again.

Chapter 2

1. No. The `Condition` attribute of the resource may have only the `Condition` name string format.

2. Yes, it is possible to use `Fn::Ref`, `Fn::GetAttr`, or other relevant intrinsic functions with conditional functions such as `Fn::If`.

3. `UpdatePolicy` is a resource attribute that handles the updates for resources such as the auto scaling group. `UpdateReplacePolicy` is used to manage the behavior of resources that are being replaced by CloudFormation during stack operations.

4. Retain, since we cannot afford to delete mission-critical databases by mistake in a template or stack operation.

5. `Fn::ImportValue` takes the values of exported outputs of other stacks.

6. Yes, but not in the same AWS Region.

7. Yes. There is an AWS-specific parameter type called `AWS::EC2::Image::Id`.

8. `AWS::NoValue` can be referred to as a null value. It is not usually used to set any value to a resource property and is mostly used in conjunction with conditional functions.

Chapter 3

1. From 9,000 and above.

2. Linting is the process of evaluating the template against linter rules and is performed by `cfn-lint`. Validation is performed by CloudFormation and checks whether the template is valid and can be processed by CloudFormation.

3. There are several steps:

    I.   CloudFormation will check whether the stack exists or not.

    II.   CloudFormation will create a ChangeSet for a new or existing stack.

    III. CloudFormation will execute the ChangeSet and listen to the stack events.

    IV.   If there is a failure, CloudFormation rolls back the changes and informs the user about the issue.

4. No. ChangeSets must have unique names; otherwise, you will get a `400 AlreadyExists` error.

5. The name of the rule file and the rule class must be the same.

6. Just add the necessary change to the template or parameters and run the stack update.

Chapter 4

1. `buildspec.yml` is a build specification file with instructions for AWS CodeBuild on how to process the build.

2. A CloudFormation artifact is the template and, in some cases, parameter files. They are stored on S3.

3. You can use CloudFormation signals, wait conditions, and update policies.

4. The easiest way to do so is to invoke `ListStackResources`.

5. `Source`, `Build`, and `Deploy`. There are various services that can be used, such as S3, CodeBuild, CodeDeploy, and CloudFormation.

Chapter 5

1. Yes, but it is not recommended. You will have to then explicitly specify the names of both roles.

2. Yes. This is managed by a property called *Maximum Concurrent Accounts*.

3. Per AWS Region (as they are defined from the first to last) and then per account (as they are defined from the first to last).

4. No. You must delete all the stack instances first.

5. The only action for the Administrator role is to assume the Execution role.

Chapter 6

1. The `cfn-init` helper script processes these configuration sections in the following order: packages, groups, users, sources, files, commands, and then services.

2. Yes, and it is recommended to do so for complex configurations or to run configuration items in a different order.

3. No. Only one configuration set can be provided.

4. Not using the `files` directive in the config set. You will have to use the `commands` directive, but it is possible to add a missing directory to the full path of the file, and `cfn-init` will automatically create it (similar to the `mkdir -p` command).

5. `WaitCondition` is a CloudFormation resource that is used to make CloudFormation wait for resource completion. For example, you can use `WaitCondition` with `cfn-signal` to make CloudFormation inform the users about resource creation only when `cfn-init` has finished running.

Chapter 7

1. `Create`, `Update`, and `Delete`.

2. Only using Lambda Layers, or simply copy the module content to the Lambda function's code.

3. CloudFormation as a requester, AWS Lambda for provisioning, CloudWatch for logs and metrics, and other AWS services, if they are used in the custom resource's logic.

4. The `responseReason` block should contain the reason for resource change failure.

5. The event is an actual payload to the Lambda function, which has to be processed. Context is metadata of the Lambda request that contains various information, such as the timestamp of the request.

Chapter 8

1. Public extensions are developed and published by the extension developer for use by other AWS users. They are visible in the registry and be activated by the user. Private extensions are developed and registered on their own accounts.

2. At the moment of this writing, resource types, hooks, and modules.

3. **CRUDL – Create, Read, Update, Delete,** and **List.**

4. `cloudformation-cli` should be used to manage extensions.

5. `cfn generate` generates code based on a specification schema.

Chapter 9

1. The rendered template is returned in the JSON format.

2. It is either a piece of a template or a full template, depending on whether the `Transform` section is declared or the `Fn::Transform` function is used.

3. The stack operation will be considered as `Failed`, and CloudFormation will start rolling back.

4. Yes, but you need to be aware of the macro evaluation order: `https://docs.aws.amazon.com/AWSCloudFormation/latest/UserGuide/template-macros.html#template-macros-use`.

5. No. At the moment of this writing, CloudFormation module extensions do not support any macros, including language extensions.

Chapter 10

1. Constructs are the building blocks of CDK. Any block of CDK, such as an `App`, `Stack`, `Asset`, or `Resource`, is considered to be a construct.

2. You have to define each stack separately by assigning a stack class to it as a value.

3. By adding subnet configuration to the VPC construct. Originally, CDK was developed by TypeScript, but there are libraries for Python, Java, C#, and JavaScript. The CDK development team is working on more languages to support in CDK.

4. No. CDK will use the default credentials and config to connect to AWS. However, it is recommended to provide an account ID and Region when using CDK in production.

Chapter 11

1. Yes, by using CloudFormation-specific resource types.

2. `sam local start-api` starts a local API server.

3. Yes. AWS SAM CLI supports deleting stacks. To delete a stack, you need to run `sam delete`.

4. It is, but you have to use the CloudFormation-specific type for DynamoDB, since `SimpleTable` doesn't have this property.

5. The application's source code and its dependencies are uploaded to S3 as a ZIP file. The template is altered to point to S3 for the source code and is saved on disk or printed to the terminal output.

Index

Packtpub.com

Subscribe to our online digital library for full access to over 7,000 books and videos, as well as industry leading tools to help you plan your personal development and advance your career. For more information, please visit our website.

Why subscribe?

- Spend less time learning and more time coding with practical eBooks and Videos from over 4,000 industry professionals

- Improve your learning with Skill Plans built especially for you

- Get a free eBook or video every month

- Fully searchable for easy access to vital information

- Copy and paste, print, and bookmark content

Did you know that Packt offers eBook versions of every book published, with PDF and ePub files available? You can upgrade to the eBook version at packtpub.com and as a print book customer, you are entitled to a discount on the eBook copy. Get in touch with us at customercare@packtpub.com for more details.

At www.packtpub.com, you can also read a collection of free technical articles, sign up for a range of free newsletters, and receive exclusive discounts and offers on Packt books and eBooks.

Other Books You May Enjoy

If you enjoyed this book, you may be interested in these other books by Packt:

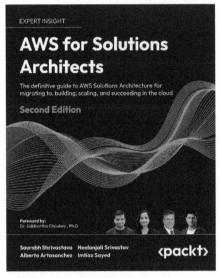

AWS for Solutions Architects - Second Edition

Saurabh Shrivastava, Neelanjali Srivastav, Alberto Artasanchez

ISBN: 978-1-80323-895-1

- Optimize your Cloud Workload using the AWS Well-Architected Framework
- Learn methods to migrate your workload using the AWS Cloud Adoption Framework
- Apply cloud automation at various layers of application workload to increase efficiency
- Build a landing zone in AWS and hybrid cloud setups with deep networking techniques
- Select reference architectures for business scenarios, like data lakes, containers, and serverless apps
- Apply emerging technologies in your architecture, including AI/ML, IoT and blockchain

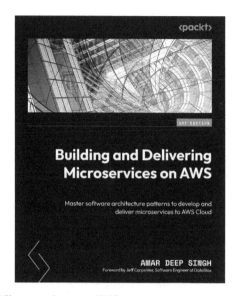

Building and Delivering Microservices on AWS

Amar Deep Singh

ISBN: 978-1-80323-820-3

- Understand the basics of architecture patterns and microservice development

- Get to grips with the continuous integration and continuous delivery of microservices

- Delve into automated infrastructure provisioning with CloudFormation and Terraform

- Explore CodeCommit, CodeBuild, CodeDeploy, and CodePipeline services

- Get familiarized with automated code reviews and profiling using CodeGuru

- Grasp AWS Lambda function basics and automated deployment using CodePipeline

- Understand Docker basics and automated deployment to ECS and EKS

- Explore the CodePipeline integration with Jenkins Pipeline and on premises deployment

Packt is searching for authors like you

If you're interested in becoming an author for Packt, please visit `authors.packtpub.com` and apply today. We have worked with thousands of developers and tech professionals, just like you, to help them share their insight with the global tech community. You can make a general application, apply for a specific hot topic that we are recruiting an author for, or submit your own idea.

Share your thoughts

Now you've finished *Mastering AWS CloudFormation – Second Edition*, we'd love to hear your thoughts! Scan the QR code below to go straight to the Amazon review page for this book and share your feedback or leave a review on the site that you purchased it from.

`https://packt.link/r/1805123904`

Your review is important to us and the tech community and will help us make sure we're delivering excellent quality content.

Download a free PDF copy of this book

Thanks for purchasing this book!

Do you like to read on the go but are unable to carry your print books everywhere?

Is your eBook purchase not compatible with the device of your choice?

Don't worry, now with every Packt book you get a DRM-free PDF version of that book at no cost.

Read anywhere, any place, on any device. Search, copy, and paste code from your favorite technical books directly into your application.

The perks don't stop there, you can get exclusive access to discounts, newsletters, and great free content in your inbox daily

Follow these simple steps to get the benefits:

1. Scan the QR code or visit the link below

https://packt.link/free-ebook/9781805123903

2. Submit your proof of purchase
3. That's it! We'll send your free PDF and other benefits to your email directly

Milton Keynes UK
Ingram Content Group UK Ltd.
UKHW051028011223
433587UK00005B/63